W9-ARG-339

SILENT COVENANTS

SILENT COVENANTS

BROWN V. BOARD OF EDUCATION

AND THE UNFULFILLED HOPES FOR RACIAL REFORM

DERRICK BELL

OXFORD
UNIVERSITY PRESS
2004

OXFORD

UNIVERSITY PRESS

Oxford   New York
Auckland   Bangkok   Buenos Aires   Cape Town   Chennai
Dar es Salaam   Delhi   Hong Kong   Istanbul   Karachi   Kolkata
Kuala Lumpur   Madrid   Melbourne   Mexico City   Mumbai   Nairobi
São Paulo   Shanghai   Taipei   Tokyo   Toronto

Published by Oxford University Press, Inc.
198 Madison Avenue, New York, New York 10016

www.oup.com

Oxford is a registered trademark of Oxford University Press

Library of Congress Cataloging-in-Publication Data
Bell, Derrick A.
Silent covenants : Brown v. Board of Ed.
and the unfulfilled hopes for racial reform / by Derrick Bell.
p.   cm.
Includes notes and index
ISBN 0–19–517272–8
1. Segregation in education—Law and legislation—United States—History.
2. School integration—United States—History.
I. Title.
KF4155 .B38 2004
344.73'0798—dc22
2003027447

Book design and typesetting: Jack Donner, BookType

1 3 5 7 9 8 6 4 2
Printed in the United States of America
on acid-free paper

For Janet Dewart Bell

CONTENTS

ACKNOWLEDGMENTS

The maturing of my views about school desegregation owe much to my contact with the late Ronald R. Edmonds, who tirelessly urged that legal concepts of equality were not linked to and could prove barriers to effective schooling. Jean Fairfax taught me that winning school cases was only one step in explaining to black parents—often with door-to-door visits—their rights under court-ordered desegregation plans. My late wife of 30 years, Jewel Hairston Bell, both taught me that persistence could prove a value, and introduced me to Rev. Jefferson P. Rogers, my friend, mentor, and the best-read person I know, who reassured me that speaking the truth as I perceive it is no less worthwhile because so few agree with my views.

I want to thank Karen Rinaldi, director of Bloomsbury, U.S.A. She recommended this project to Oxford University Press's publisher of the Academic Division Niko Pfund, who expressed a level of enthusiasm not likely to be equaled in either sales or acclaim. My editors at Oxford, Dedi Felman and Helen Mules earned credit for translating my unorthodox views into readable and understandable text. The list of students and colleagues who contributed research and suggestions to this book is a long one and includes: Jack Boger, Gail Bowman, Tracy Burnett, Lenora Fulani, Gail Foster, David Gray, Phoebe Hoss, Gwen Jordan, Una Kim, Brandon Lofton, Frank Michelman, Geoff Miller, Markita Morris, Joy Radice, Nirej Sekhorn, Rogers Smith, Stephen Steinberg, Melissa Tidwell, and Dennis Ventry. My thanks for the support provided by the New York University School of Law and Dean Richard Revesz. And finally to Richard Delgado, Jean Stafancic, and Deborah Gershenowitz of NYU Books for their understanding that far exceeded professional courtesy.

The world is moved by diverse powers and pressures creating cross currents that unpredictably, yet with eerie precision, determine the outcome of events. Often invisible in their influence, these forces shape our destinies, furthering or frustrating our ambitions and goals. The perfection for which we strive is elusive precisely because we are caught up in the myriad of manifestations of perfection itself.

—DB

INTRODUCTION

GRADUATION DAY AT YALE UNIVERSITY in late May 2002 was blessed with warm, clear weather. It is the hope for such a beautiful morning that enables outdoor commencements to survive the rain-soaked disappointment of those hopes on far too many better-forgotten occasions. Yale's Old Campus was filled with faculty, administrators, soon-to-be graduates, and their well-dressed families and friends. Under the canopy-covered stage, there were ten individuals designated to receive honorary degrees because of their significant achievements.

I was there at the invitation of one of those honorees, Robert L. Carter, my mentor and friend for more than forty years. Then eighty-five, a senior judge on the federal district court with thirty years of service, Carter had previously enjoyed a long and distinguished career as an NAACP civil rights attorney and, for a few years, a partner in a large law firm. All of these accomplishments would be worthy of the praise and warm applause that other candidates received. When, though, Yale University president Richard Levin announced that Judge Carter was an important member of the legal team that planned the strategies and argued the landmark case of *Brown v. Board of Education*,[1] noting that the decision was only two years short of its fiftieth anniversary, the audience leaped to its feet and, with great enthusiasm, applauded and cheered.

On that happy day, Judge Carter was the recipient of the audience's appreciation for his work in helping litigate a case in which the Supreme

Court had held racial segregation in the public schools unconstitutional. The mainly white audience that had assembled for the commencement exercises at one of the nation's premier universities was not unsophisticated. For them, and so many others regardless or status or race, *Brown v. Board of Education* evoked awe and respect. If asked, most would have agreed that the decision was the finest hour of American law. In their view, this long-awaited and now much-appreciated decision had erased the contradiction between the freedom and justice for all that America proclaimed, and the subordination by race permitted by our highest law.

Even as I stood and joined in the applause, I wondered. How could a decision that promised so much and, by its terms, accomplished so little, have gained so hallowed a place among some of the nation's better-educated and most-successful individuals that its mere mention in connection with one of its lawyer advocates sparked a contained but very real demonstration?

* * *

I had every reason to be leading the applause rather than musing about the causes of the crowd's enthusiasm. After all, on May 17, 1954, the day on which the Supreme Court handed down a decision we hoped would remove the protective cloak of law from policies of racial discrimination that for generations had burdened the lives of black people, I was on a ship heading home from a year's military duty in Korea. While there, I had applied to law school, planning to enroll when I completed the two years of active duty required when I signed up for ROTC in college.

I entered law school that fall. The only black in a class of about 140 white males, I was determined not to be among the two-thirds of first-year law students who, routinely in those days, failed to graduate. My hard work paid off and, after the first year, my grades led to an invitation to join the law review. Quite soon, I began submitting so much writing on racial issues that the law review's faculty advisor asked me—only half in jest—whether it was my intention to change the name of the publication to the University of Pittsburgh Civil Rights Journal.

Nothing in my legal education altered my assumption that the *Brown* decision marked the beginning of the end of Jim Crow oppression in all its myriad forms. For black Americans long burdened by our subordinate status, there was, to paraphrase the spiritual, "a great day a-coming." Among black people at every level, that was the majority view. A few months before graduating in 1957, I took a train to Philadelphia to meet with Judge William H. Hastie, the first black federal judge and a hero of mine because of his longtime civil rights activism.

Judge Hastie greeted me warmly in his chambers and commended me on my academic achievements. He said that I was one of the few black law students in the country who held an editorship position on law review at a mainly white school. When I told him that I hoped to follow in his footsteps and become a civil rights lawyer, Hastie nodded appreciatively. He added, though, that while there might well be some mopping up to do, the *Brown* decision had redefined rights to which blacks were entitled under the Constitution. "Son," he said, "I am afraid that you were born fifteen years too late to have a career in civil rights."

Despite Judge Hastie's optimism, the Supreme Court's *Brown* decision did not alter the all-white and virtually all-male hiring practices of large law firms. I graduated near the top of my class at the University of Pittsburgh Law School, but unlike several of my classmates, I received no job offers from local law firms. Through the intervention of a few of my law teachers, I was able to gain a position with the U.S. Department of Justice and served for several months in the newly formed Civil Rights Division. Later, Thurgood Marshall, then Director Counsel of the NAACP Legal Defense Fund (LDF), invited me to join the staff. From 1960 until 1965, I handled and eventually came to supervise most of the southern school litigation that at one point reached three hundred cases. Rejoining the government in 1966, I helped supervise enforcement of Title VI of the 1964 Civil Rights Act, authorizing the termination of federal funds to school districts that were found in noncompliance with the *Brown* mandate.

For the first decade of my legal career, I, like most civil rights professionals, believed with an almost religious passion that the *Brown* decision was the equivalent of the Holy Grail of racial justice. And why not? The Constitution is said to be America's civil religion. If *Brown*'s revised reading of the Constitution were fully enforced in the public schools across the country, it would serve eventually to eliminate racial discrimination in all aspects of life. Joining a law faculty in 1969 provided time for reflection and writing that led to a broader perspective on the by-then quarter-century-long campaign to desegregate the public schools.

By this point, my enthusiasm for gaining compliance with *Brown* through court orders requiring the balancing of races in each school had waned with experience. *Brown* remained Holy Writ, but I now felt we were misreading its message. As happens all too often in religion, disciples lose sight of the basic truths amid all the doctrines that tend to stifle those truths rather than nourish them.

In a 1976 article, I considered the fact that our clients' aims for better schooling for their children no longer meshed with integrationist ideals. Arguing that civil rights lawyers were misguided in requiring racial balance of each school's student population as the measure of compliance and the guarantee of effective schooling, I urged that educational equity rather than integrated idealism was the appropriate goal. In short, while the rhetoric of integration promised much, court orders to ensure that black youngsters actually received the education they needed to progress would have achieved more.[2]

In a later essay in 1980, I noted the major role of fortuity in civil rights gains and why those gains tended to be fleeting even when enunciated in terms of permanence.[3] The *Brown* decision, I contended, was a prime but far from the only example of what I called the "interest-convergence" theory. Even so, I continued to view *Brown* as basically a positive decision, but as the years passed, my understanding of the complexity of race in America and our efforts to remedy its injustices raised new doubts.

*   *   *

Over the decades, the *Brown* decision, like other landmark cases, has gained a life quite apart from the legal questions it was intended to settle. The passage of time has calmed both the ardor of its admirers and the ire of its detractors. Today, of little use as legal precedent, it has gained in reputation as a measure of what law and society might be. That noble image, dulled by resistance to any but minimal steps toward compliance, has transformed *Brown* into a magnificent mirage, the legal equivalent of that city on a hill to which all aspire without any serious thought that it will ever be attained.

Considered within the context of American political, economic, and cultural life, the *Brown* decision is a long-running racial melodrama. As with a film or play, the decision stimulated varying feeling. It energized the law, encouraged most black people, enraged a great many white people, and, like so many other racial policies, served the nation's short-term but not its long-term interests. Generating an emotionally charged concoction of commendations and condemnations, the *Brown* decision recreated the nineteenth century's post–Civil War Reconstruction/Redemption pattern of progress followed by retrogression. It stirred confusion and conflict into the always-vexing question of race in a society that, despite denials and a frustratingly flexible amnesia, owes much of its growth, development, and success to the ability of those dominant members of society who use race to both control and exploit most people, whatever their race.

As had happened in the past, the law employing the vehicle of a major judicial decision offered symbolic encouragement to the black dispossessed. The substantive losses so feared by its white adversaries evolved almost unnoticed into advances greater for whites than for blacks. And a half-century later, as must now be apparent to all, the nation's racial dilemma—modernized and, one might say, "colorized,"— has become more complex rather than simplified. The ever-widening racial disparities in all aspects of life overshadow the gains in status achieved by those black Americans who, by varying combinations of hard work and good fortune, are viewed as having "made it." Indeed, although it did not achieve what its supporters hoped for, historians and other social scientists, safely removed from the fray, may come to view *Brown* as the perfect precedent. As a dictionary would define perfect, it was: "pure, total; lacking in no essential detail; complete, sane, absolute, unequivocal, unmitigated, an act of perfection."

They will have a point. In law, perfection in the social reform area is a legal precedent that resolves issues in a manner that: (1) initially or over time gains acceptance from broad segments of the populace; (2) protects vested property in all its forms through sanctions against generally recognized wrongdoers; (3) encourages investment, confidence, and security through a general upholding of the status quo; and (4) while recognizing severe injustices, does not disrupt the reasonable expectations of those not directly responsible for the wrongs. Such reform is arranged of seeming necessity within the context of a silent covenant. That is, the policymakers who approve the policy do so with the knowledge, unspoken but clearly understood, that they or those who follow them stand ready to modify or even withdraw the reforms where adverse reaction or changed circumstances threaten any of the first three components.

Arguably, the *Brown* decision eventually met each of these standards. The question is whether another approach than the one embraced by the *Brown* decision might have been more effective and less disruptive in the always-contentious racial arena. The claim that the perfect is the enemy of the good sounds like a bureaucratic excuse for failing to do what needs to be done. At least in the first *Brown* decision, the Supreme Court did not settle for the pragmatic approach. Overcoming fears of predictable resistance, the Court sought to change society with one swift blow. A year later, the Court, in *Brown II*, reacted to the outraged cries of "never" coming from the South and the absence of support from the executive and legislative branches, and backed away from its earlier commitment. In evident response to the resistance, the Court issued a fall-back decision that became a prelude to its refusal to issue orders requiring any meaningful school desegregation for almost fifteen years.

In gauging the continuing impact and influence of the *Brown* decision as melodrama, we can begin with that prestigious gathering at Yale's commencement. It was a striking illustration of the strong sense possessed by so many people that racial injustices could be overcome through peaceful litigation. This country, after all, was a good place. Surely, blacks once benighted by racial discrimination could now throw off the shackles of segregation and get down to work. Soon, we would no longer even consider race save as an unhappy, better-forgotten historic relic of genocide, slavery, and segregation.

Professor Michael Seidman explains how *Brown* brought about a transformation without real change. He reminds us that the Court in *Brown* faced a massive contradiction between the nation's oft-cited commitment to equality and the great value whites placed on the racial preferences and priorities given tacit approval by the Court in *Plessy v. Ferguson*,[4] the decision that approved segregation. Given their lack of political and economic power, it appeared that the black demand for equality could never be satisfied. As Seidman puts it, though, the contradictions in the ideology of the separate-but-equal doctrine were permanently destabilizing and threatened any equilibrium.

By purporting to resolve those contradictions, *Brown* served to end their destabilizing potential. The Court, Seidman claims,

> resolved the contradictions by definitional fiat: Separate facilities were now simply proclaimed to be inherently unequal. But the flip side of

this aphorism was that once white society was willing to make facilities legally non-separate, the demand for equality had been satisfied and blacks no longer had just cause for complaint. The mere existence of *Brown* thus served [to] legitimate current arrangements. True, many blacks remained poor and disempowered. But their status was no longer a result of the denial of equality. Instead, it marked a personal failure to take advantage of one's definitionally equal status.[5]

Brown, then, served to reinforce the fiction that, by the decision's rejection of racial barriers posed by segregation, the path of progress would be clear. Everyone can and should make it through individual ability and effort. One would have thought that this reinforcement of the status quo would placate if not please even the strongest supporters of segregation. To the contrary, the *Brown* decision provided politicians with a racial issue through which to enrage and upset large groups of white people, initially in the South, but far more generally as efforts to implement the decision moved across the country.

In effect, they demanded the name of segregation as well as the game of racial preference. Courts initially responded to this resistance with caution intended to give time for the process to work, and later with a series of stronger and more specific orders intended as much to uphold judicial authority as to effectively carry out the mandate of *Brown*. These orders were carried out eventually, but the fear of sending their children to desegregated schools led many white parents either to move to mainly white school districts or to enroll their children in private, all-white schools. With their departure went the primary reason for racial-balance remedies.

Beyond the schools, resistance to desegregation of public facilities included forcible refusal by elected officials to comply with court orders and violent response by portions of the public to peaceful civil rights protestors. The coverage of this resistance by the media in general, and particularly by television, showed the nation that it was intimidation and violence that enabled the segregationists to boast that Negroes were the contented beneficiaries of the southern way of life. Paradoxically, then, as I will discuss in more detail, the major value of the *Brown* decision may have come as a result of well-publicized forms of white resistance that appalled many who otherwise would have remained on the sidelines. Clearly, the Civil Rights Act of

1964 and the 1965 Voting Rights Acts were responses to the courage of thousands of black people and their white allies who refused to be intimidated by segregationist violence and disorder.

While civil rights lawyers worked to remove the most obvious legal symbols of segregation, we left it to A. Philip Randolph and the National Urban League to address the major changes in the economic outlook of a great many black people. Living in inner-city areas across the country, they were finding it increasingly difficult to find jobs. Employers were moving to the suburbs where public transportation was almost nonexistent but discrimination in hiring was rampant. Without work, family instability followed. Those able to leave the old neighborhoods did so, taking with them the stability of middle-class educations and aspirations. Public services, including schools, hospitals, and community centers, all but collapsed under the burden. For those left behind, joblessness and hopelessness were eased with alcohol and drugs, sedatives that quickly worsened conditions for individuals and their communities. Neither the *Brown* decision nor our efforts to give it meaning had any relevance to the plight of those whom we had not forgotten, but had no real idea how to help.

President Lyndon Johnson launched his War on Poverty in the mid-1960s, and Dr. Martin Luther King came to recognize that desegregated facilities meant little to those unable to afford their cost. Johnson's campaign was sidetracked by the Vietnam War, and Dr. King's Poor People's Movement ended with his assassination. Through it all, we continued our striving for racial equality even as resistance to our efforts stiffened, and elected officials and those who hoped to gain election found other issues more attractive, more likely to gain the support of whites even if they ignored the needs of blacks and working-class whites.

During this time of transition, the anniversary of *Brown* on May 17 became the "Flag Day" of the civil rights movement, a time to gather, renew our commitment, and join in the strains of "We Shall Overcome." The decision itself became an archetype of a landmark decision. Landmark decisions are, at bottom, designed through reference to constitutional interpretations and supportive legal precedents to address and hopefully resolve deeply divisive social issues. They are framed in a language that provides at least the appearance of doing justice without unduly upsetting large groups whose potential for noncompliance can frustrate relief efforts and undermine judicial authority. For reasons that may not even have been apparent to the members of the Supreme Court, their school desegregation decisions achieved over time a far loftier place in legal history than they were able to accomplish in reforming the ideology of racial domination that *Plessy v. Ferguson* represented.

Brown teaches that advocates of racial justice should rely less on judicial decisions and more on tactics, actions, and even attitudes that challenge the continuing assumptions of white dominance. History as well as current events call for realism in our racial dealings. Traditional statements of freedom and justice for all, the usual fare on celebratory occasions, serve to mask continuing manifestations of inequality that beset and divide people along lines of color and class. These divisions have been exploited to enable an uneasy social stability, but at a cost that is not less onerous because it is all too obvious to blacks and all but invisible to a great many whites.

Underlying these fairly apparent manifestations of racial reaction and interaction, I perceive more subtle but far from invisible occurrences that influence both racial progress and racial retrogression. First, from the nation's beginnings, policymakers have been willing to sacrifice even blacks' basic entitlements of freedom and justice as a kind of political catalyst that enables whites to reach compromises that resolve differing and potentially damaging economic and political differences. Second, policymakers recognize and act to remedy racial injustices when, and only when, they perceive that such action will benefit the nation's interests without significantly diminishing whites' sense of entitlement.

These seemingly diverse policies are actually two sides of the same coin, each promoting in its own way the maintenance of white dominance. Blacks are not neutral observers in their subordinate status, but even their most strenuous efforts seldom enable them to break free of a social physics in which even the most blatant discrimination is ignored or rationalized until black petitions find chance harmony with white interests. Racial justice, then, when it comes, arrives on the wings of racial fortuity rather than hard-earned entitlement. Its departure, when conditions change, is preordained.

The landscape for meaningful racial reform is neither smooth nor easily traveled. History's lessons have not been learned, and even at this late date may not be teachable. Racial reforms that blacks view as important are opposed by many whites as a threat to their status, an unfair effort to make them pay for wrongs that neither they nor their families have committed. Color blindness, now as a century ago, is adopted as the easy resolution of issues of race with which the nation would rather not wrestle, much less try seriously to resolve. It is an attractive veneer obscuring flaws in the society that are not corrected by being hidden from view. *Brown v. Board of Education* was a dramatic instance of a remedy that promised to correct deficiencies in justice far deeper than the Supreme Court was able to understand. Understanding those deficiencies more fully and suggesting how we should address them is the challenge of this book.

1

PLESSY'S LONG SHADOW

THE SUPREME COURT'S 1896 DECISION in *Plessy v. Ferguson*[1] served to bring the law into a dismal harmony with the nation's view of race in life. The Court decided that segregation in public facilities through "separate but equal" accommodations for black citizens would satisfy the equal protection clause in the Fourteenth Amendment.

The years since the sporadically enforced policies of Reconstruction ended in 1876 had been hard for those former slaves and their offspring whose slavery had legally ended with the passage of the Thirteenth Amendment in 1865. To ensure their rights to due process and the equal protection of the law, the Fourteenth Amendment in 1868 provided that "all persons born or naturalized in the United States, . . . are citizens of the United States and of the State wherein they reside." Despite legislation intended to provide enforcement of these rights, the laws were poorly enforced and most were subsequently declared unconstitutional.

Corrupting law but relying on intimidation and violence, southern governments stripped blacks of political power. Given meaningful if unspoken assurances that the federal government would not protect black civil rights, conservative southerners regained power utilizing racial fear and hatred to break up competing populist groups of poor black and white farmers. In addition to the disenfranchisement of blacks, whites sought to secure their power through intensive anti-Negro propaganda campaigns championing white supremacy. Literary and scientific leaders published tracts and books intended to "prove" the inhumanity of the Negro. In this hostile climate, segregation laws that had made a brief appearance during Reconstruction were revived across the South, accompanied by waves of violence punctuated by an increase in lynchings and race riots.

In an effort both to protest the indignity of segregation and challenge its validity, Homer Plessy, acting for a New Orleans civil rights group, attempted to ride in a railroad car reserved for whites. He was arrested and convicted of violating Louisiana's 1890 segregation law. On appeal, the Supreme Court acknowledged that the Fourteenth Amendment required absolute equality of the two races before the law, adding: "but in the nature of things it could not have been intended to abolish distinctions based upon color, or to enforce social, as distinguished from political equality, or a commingling of the two races upon terms unsatisfactory to either."

Segregation laws were widespread in the dozen or so years before the *Plessy* decision. Now, with the Court's implicit approval, the first decade of the twentieth century witnessed the enactment of a wide variety of segregation statutes. No detail seemed too small as laws required segregation at work, at play, and at home. Public schools were always separate and almost always vastly unequal. Public conveyances, eating and hotel facilities, bathrooms, water fountains, prisons, cemeteries, parks, and sporting and entertainment events were all covered. New Orleans even deemed it in its public interest to enact an ordinance separating Negro and white prostitutes.

The society, through law, created two worlds so separate that communication between them was almost impossible. John Hope Franklin reported that separation bred suspicion and hatred, fostered rumors and misunderstandings, and created conditions that made any steps toward its reduction extremely difficult. Segregation was so complete that a southern white minister explained that it "made of our eating and drinking, our buying and selling, our labor and housing, our rents, our railroads, our orphanages and prisons, our recreations, our very institutions of religion, a problem of race as well as a problem of maintenance."[2]

The tree of segregation had deep roots, and public acceptance went beyond the South to encompass hundreds of communities across the nation. It grew by means of practices police were ready to enforce. The purpose of these policies was not simply to exclude or segregate but to subordinate those who, based on their color and without regard to their accomplishments, were presumed to be inferior to any white person no matter how low or ignorant. World War II, fought to ensure freedom in the world, had little immediate effect on segregation laws that remained in force and were fully enforced. Actually, of course, segregation was the name, but domination was the game. Intimidation, including often-random murder, was the means of enforcement. In 1896, the year in which the Supreme Court rejected in *Plessy v. Ferguson* Homer Plessy's argument that segregation stamped the colored race with a badge of inferiority, seventy-seven Negroes were lynched.

As part of its "massive resistance" strategy in the years after the *Brown* decision, southerners worked hard to convince the nation that blacks were content living under segregation. A state commission created to justify the southern way of life called an elderly black man before it to testify to his experience living under the separate but equal southern way of life. The man, called Tom by the commission chairman, was dressed in an old suit, but he stood straight and walked to the witness chair with a steady gait. He was obviously under great pressure.

"Tom," the chairman said, "you've lived in a rural area of this great state all your life. Now, you have a little farm, got a nice mortgage on it, sell your produce to black and white alike. You tell the commission and the national television audience. Tell them that separate but equal is not so bad."

The questions were leading, and unless he answered as he was expected to, Tom could put everything he had at risk. Tom sat in the witness chair, silent but thoughtful. He surely understood the significance of his answer.

"Tom," the chairman asked again, more firmly, less friendly, "Do you want me to repeat the question?"

Tom slowly shook his head and then, sitting erect and looking directly at the chairman, he said: "Segregation is like the one-legged man who went into a shoe store. He only needed one shoe, but the store made him buy two. So, he put on the separate shoe and wore it and wore it till he wore it clean out. But you know Mr. Chairman, he never had a chance to wear that equal shoe at all."

2

BROWN'S HALF LIGHT

THE EVENING OF MAY 17, 1954, was a night for celebration. An office full of ecstatic NAACP workers in Manhattan, as well as black people throughout the country, were doing just that as they hailed the bright new era all assumed would arrive with the landmark decision in *Brown v. Board of Education* handed down by the Supreme Court earlier that day. The case was not easily won. It was the culmination of two decades of planning and litigation. At the very least, a party was in order.

The NAACP staff hailed the high court's opinion with cheers, toasts, and impromptu dancing, but according to one report, Thurgood Marshall, one of the chief architects of the litigation wandered morosely through the happy throng frowning. "You fools go ahead and have your fun," he said, "but we ain't begun to work yet."[1] Marshall's prediction was both prophetic and a highly accurate commentary on the black experience. Even so, the staff had reason to celebrate. The organization was doing what its founders had intended.

The National Association for the Advancement of Colored People (NAACP) was founded in 1909. Its founders, an interracial group of liberal lawyers and socialists, concerned with the nonenforcement of the Fourteenth and Fifteenth Amendments, saw the need for an organization that would effectively press for political, legal, and educational rights. They sought an end to segregation, the right to work, and the right to protection from violence and intimidation. The need for the NAACP was clear.

In the previous year, in addition to the several dozen blacks lynched each year, thousands of whites rioted in Springfield, Illinois. They killed six blacks, two by lynching, and burned and destroyed black homes and businesses. Two thousand blacks left the city but none of the alleged riot leaders were punished, although the city obtained indictments following the restoration of order. The white community launched a political and economic boycott to drive out the remaining black residents.[2]

After its founding, the NAACP established a legal redress committee, and in the next decades several of its cases reached the Supreme Court. It successfully challenged a municipal ordinance requiring residential segregation,[3] and overturned a conviction of a black man that had been obtained in a mob-dominated proceeding.[4] During the 1920s, the NAACP was involved in the defense of blacks charged in interracial crimes, additional challenges to racially restrictive zoning and covenants, and ongoing attacks on the white primary in Texas.[5]

During this period, the NAACP magazine, *The Crisis*, begun and edited by W. E. B. Du Bois, began publishing the results of serious studies of the financing of Negro schools in several southern states. The disparities were shocking. Georgia in 1926 had an average per-pupil expenditure of $36.29 for whites and $4.59 for blacks, and average teachers' salaries of $97.88 per month for whites and $49.41 for blacks. North Carolina was seen as the most enlightened state, in which disparities were on the order of 2 to 1 rather than from 5–8 to 1 in other southern states.[6]

After a great deal of disagreement as to how best to use quite-limited funds, the NAACP launched a program in the mid-1930s to equalize teacher salaries. There were many obstacles, not the least of which was the difficulty in finding teachers willing to risk their positions in order to challenge their employers. In addition, there were few local black lawyers able and willing to handle the litigation. School boards resisted with all manner of procedural roadblocks, and courts were far from objective even though the salary disparities' violation of the "separate but equal" standard was clear. Slowly, the NAACP's legal staff, now under the direction of Thurgood Marshall, determined that a direct attack on segregation was more feasible than individual suits intended to equalize facilities and salaries.

The long and laboriously prepared road leading to the Supreme Court's repudiation of state-sanctioned segregation gained real momentum following victories by the NAACP lawyers in several cases requiring the admission of black plaintiffs into previously all-white, state-run graduate schools. The Supreme Court held that the "separate but equal" rationale for racial segregation required relief even though the state provided allegedly equal segregated facilities within the state, or was willing to pay tuition to blacks who enrolled in out-of-state schools.[7]

Encouraged by these decisions, Thurgood Marshall launched a full-scale assault on segregated schools in a case to desegregate the University of Texas Law School. But as in the other graduate school cases, the Court granted relief to the plaintiff without reaching the issue of the constitutionality of separate but equal educational facilities.[8] The NAACP had won several battles, but the overriding goal remained the total destruction of state-enforced segregation.

In carefully planned and executed litigation, Marshall was able, in *Brown*, to get the Court to hear four school desegregation cases, which it consolidated in *Brown v. Board of Education*.[9] The facts and local conditions were different, but all posed a common legal question: whether public schools under the Constitution could operate on a racially segregated basis.

The school boards relied on the "separate but equal" doctrine announced by the Supreme Court in 1896.[10] Plaintiffs argued that segregated public schools were not and could not be made equal, thus denying their clients the substance of the most important protection promised by the Fourteenth Amendment, the equal protection of the laws.

Having avoided the question for so long, the Court first searched diligently in the legislative history of the Fourteenth Amendment for the framers' view on this issue. There was much to argue on either side, but Chief Justice Earl Warren concluded that the evidence was "inconclusive." For one thing, the status of public education had greatly changed in the intervening decades. In the young nation there were few public schools and most blacks were illiterate; therefore, any views concerning education held by those who drafted or voted for the Fourteenth Amendment would have little contemporary relevance.

Thus Chief Justice Warren decided that the Court could not "turn the clock back to 1868 when the Fourteenth Amendment was adopted, or even to 1896 when the Court had approved state mandated segregation if facilities were separate but equal." Rather, public education had to be considered "in the light of its whole development and its present place in American life throughout the nation. Only in this way can it be determined if segregation in public schools deprived these plaintiffs of the equal protection of the laws."[11]

Then, in terms that have been frequently quoted, Chief Justice Warren described public education as "perhaps the most important function of state and local governments." He noted that both compulsory school attendance laws and the great expenditures for education demonstrate our recognition of the importance of education to our democratic society. Pointing out that an education is required in the performance of our most basic public responsibilities, including service in the armed forces, he concluded that it was the very foundation of good citizenship.

Expressing doubt that any child can be expected to succeed in life if denied the opportunity for an education, Chief Justice Warren found that where the state has undertaken to provide schooling to its children, it must be made available to all on equal terms. With this foundation, Warren reached the major issue in the case: Does segregation of children in public schools solely on the basis of race, even though the physical facilities and other "tangible" factors may be equal, deprive the children of the minority group of equal educational opportunities?

His answer came quickly: "We believe that it does." It is particularly important for children in elementary and secondary schools, he said, because: "[t]o separate them from others of similar age and qualifications solely because of their race generates a feeling of inferiority as to their status in the community that may affect their hearts and minds in a way unlikely ever to be undone."[12]

The opinion concluded in terms of triumph, or so they must have sounded to the NAACP lawyers: "In the field of public education, the doctrine of 'separate but equal' has no place. Separate educational facilities are inherently unequal." Thus, the plaintiffs' rights under the equal protection clause were deemed violated by the segregation they complained of.

Departing from earlier precedents holding that violations of individual constitutional rights should be immediately remedied, Warren explained that because of the "wide applicability of this decision, and because of the great variety of local conditions, the formulation of decrees in these cases present problems of considerable complexity." Having found that segregation in public schools is a denial of the equal protection of the laws, the Court postponed action and scheduled the cases for further argument on questions of relief.

*   *   *

The following year, after considering the further arguments it had requested on the issue of relief, the Court issued a second decision in *Brown v. Board of Education* (*Brown II*)[13] This time, working from the ideological foundation that segregated education denied the constitutional guarantee of equal protection of the laws, the Court addressed itself to the question of what remedy should be granted. The attorney general and those states requiring or permitting segregated public schools both urged that the cases be remanded to the district courts. Rejecting the NAACP's requests that desegregation be ordered immediately, the Court opted for a procedure that would permit each lower court to resolve for itself the administrative and academic problems presented by compliance.

The Court expected a "prompt and reasonable start toward full compliance, with defendants carrying the burden of showing that requests for additional time are necessary in the public interest and consistent with good faith compliance at the earliest practicable date." Enumerating a number of possible problems in transportation, personnel, and revision of school districts in attendance areas, the Court returned the cases to the district courts with the admonition that orders and decrees be entered to admit plaintiffs to public schools on a racially nondiscriminatory basis "with all deliberate speed. . . ."[14]

*   *   *

The "all deliberate speed" instruction was an unknown and never really defined legal standard that those committed to segregation interpreted as never. Black people were disappointed rather than dismayed when the Court delayed specific relief for a year and then, in 1955, returned the cases to the lower courts for enforcement. Reflecting that disappointment, civil rights lawyer-historian Loren Miller wrote at the time, "The harsh truth is that the first *Brown* decision was a great decision; the second *Brown* decision was a great mistake."[15]

J. Harvie Wilkinson III, now a federal judge but writing as a University of Virginia professor two decades after *Brown*, offered practical details of why *Brown II* was a mistake. *Brown II*, he felt, left federal judges far too exposed; it "gave trial judges little to wrap in or hide behind. The enormous discretion of the trial judge in interpreting such language as 'all deliberate speed' and 'prompt and reasonable start' made his personal role painfully obvious." The judge who, in trying to enforce *Brown*, did more than the bare minimum, would be held unpleasantly accountable by the very active, vocal, and powerful opposition that surrounded him. Wilkinson explained:

> Segregationists were always able to point to more indulgent judges elsewhere. *Brown II* thus resembled nothing more than an order for the infantry to assault segregation without prospect of air or artillery support. That some of the infantry lacked enthusiasm for the cause only made matters worse. . . . Given the vague and sparse character of *Brown II* and the Court's low profile thereafter, stagnation was inevitable.[16]

Having promised much in its first *Brown* decision, the Court in *Brown II* said in effect that its landmark earlier decision was more symbolic than real. As the designated, subordinate "other" in the society without real economic and political power, blacks, of necessity, have recognized and tried to give substance to the potential in symbols. Even so, looking back across fifty years of measurable progress mixed with unmeasurable frustration, one might expect that even its supporters would be disappointed by recognition of what the *Brown* decision did not do and probably could not have done.

Its advocates expected that the *Brown* decision would cut through the dark years of segregation with laserlike intensity. The resistance, though, was open and determined. At best, the *Brown* precedent did no more than cast a half-light on that resistance, enough to encourage its supporters but not bright enough to reveal just how long and difficult the road to equal educational opportunity would prove to be. Contending with that resistance made it unlikely that any of those trying to implement *Brown*, including myself, would stop to consider that we might be on the wrong road.

3

BROWN RECONCEIVED
An Alternative Scenario

HAVING READ AN EARLY DRAFT OF THIS MANUSCRIPT, longtime friend and Harvard University professor Frank Michelman asked: "Was there any way that they, as a Court acting subject to certain public expectations about the differences among courts, legislatures, and constitutional conventions, could have framed their intervention differently from, and better than, the way they actually chose?"

I think the answer is yes. Despite decades of efforts to reverse *Plessy v. Ferguson* and the NAACP lawyers' well-researched legal arguments supported by reams of social science testimony, the Supreme Court might have determined to adhere to existing precedents. Suppose that, while expressing sympathy for the Negroes' plight, the Court had decided that *Plessy v. Ferguson* was still the law of the land? Suppose, moreover, they understood then what is so much clearer now: namely, that the edifice of segregation was built not simply on a troubling judicial precedent, but on an unspoken covenant committing the nation to guaranteeing whites a superior status to blacks?

On this understanding, could the Court have written a decision that disappointed the hopes of most civil rights lawyers and those they represented while opening up opportunities for effective schooling capable of turning constitutional defeat into a major educational victory? Again, I think the answer is yes. And I have imagined such an alternative.

The Supreme Court of the United States
May 17, 1954

Today we uphold our six decades old decision in Plessy v. Ferguson, *163 U.S. 537 (1896). We do so with some reluctance and in the face of the arguments by the petitioners that segregation in the public schools is unconstitutional and a manifestation of the desire for dominance whose depths and pervasiveness this Court can neither ignore nor easily divine. Giving full weight to these arguments, a decision overturning* Plessy, *while it might be viewed as a triumph by Negro petitioners and the class they represent, will be condemned by many whites. Their predictable outraged resistance could undermine and eventually negate even the most committed judicial enforcement efforts.*

No less a personage than Justice Oliver Wendell Holmes acknowledged the limits of judicial authority when, speaking for the Court in a 1903 voting rights case from Alabama, he denied the relief sought by black voters because if, as the black petitioners alleged, the great mass of the white population intended to keep the blacks from voting, it would do little good to give black voters an order that would be ignored at the local level. "Apart from damages to the individual," Holmes explained, "relief from a great political wrong, if done, as alleged by the people of a state and the state itself, must be given by them or by the legislative and political department of the Government of the United States."[1]

While giving racial discrimination the sanction of law, Justice Holmes refused either to interfere or to acknowledge the status-affirming role for whites reflected in their refusal to grant blacks even the basic citizenship right to vote. The Court in Plessy v. Ferguson *had done the same seven years earlier when, by distinguishing between the denial of political rights and the separation of the races on a social basis, the Court rejected Homer Plessy's argument that this law-enforced separation branded blacks with a "badge of inferiority."*[2]

Respondents' counsel, John W. Davis, a highly respected advocate, urges this Court to uphold "separate but equal" as the constitutionally correct measure of racial status because, as he put it so elegantly: "somewhere, sometime to every principle comes a moment of repose when it has been so often announced, so confidently relied upon, so long continued, that it passes the limits of judicial discretion and disturbance."[3]

Elegance, though, must not be allowed to trample long-suppressed truth. The "separate" in the "separate but equal" standard has been rigorously enforced. The "equal" has served as a total refutation of equality. Within the limits of judicial authority, the Court recognizes these cases as an opportunity to test the legal legitimacy of the "separate but equal" standard, not as petitioners urge by overturning Plessy, *but by ordering for the first time its strict enforcement.*

Counsel for the Negro children have gone to great lengths to prove what must be obvious to every person who gives the matter even cursory attention: With some notable exceptions, schools provided for Negroes in segregated systems are unequal in facilities—often obscenely so. Unfortunately, this Court in violation of Plessy's *"separate but equal" standard, rejected challenges to state-run schools that were both segregated and ruinously unequal.*

Hardly three years after setting the "separate but equal" standard, this Court blunted the equal prong with "practical considerations." When black parents sought to enjoin a Georgia school board from collecting school tax levies from them for a black high school it had closed while continuing to operate the white high school, Justice Harlan, speaking for the Court, reasoned that enjoining the board from operating a high school for whites would deprive whites of a high school education without regaining the black high school that had served sixty, and that had been turned into a primary school for three hundred children. Given the board's limited resources, he found their decision reasonable.[4]

Justice Harlan returned to his dissenting role in race cases when the Court upheld a Kentucky statute subjecting Berea College, a private college that admitted both white and black students, to a heavy fine.[5] *Because the state had chartered the private school and could revoke the charter, it could also amend it to prohibit instruction of the two races at the same time and in the same place. Harlan pointed out that the precedent could bar minority association with whites in churches, markets, and other public places, a warning that by 1908 had become fact in many jurisdictions.*[6]

In recent years, this Court, acknowledging the flouting of the "separate but equal" standard at the graduate school level, ordered black plaintiffs into previously all-white graduate programs. In Sweatt v. Painter,[7] *the most significant of these cases, Texas denied admission to a black law school applicant, Herman Marion Sweatt. When Sweatt filed suit, the state sought to meet the separate but equal standard by setting up a small law school in three basement rooms eight blocks from the University of Texas Law School. It would have no regular faculty or library and was not accredited. This Court, in ordering Sweatt's admission, considered both its inadequate facilities and the intangible assets of the white law school, including its reputation and the value of interaction with its faculty, student body, and alumni, which include most of the state's lawyers and judges.*

Encouraged by those decisions, petitioners now urge that we extend those holdings to encompass segregation in literally thousands of public school districts. In support, their counsel speak eloquently both of the great disparities in resources and of the damage segregation does to Negro children's hearts and minds. We recognize and do not wish to rebut petitioner's evidence of this psychological damage.

Rather, we suggest that segregation perpetuates the sense of white children that their privileged status as whites is deserved rather than bestowed by law and tradition. We hold that racial segregation afflicts white children with a lifelong mental and emotional handicap that is as destructive to whites as the required strictures of segregation are to Negroes.

Again, it would seem appropriate to declare wrong what is clearly wrong. Given the history of segregation and the substantial reliance placed on our decisions as to its constitutionality, though, a finding by this Court in these cases that state supported racial segregation is an obsolete artifact of a bygone age, one that no longer conforms to the Constitution, will set the stage not for compliance, but for levels of defiance that will prove the antithesis of the equal educational opportunity the petitioners seek.

The desegregation of public schools is a special matter, the complexity of which is not adequately addressed in the petitioners' arguments. In urging this Court to strike down state-mandated segregation, the petitioners ignore the admonishment of W. E. B. Du Bois, one of the nation's finest thinkers. Commenting on the separate school–integrated school debate back in 1935, Dr. Du Bois observed that: "Negro children needed neither segregated schools nor mixed schools. What they need is education."[8]

We are aware as well that despite the tremendous barriers to good schools posed by the Plessy *"separate but equal" standard, some black schools, through great and dedicated effort by teachers and parents, achieved academic distinction. Many of the most successful blacks today are products of segregated schools and colleges. In urging what they hope will be a brighter tomorrow, petitioners need not cast aside the miracles of achievement attained in the face of monumental obstacles. While truly harmed by racial segregation, there is far too much contrary evidence for this Court to find that Negroes are a damaged race.*

We conclude that Dr. Du Bois's opinion is right as regards educational matters, and that as regards legal matters, his still-accurate admonition can be given meaning within the structure of the Plessy v. Ferguson *holding.*

The three phases of relief that we will describe below focus attention on what is needed now by the children of both races. It is the only way to avoid a generation or more of strife over an ideal that, while worthwhile, will not provide the effective education petitioners' children need and that existing constitutional standards, stripped of their racist understandings, should safeguard.

While declaring racial segregation harmful to Negro children, the unhappy fact is that as the nation's racial history makes clear, racial division has been a source of much undeserved benefit to whites and a great deal of misery to Negroes. And as is always the case, oppression is harmful to the oppressor as well as the oppressed. We accept the expert testimony submitted in this case that a great many white as well as Negro children have been harmed by segregation.

Pressured by this litigation, the school boards assure this Court that they are taking admittedly tardy steps to equalize facilities in Negro schools. We find these measures worthwhile, but woefully inadequate to remedy injustices carried on for most of a century. This being the case, more important than striking down Plessy v. Ferguson *is the need to reveal its hypocritical underpinnings by requiring its full enforcement for all children, white as well as black. Full enforcement requires more than either equalizing facilities or, as in the case of Delaware, one of the five cases before the Court, ordering plaintiffs, because of the inadequacy of the Negro schools, to be admitted into the white schools.*

Realistic rather than symbolic relief for segregated schools will require a specific, judicially monitored plan designed primarily to provide the educational equity long denied under the separate but equal rhetoric. This Court finds that it has the authority to grant such relief under the precedent of Plessy v. Ferguson. *As a primary step toward the disestablishment of the dual school system, this Court will order relief that must be provided all children in racially segregated districts in the following components:*

1. Equalization. *Effective immediately on receipt of this Court's mandate, lower courts will order school officials of the respondent school districts to:*

(A) ascertain through appropriate measures the academic standing of each school district as compared to nationwide norms for school systems of comparable size and financial resources. These data, gathered under the direction and supervision of the district courts, will be published and made available to all patrons of the district, white as well as black.

(B) equalize all schools within the district, including resources, physical

facilities, teacher-pupil ratios, teacher training, experience, and salary, with the goal of each district, as a whole, measuring up to national norms within three years. School districts will report progress to the court annually.

2. Representation. *The battle cry of those who fought and died to bring this country into existence was: "taxation without representation is tyranny." Effective relief in segregated school districts requires no less than the immediate restructuring of school boards and other policy-making bodies to insure that those formally excluded by race from representation have persons selected by them in accordance with the percentage of their children in the school system. This restructuring must take effect no later than the start of the 1955–1956 school year.*

3. Judicial Oversight. *To effectuate the efficient implementation of these orders, federal district judges will establish three-person monitoring committees, with the Negro and white communities each selecting a monitor and a third person with educational expertise selected by an appropriate federal agency. The monitoring committees will work with school officials to prepare the necessary plans and procedures enabling the school districts' compliance with phases 1 and 2. The district courts will give compliance oversight priority attention and will address firmly any actions intended to subvert or hinder the compliance program.*

School districts that fail to move promptly to comply with the equalization standards set out above will be deemed in noncompliance. Following a judicial determination to this effect, courts will determine whether such noncompliance with the "separate but equal" standard justifies relief such as we have ordered in the graduate school cases, including orders to promptly desegregate their schools by racially balancing the student and faculty populations in each school.

In this Court's view, the petitioners' goal—the disestablishment of the dual school system—will be more effectively achieved for students, parents, teachers, administrators, and other individuals connected directly or indirectly with the school system by these means rather than by a ringing order for immediate desegregation that we fear will not be effectively enforced and will be vigorously resisted. Our expectations in this regard are strengthened by the experience in the Delaware case, where school officials unable to finance the equalization of separate schools opted to desegregate those schools.

We recognize that this decision comports with neither the hopes for orders requiring immediate desegregation by petitioners nor the states' contentions that we should simply reject those petitions and retain the racial status quo.

Our goal, though, is not to determine winners and losers. It is, rather, our obligation to unravel the nation's greatest contradiction as it pertains to the public schools. Justice John Marshall Harlan, while dissenting in Plessy, *perhaps unwittingly articulated this contradiction in definitive fashion when he observed:*

> *The white race deems itself to be the dominant race in this country. And so it is, in prestige, in achievements, in education, in wealth and in power. So, I doubt not, it will continue to be for all time, if it remains true to its great heritage and holds fast to the principles of constitutional liberty. But in view of the Constitution, in the eye of the law, there is in this country no superior, dominant, ruling class of citizens. There is no caste here. Our Constitution is color-blind, and neither knows nor tolerates classes among citizens.*[9]

The existence of a dominant white race and the concept of color blindness are polar opposites. The Fourteenth Amendment's equal protection clause cannot easily ferret out the racial injustice masquerading in seemingly neutral terms like "separate but equal" and "color blindness." It has proven barely adequate as a shield against some of the most pernicious modes of racial violence and economic domination. The clause, perhaps unfortunately given its origins, most comfortably serves to adjudicate relationships between legally recognized categories of business or other entities (rather than squarely addressing the validity of the state's exercise of coercion against a whole group).

This Court does not ignore the value of simply recognizing the evil of segregation, an evil Negroes have experienced firsthand for too long. There is, we also agree, a place for symbols in law for a people abandoned by law for much of the nation's history. We recognize and hail the impressive manner in which Negroes have taken symbolic gains and given them meaning by the sheer force of their belief in the freedoms this country guarantees to all. Is it not precisely because of their unstinting faith in this country's ideals that they deserve better than a well-intended but empty and probably unenforceable expression of equality, no matter how well meant? Such a decision will serve as sad substitute for the needed empathy of action called for when a history of racial subordination is to be undone.

The racial reform–retrenchment pattern so evident in this Court's racial decisions enables a prediction that, when the tides of white resentment rise and again swamp the expectations of Negroes in a flood of racial hostility, this Court, and probably the country, will vacillate; then, as with the

Emancipation Proclamation and the Civil War amendments, it will ratio-nalize its inability and—let us be honest—its unwillingness to give real meaning to the rights we declare so readily yet so willingly sacrifice when our interests turn to new issues and more pressing concerns.

It is to avoid still another instance of this outcome that we reject the peti-tioners' plea that the Court overturn Plessy forthwith. Doing so would systematically gloss over the extent to which Plessy's simplistic "separate but equal" form served as a legal adhesive in the consolidation of white supremacy in America. Rather than critically engaging American racism's complexities, this Court would substitute one mantra for another: where "separate" was once equal, "separate" would be now categorically unequal. Restructuring the rhetoric of equality (rather than laying bare Plessy's white-supremacy underpinnings and consequences) constructs state-supported racial segregation as an eminently fixable aberration. And yet, by doing nothing more than reworking the rhetoric of equality, this Court would fore-close the possibility of recognizing racism as a broadly shared cultural condition.

Imagining racism as a fixable aberration, moreover, obfuscates the way in which racism functions as an ideological lens through which Americans perceive themselves, their nation, and their nation's other. Second, the vision of racism as an unhappy accident of history immunizes "the law" (as a logical system) from antiracist critique. That is to say, the Court would position the law as that which fixes racism rather than that which participates in its consolidation. By dismissing Plessy without dismantling it, the Court might unintentionally predict if not underwrite eventual failure. Negroes, who, despite all, are perhaps the nation's most faithful citizens, deserve better.

* * *

Had this been the *Brown* decision handed down in 1954, both civil rights and school board lawyers would probably, for differing reasons, have condemned it. Yet it makes sense today. As Duke University law professor Jerome Culp suggests:

> A gradualist approach would have been less acrimonious and would have avoided the emergence of political forces in both political parties—forces that have helped to elect every nonincumbent Repub-lican president since that time, and have created a minor political force inside the Democratic party for cutting back the requirement of racial justice."[10]

Yet later in the same article, Professor Culp acknowledges that the *Brown* opinion's nongradualist approach "did challenge the fundamental assumption of inferiority that underlay the *Plessy* regime and had supported the racial status quo."[11] To assess whether the symbolism inherent in the *Brown* opinion was of more value than my pragmatic approach, I will review in chapters 4 through 6 the racial background of the *Brown* decision in respect to policies around slavery and emancipation, as well as the fear during the post–World War II years of the spread of communism. I will then lay out my developing understanding of how these influences have played out over the years since.

4

THE RACIAL-SACRIFICE COVENANTS

IN PREHISTORIC TIMES, a people fearing that they had irritated their gods would seek to make amends by sacrificing a lamb, a goat, or sometimes a young virgin. Somehow, the shedding of innocent blood effected a renewed connection between the people and their gods. A similar though seldom recognized phenomenon has occurred throughout American racial history. To settle potentially costly differences between two opposing groups of whites, a compromise is effected that depends on the involuntary sacrifice of black rights or interests. Even less recognized, these compromises (actually silent covenants) not only harm blacks but also disadvantage large groups of whites, including those who support the arrangements. Examples of this involuntary racial-sacrifice phenomenon abound and continue. A few of the more important are: the slavery understandings, the Constitution, universal white male suffrage, the *Dred Scott v. Sandford* case, the Hayes-Tilden compromise, and the southern disenfranchisement compromise. Contemporary sacrifices of black rights and interests underlie policies on the death penalty, drug-penalty sentencing rules, and reliance on standardized test scores in college and graduate school admissions procedures.

The Slavery Understanding

Historian Edmund Morgan explains that plantation owners in the early seventeenth century recognized that they needed a stable work force to grow and profit from tobacco. Because Native Americans would escape or die, and the indentures of whites came to an end, the solution, over a decade or so, was to sentence African laborers to slavery—indenture for life. The landowners convinced working-class whites to support African enslavement as being in their interests, even though these yeoman workers could never compete with wealthy landowners who could afford slaves.[1]

Slaveholders appealed to working-class whites by giving them the chance to vote and by urging them, owing to their shared whiteness, to unite against the threat of slave revolts or escapes. The strategy worked. Wealthy whites retained all their former prerogatives, but the creation of a black subclass enabled poor whites to identify with and support the policies of the upper class. With the safe economic advantage provided by their slaves, large landowners were willing to grant poor whites a larger role in the political process. Thus, paradoxically, slavery for blacks led both to greater freedom for poor whites and an economic structure that would keep them poor.

In the main, poor whites in the seventeenth century were willing to subordinate their economic hopes for feelings of racial superiority. In their poverty, whites vented their frustrations at what had been a mainly unsatisfying trade-off. They hated the slaves rather than their masters, who held both black slave and free white in economic bondage. Slavery ended, but the economic disparities between rich and working-class whites, camouflaged by racial division, continued unabated. When Americans formed a new government, even its vaunted commitment to principles of individual liberty were not strong enough to overcome the by-then settled policies of African slavery and their adverse economic impact on white workers.

The Constitution

By 1776, when the American colonies were ready in the name of individual rights to rebel against English domination, slavery had been established for more than a century. The Revolutionary period thus revealed the white majority's increasing ambivalence regarding the status of blacks. Clearly, recognition of individual rights demanded by white Americans for themselves stood in contradiction to the suppression of those rights for blacks, both free and slave, living in their midst. Lawyer-historian Staughton Lynd concluded that the contradictions were rationalized by economic concerns and resolved by the almost universal belief in Negro inferiority.[2]

Prior to the Revolutionary War, most of the colonies levied taxes on the importation of slaves and enjoyed a comfortable revenue from this source. Indeed, the war through which the nation gained its independence was financed in substantial part out of the profits of slavery. But one by one, many of the colonies imposed statutory restrictions on the importation of slaves or banned the trade entirely. In the main, these statutes reflected the colonists' constant fear of slave insurrections. In the northern colonies, the acts were also the result of white immigrants' opposition to slave labor and, to some extent, the activities of abolitionists.

At the first Continental Congress in 1774, efforts to halt the importation of slaves came to little. Even the criticism of the slave traffic included in Jefferson's first draft of the Declaration of Independence was stricken in the final version. By the close of the Revolutionary War, the pressures to fully reopen the profitable African slave trade were great, particularly since, as a result of the fighting, the slaves, "by pillage, flight, and actual fighting, had become so reduced in numbers . . . that an urgent demand for more laborers was felt in the South."[3]

The Congress of the Confederation took virtually no action against the slave trade. Indeed, the only legislative activity in regard to the trade prior to the Constitutional Convention in 1787 came from the individual states. During this period, pressured by abolitionists' moral appeals, fear of slave revolts, and the opposition of white laborers, Connecticut, Vermont, Pennsylvania, Delaware, and Virginia prohibited by law the further importation of slaves. Out of fear that the addition of more slaves would drive down their prices, the New England and middle states, including Maryland, practically ceased their importation.[4]

Those who gathered in Philadelphia in 1787 to write the constitution establishing the framework of the new federal government, certainly knew that slavery was an accepted American institution, but they were divided on how to handle the issue. Among the framers were some who abhorred the "peculiar institution." Thomas Jefferson, himself a slaveowner, while not present in Philadelphia, had often expressed his view that slavery "brutalizes slave owner as well as slave" and, worst of all, tends to undermine the "only firm basis of liberty, the conviction in the minds of the people that liberty is the gift of God."[5]

Gouverneur Morris, one of the convention's most outspoken opponents of slavery, conceded his ambivalence in the convention debates of July 5 and 6 when he said that "Life and liberty were generally said to be of more value, than property," but that "an accurate view of the matter would nevertheless prove that property was the main object of Society."[6] Some of the delegates were sympathetic to the petitions for freedom of Africans and abolitionists speaking in their behalf. Some were not. They debated the issue at length and their negotiations led to compromises.

The unresolvable dilemma for abolitionists was stated succinctly by another delegate, Charles Cotesworth Pinckney: "Property in slaves should not be exposed to danger under a Government instituted for the protection of property." This was not merely a theoretical consideration for the North. As Madison recalled as late as 1833, a compromise on the slavery issue would also advance the interests of many northerners, including merchants, shipowners, and manufacturers. But personal interest aside, as Professor Lynd pointed out, "The belief that private property was the indispensable foundation for personal freedom made it more difficult for northerners to confront the fact of slavery squarely."[7]

Compromises reached, the delegates handled the question of slavery as an economic and political rather than a moral matter. This morally neutral approach was deemed necessary in light of the sensitivity of southern delegates, who would brook no interference with their institution. Even so, the delegates apparently recognized that slavery was ultimately incompatible with the doctrines of freedom and liberty that characterized this "revolutionary generation." The delegates hypocritically avoided the word "slaves," referring instead to "persons" whom the states shall think it proper to import, or "persons" bound to service or labor. Evasion, though, was insufficient to disguise the sacrifice of those who would suffer the cruelty of slavery.

While insuring that the foundation of our basic law would recognize rights to life and liberty for every citizen, the framers knew that the new nation would continue the systematic denial of rights to those of African descent. The other factor which led the North to acquiesce to a slavery-permitting federal government grew out of the difficulty even the most liberal of the framers had in imagining a society in which whites and blacks would live together as fellow citizens. As Jefferson suggested, honor and intellectual consistency drove them to favor abolition; personal distaste, to fear it. At another point, Jefferson wrote: "Nothing is more certainly written in the book of fate, than that these people are to be free; nor is it less certain that the two races, equally free, cannot live in the same government."

Professor Lynd concludes:

> Unable to summon the moral imagination required to transcend race prejudice, unwilling to contemplate social experiments which impinged on private property, the Fathers, unhappily, ambivalently, confusedly, passed by on the other side. Their much-praised deistic coolness of temper could not help them here. The compromise of 1787 was a critical, albeit characteristic, failure of the American pragmatic intelligence.[8]

In at least ten provisions the framers, in compromises with the southern delegates and other defenders of slavery, agreed to language that both gave legitimacy to slavery and provided for its protection.[9] The framers decided that the hopes of blacks, free and slave, for inclusion in the new government guaranteeing liberty for all, must be sacrificed to resolve conflicts between whites of differing views.

Black people knew what they had lost in the negotiating process. Then and later, they understood, as Frederick Douglass put it in an 1849 speech, that the Constitution, while cunningly framed, "was made in view of the existence of slavery, and in a manner well calculated to aid and strengthen that heaven-daring crime." Even after the Civil War and the enactment of the post–Civil War amendments, Douglass in 1887 refused to join in the Constitution's centennial celebrations because "[s]o far as the colored people of the country are concerned, the Constitution is but a stupendous sham . . . keeping the promise to the eye and breaking it to the heart. . . . They have promised us law and abandoned us to anarchy.[10]

Universal White Male Suffrage

At least the framers debated slavery. There was, by contrast, little discussion of the political rights of white men who were not landowners or in possession of status based on earnings and savings. All agreed that the new government should be firmly in the hands of the elite. Indeed, the convention itself was motivated by small landholders who rose up in opposition to both high taxes and stringent economic conditions. To prevent foreclosures, armed bands of men forced the closing of several courts as a means of preventing execution of fore-closures and other creditor-initiated court actions. From August 1786 until February 1787, Daniel Shays, a Revolutionary War veteran, and other local leaders in western Massachusetts led several hundred men in forcing the Supreme Court in Springfield to adjourn. In January 1787, Shays led a force of about twelve hundred men in an attack on the federal arsenal at Springfield. The attack failed and Shays fled to Vermont. The willingness of small farmers to fight led the Massachu-setts legislature to enact laws easing the economic condition of debtors.

The framers were not much interested in providing a provision for universal suffrage in the Constitution, and none was provided. Thus, each state set its own voting requirements, which usually included residence and property ownership. In the first half of the nineteenth century, advocates and opponents of expanding the right to vote often resolved their differences through compromises that banned blacks from the polls while opening them to white men.[11] By 1840, 93 percent of the northern free black population lived in states that completely or practically excluded them from the right to vote. Only in New England, where many free blacks had lived for decades and where, in any event, their numbers were few, could blacks vote on an equal basis with whites. New York set property and residence require-ments for black voters not required for whites, and New Jersey, Connecticut, and Pennsylvania eventually barred blacks entirely, although at an earlier time theoretically they had the right to vote.

Even that "right," as Alexis de Tocqueville found, was more theo-retical than real. In his 1832 journal he wrote:

> I said one day to an inhabitant of Pennsylvania: "Be so good as to explain to me how it happens that in a state founded by Quakers, and celebrated for its toleration, free blacks are not allowed to exercise civil rights. They pay taxes; is it not fair that they should vote?"
>
> "You insult us," replied my informant, "if you imagine that our legislators could have committed so gross an act of injustice and intolerance."

"Then the blacks possess the right of voting in this country?"

"Without a doubt."

"How come it, then, that at the polling-booth this morning I did not perceive a single Negro?"

"That is not the fault of the law. The Negroes have an undisputed right of voting, but they voluntarily abstain from making their appearance."

" A very pretty piece of modesty on their part" rejoined I.

"Why, the truth is that they are not disinclined to vote, but they are afraid of being maltreated; in this country the law is sometimes unable to maintain its authority without the support of the majority. But in this case the majority entertains very strong prejudices against the blacks, and the magistrates are unable to protect them in the exercise of their legal rights."

"Then the majority claims the right not only of making the laws, but of breaking the laws it has made?"[12]

Professor Leon Litwack reports that the adoption of white male suffrage led directly to the political disenfranchisement of the Negro. Those who opposed an expanded electorate for both whites and Negroes warned that it would, among other things, grant the Negro political power. Even the friends of equal suffrage harbored reservations. One Pennsylvanian, for example, opposed disenfranchisement but conceded that Negroes "in their present depressed and un-cultivated condition" were not "a desirable species of population," and he "should not prefer them as a matter of choice." Such admissions as these by "friends" hardly added to the popular acceptance of Negro suffrage. Those courageous enough to actually advocate for the right of Negroes to vote found themselves labeled as either radical amalgamationists or hypocrites for advancing so dangerous a doctrine. Deploying various political, social, economic, and pseudo-anthropological arguments, white suffragists moved to deny the vote to the Negro. From the admission of Maine in 1819 until the end of the Civil War, every new state restricted suffrage to whites in its constitution.

Without formality, whites of widely varying viewpoints on the issue of universal suffrage, through their general agreement that blacks should not be permitted to vote, were able to compromise on other differences. It is as though the presence of blacks was a reminder to all whites that, whatever their differences, they must unite to protect themselves against the black citizens in their midst. Thus, racially catalyzed, they moved quickly to resolve even disagreements on matters having nothing to do with race. Somehow race, while not on the table, influenced policy decisions often to the disadvantage of working-class whites.

Dred Scott v. Sandford

Over time, the economic and political friction between free and slave states worsened. Congress had expended great effort to balance the conflicting economic interests of slave and free states in the Missouri Compromise of 1820. The sectional controversy over the extension of slavery continued to escalate over the next forty years and was marked by additional congressional efforts to balance the interests of pro- and antislavery forces. The interests of slaves and free blacks usually were not either the principal concerns of the two factions or the basis of compromises that they reached.

In the courts, controversy broke out over scores of lawsuits seeking to use the judicial forums of free states to win freedom for slaves who escaped or were brought by their masters from slave states. Earlier in the 1820s and 1830s, courts in slave states recognized that slaves could be freed if they were taken by their masters and remained in free states for more than short periods of time. As tensions grew, free states that earlier accommodated the slave-protective interests of slaveholding states began to refuse to recognize the enslaved status of anyone within their borders, even of those slaves merely passing through with their masters or those fleeing and required under federal law to be returned. Southern states retaliated by refusing to follow their earlier decisions recognizing the freed status of slaves gained while in free territory.

Dred Scott v. Sandford was the culmination of a very controversial case in which a southern state court rejected its earlier leniency in such litigation.[13] Scott was owned by an army surgeon, Dr. John Emerson, who moved him first from a military post in Missouri to the free state of Illinois where he resided for two years, and then to a portion of Louisiana where, under the Missouri Compromise, slavery was forever forbidden. Emerson granted Scott the right to marry Harriet, a slave, and two children, Eliza and Lizzie, were born to the couple. Two years later, in 1838, Emerson moved Scott and his family back to Missouri where, in 1852, Scott sued Emerson for his freedom under common law rules providing that the lengthy period in free territory had ended his bondage. Scott won in the trial court, but the Missouri Supreme Court reversed, overturning a number of its earlier decisions to find that Dred Scott had not been rendered free as a result of having spent four years in nonslave areas.[14]

Emerson died, and Scott and his family were bequeathed to John F. A. Sandford, a citizen of New York. Scott then sued in federal court under rules of diversity that give federal courts jurisdiction when a citizen of one state sued a citizen of another. Having lost in the lower court, Scott appealed to the U.S. Supreme Court, where the case was heard twice. Chief Justice Roger Taney could have rejected Dred Scott's claim on the procedural ground that, as a noncitizen, he could not invoke the Court's diversity jurisdiction. In his effort to settle the slavery issue once and for all, Taney was willing to sacrifice any entitlement to citizenship for all blacks, whatever their status. He ruled that Dred Scott could not be freed by his master's sojourn in a free territory and, indeed, because of his race, was not eligible to become a citizen under any circumstances.

Taney ruled that the carefully negotiated arrangements under the Missouri Compromise would deprive slave owners of their property in violation of the Constitution's due process clause. The ruling that Congress had no power to exclude slavery from the territories seeking admission to the Union deprived the factions of an arena where their differences could be negotiated. Taney's decision was in many ways a continuation of, rather than a departure from, the legal thinking and judicial and legislative actions of the era. He listed a number of exclusionary laws and practices to support his decision. Colonial laws barred interracial marriages and in many ways indicated that blacks were outside the realm of full citizens.

Taney said it would be impossible to enumerate all the various laws marking the depressed condition of the black race. The first Congress, he pointed out, provided for a militia in which every "free, able-bodied white male citizen" should be enrolled; the first Naturalization Law of 1790 confined the right of citizenship "to aliens being free, white persons." He concluded from a review of these laws and policies that blacks "had for more than a century before been regarded as beings of an inferior order, and altogether unfit to associate with the white race, either in social or political relations; and so far inferior that they had no rights which the white man was bound to respect. . . ."[15]

Taney ignored contrary evidence that laws in some states condemned as kidnapping the practice of hunting down free Negroes and reducing them to slavery. Free Negroes could enter into contracts, purchase real estate, bequeath property, and seek redress in the courts. Even so, the phrase that "Negroes had no rights that whites need respect" probably reflected the rejection blacks all to often experienced as they attempted to practice the rights that in theory they had under the law.

Today, *Dred Scott* is universally condemned by scholars across the political spectrum. Their desire to put distance between the Supreme Court and what they deem its worst decision is understandable but, I think, misplaced. Taney, as reviled today as the framers are revered, attempted to do what they had done: sacrifice the freedom interests of blacks to resolve differences among policy-making whites. Recall that the framers, to ensure that proslavery states would join the new government, ignored abolitionists' petitions urging the banning of slavery. Taney's effort failed because sacrificing the opportunity for blacks to gain citizenship rights did not solve and probably worsened the divisions between northern business interests favoring free territories and southern plantation owners wishing to expand the areas open to slavery. According to many historians, the Court's miscalculation in *Dred Scott* helped precipitate the Civil War.[16]

Government Professor Mark A. Graber points out that, prior to the passage of the Civil War amendments, descendants of American slaves could not be U.S. citizens. In Graber's view, Chief Justice Taney's conclusions were well within the mainstream of antebellum constitutional thought.[17] Peter Bergman maintains that *Dred Scott* was not the "classically worst " assertion of judicial supremacy, but was rather a "sincere" judicial effort to solve a nation-wrecking problem. Bergman concludes: "The Court's fault, if it may be so described, lay in accepting the buck which Congress and the statesmen had passed, and in failing to anticipate the partisan political use which its efforts could be made to serve."[18] The failed compromise of black rights in the *Dred Scott* case led to one of the most destructive wars in history. The Union was saved at a terrible cost in blood, and the industrial system, freed of its plantation competition, was able to advance its exploitation of labor, white as well as black.

It is interesting to compare *Dred Scott*, the decision everyone loves to hate, with *Brown v. Board of Education*, the decision that virtually everyone admires. Slavery advocates applauded the *Dred Scott* decision that sacrificed black rights, but it enraged abolitionists and northern industrialists whose efforts pushed the nation toward the Civil War that no one wanted. Racial-reform advocates hailed the *Brown* decision that sought to overturn past compromises of black rights, but the decision enraged large numbers of whites, who mounted a political rebellion that over the years seriously undermined the Court's good intentions. Both cases indicate how difficult it is to rearrange racial compromises without harming blacks, who feel the pain of loss, and working-class whites, who are oblivious to it.

The Hayes-Tilden Compromise

Possibly the definitive example of black rights becoming grist in the mill of white interests occurred during the hotly disputed Hayes-Tilden presidential election of 1876. In the following year, a possible second Civil War was averted by a compromise that even conservative historians now concede was a shameful moment.[19] Once again, economic and political elites were its beneficiaries, while blacks were devastated and the white working class, despite their poor circumstances, savored their superior status over blacks.

Blacks had made impressive gains in the postbellum period. The personal and real property holdings, skilled jobs, businesses acquired, and money saved by blacks are recorded.[20] Detailed information concerning the achievements by blacks in the crafts and the professions appear in the many studies of Reconstruction in particular states.[21] In politics, blacks held many local and state offices throughout the South, and between 1870 and 1901 the region sent twenty blacks to the House of Representatives and two to the Senate.[22]

With the exception of North Carolina, there was no general public educational system in the South prior to abolition. As W. E. B. Du Bois explained in his masterful work, *Black Reconstruction*, there were many germs of a southern public school system before the Civil War, but property owners saw no value in being taxed to educate the laboring class and thus make their exploitation more difficult. And white laborers saw no need for schooling, viewing it as a luxury connected with wealth. They accepted their subordination to the slaveholders. Only by becoming slaveholders themselves could they escape from their condition. On the other hand, blacks, whether slave or free, saw education as both a self-sustaining proof of their humanity and a stepping stone to wealth and respect.

As a result, Du Bois found the first great mass movement in the South for state-financed public education came from Negroes.[23] "It is fair to say that the Negro carpetbag governments established the public schools of the South."[24] They did so with the help of the Freedmen's Bureau and missionary societies, and despite local hostility that often took the form of violence.

These efforts toward black self-sufficiency, far from silencing the stereotypes of blacks as shiftless and crime-prone, threatened white dominance. Southern Democrats went so far as to give up the presidency in return for commitments that would enable whites to again control the South. By 1876, the demolition of radical Reconstruction was already well advanced. The federal government had proven itself unwilling or unable to halt the violence and terrorism by which southern whites regained political control in most southern states. The Democrats had regained great strength both in the South and much of the North. They fully expected that their presidential candidate, Samuel J. Tilden, the reform governor of New York, would be elected. Republicans were divided by scandal and disparate views on economic issues, but all had tired of their lengthy involvement in southern affairs and were more than ready to bury the hatchet on terms that would insure continued development of business interests in the South.

When the election returns were counted, Tilden had a plurality of 250,000 votes in the nation, and appeared to have won the electoral count by one vote. But the returns from three southern states, South Carolina, Florida, and Louisiana (the last three states in which blacks still played a major political role), were challenged. Recounts of the votes did not resolve the challenge that then was submitted to a special electoral commission composed of five members from the Senate, five from the House, and five from the Supreme Court. As it turned out, eight of the fifteen were Republicans, and each disputed issue was resolved in favor of the Republicans by a strictly party vote of 8 to 7.

But Democrats need not have accepted this resolution. They did so because of several understandings between Democratic and Republican leaders, principal of which was that if the Republican Hayes were elected, the national administration would withdraw the remaining federal troops from the South. It was also agreed that Hayes would include southern Democrats in his cabinet and would support efforts of southern capitalists to obtain subsidies for railroad construction in the South. As president, Hayes willingly carried out these promises to the southerners. The demise of blacks as a political force proceeded rapidly thereafter. Most whites became both the victors and victims of one-party rule.

The Southern Disenfranchisement Compromise

Following the Hayes-Tilden compromise, the federal government was no longer a factor in southern politics. Without the Republican Party as opponent, southern Democrats resorted to all manner of devices to keep blacks away from the polls. Intimidation and physical violence were the chief tools of suppression. As John Hope Franklin explains, though, without the opposition of Republicans, wealthy Democrats flourished at the expense of farmers. Sharp class lines appeared as poor white farmers being driven to economic ruin opposed the economic pressures long exerted by those who dominated the Democratic Party.

Radical agrarian groups flourished all over the United States after the Civil War, but in the South they were kept within bounds during Reconstruction because of the fear of Negro rule. Prostrated by depression, both black and white farmers organized in the late 1880s, and for a time there was close cooperation between the white and black groups. This cooperation made white solidarity more difficult to maintain. The Populist or People's Party became the political vehicle for the farmers and, in the 1892 election, gained substantial power in several southern states, despite the violence Democrats resorted to in an effort to retain control.

To thwart the Populist Party's efforts to unite black and white farmers, Democrats reversed their opposition to black voting and began ordering blacks to the polls to vote Democratic or face retaliation, such as losing their jobs. Frustrated by the means by which Democrats obtained black votes and fearing that the Democratic

Party might impose literacy and other measures that would be used against poor, ignorant whites, Populists began supporting state constitutional amendments excluding blacks from the franchise. The disenfranchisement movement grew—the Fifteenth Amendment notwithstanding—when it became evident that white factions would compete with one another for the Negro vote, thus giving blacks the balance of power.[25]

The readiness of both the Democratic and Populist Party members to sacrifice black voters in their efforts to gain and hold political power is reflected in the political career of Tom Watson. A Populist leader in 1892, Watson was a staunch advocate of a union between Negro and white farmers, and tried unsuccessfully to convince poor whites of the adverse economic effects of segregation:

> You are kept apart that you may be separately fleeced of your earnings. You are made to hate each other because upon that hatred is rested the keystone of the arch of financial despotism which enslaves you both. You are deceived and blinded that you may not see how this race antagonism perpetuates a monetary system which beggars you both.[26]

Watson's arguments failed, and he later turned to race-baiting, an all-too-familiar tactic that won him election to the U.S. Senate from Georgia. John Hope Franklin notes how the Populist movement collapsed in the 1890s as poor whites heeded conservative assurances that "Negro rule" must be avoided at all costs.[27] The issue of race, as Franklin quoted a dejected leader of poor whites, "was an everlasting, overshadowing problem which served to hamper their [i.e., poor whites'] progress and prevent them from becoming realistic in social, economic and political matters."

Even today, the pattern of pandering for white votes by asserting the dangers to whites' well-being if racial injustices are remedied is as viable, if more subtle, as it was a century ago. In the wake of the *Brown* decision, southern Democratic politicians who began their career with populist themes switched to overt race-baiting. George Corley Wallace, a farmer's son who worked his way through the University of Alabama Law School, was typical. As a two-term state legislator and then a local judge, Wallace was a moderate on integration. After losing an election in 1958 for the governorship to a segregationist candidate endorsed by the Ku Klux Klan, Wallace abandoned his moderate stand on integration. He is supposed to have pledged that he would "never be out-niggered again."

True to his word, Wallace defied the U.S. Commission on Civil Rights investigation of black voting rights, and was elected governor in 1962 on a campaign of segregation and economic issues. In his first year in office, he kept a pledge to "stand in the schoolhouse door," blocking the admission to the University of Alabama of Vivian Malone and James Hood, black students who a federal court had ordered admitted to the all-white school. He yielded in the face of a federalized national guard, but resisted desegregation efforts in Tuskegee, Birmingham, Huntsville, and Mobile. In the process, he became a national symbol of resistance to school desegregation, and parlayed his notoriety into a third-party candidacy for the presidency in 1968, winning 13 percent of the vote and five southern states.

Wallace was reelected governor in 1970, and was permanently paralyzed in an assassination attempt while campaigning for president in 1972. In the 1980s with blacks voting in Alabama and desegregation a fact of life, he renounced his segregationist ideology, sought reconciliation with civil rights leaders, and gained re-election as governor in 1982 with substantial support from black voters. By that point, of course, as a result of the federal civil rights acts and years of protests, blacks had become a major force in Alabama politics. The segregationist stance that won Wallace election in 1962 would not have served him well two decades later.

Wallace's personal reform, however motivated by self-interest, highlights the continuing readiness of politicians to garner white votes by targeting blacks as the source of white fears and anxieties. Traditionally, the Democratic Party, while relying on black votes, goes out of its way not to acknowledge that reliance. In recent elections, Democrats often shed liberal credentials and actually turn their backs on black voters in a frantic effort to gain white votes they deem essential to election. The tactic has not been impressively successful.

As for whites, while the economic and political benefits they have gained from segregation and subsequent policies of racial domination are demonstrable, the very real economic costs are unacknowledged. There is no doubt that the loss of protection for their political rights as Reconstruction ended presaged the destruction of economic and social gains which blacks in some areas had achieved. Blacks lost busi-

nesses and farms, progress in the public schools was halted, and the
Jim Crow laws that would eventually segregate blacks in every aspect
of public life began to emerge out of a series of unofficial racial
compromises between white elites and poorer whites who demanded
laws segregating public facilities.

Yale historian C. Vann Woodward reports that, after first resisting
these demands, southern leaders in the post-Reconstruction era
enacted segregation laws mainly at the insistence of poor whites, who,
given their precarious social and economic status, demanded these
barriers to retain a sense of racial superiority over blacks.[28] He
observed that "[i]t took a lot of ritual and Jim Crow to bolster the
creed of white supremacy in the bosom of a white man working for a
black man's wages."[29] Woodward's quote describes more than it
explains. Why would whites conflate Jim Crow laws with real
economic well-being? The full answer is probably complex, but as we
have discussed, whites' confusion of race and self-interest is not a
recent phenomenon, dating back to early colonial times.

Contemporary Racial-Sacrifice Covenants

Contemporary examples of the sacrifices of black rights and interests
are less obvious but hardly less harmful. Crime is a serious issue, and
no politician wants to be tagged as "soft on crime." As a result, those
holding or seeking office sacrifice the right to just criminal prosecu-
tions by refusing to amend drug and other criminal laws and
procedures that result in severe sentences for nonviolent offenses,
sentences that are disproportionately meted out to black men and
women.

The prime example is the death penalty. In April 2003, 3,525
inmates were on death row. As traditionally has been the case, those
being executed or awaiting execution are poor, over half are racial
minorities, and most were sentenced to death for a crime against a
white victim.[30] The statistical evidence of racial bias in the imposition of the death penalty is overwhelming. Most indicate that, where
the victim is white, the odds of receiving the death penalty are four
times greater for a black defendant than for a white one.[31] But despite
such overwhelming evidence of racial bias, the response of the courts
has been to deny relief on the grounds that patterns of racial discrimination are insufficient to prove discrimination in a particular case.

This is what the Supreme Court told the defendant Warren McCleskey, charged with murdering a white police officer in the course of a store robbery. In his case, defense counsel introduced the most complete and unequivocal statistical study of racial discrimination in the death penalty ever produced.[32] The Court, speaking through Justice Powell in a close 5 to 4 decision, did not question the accuracy of the statistical evidence, but set an evidentiary standard impossible to meet. Otherwise, Justice Powell feared that acceptance of statistical proof would have a domino effect not only on Georgia's capital system but also on much of the nation's criminal and even civil process. In short, the Court majority sacrificed the entitlement of black capital defendants to an unbiased sentencing process rather than expose the unfairness that exists throughout the criminal justice system. In dissent, Justice Brennan condemned Justice Powell's fear of "too much justice." Brennan wrote that "[t]he prospect that there may be more widespread abuse than *McCleskey* documents may be dismaying, but it does not justify complete abdication of our judicial role."[33]

While the *McCleskey* decision has not been overturned, the many flaws in the application of the death penalty have led to a moratorium movement with increased scrutiny of death penalty convictions in several states. Public support for the death penalty has declined, but most elected officials would rather not support abolition or reform for fear such a stance will render them vulnerable to political opponents. Evidently, they find the sacrifice of racial justice in order to protect their political careers an easy choice.

This is certainly the case when it comes to reforming the harsh punishments imposed for offenses involving crack cocaine compared with powder cocaine. Data from the U.S. Sentencing Commission shows that most people arrested on crack cocaine charges are black and most people accused of powder cocaine charges are white. Under federal law, a convicted drug offender receives the same five-year sentence for five hundred grams of powder as for five grams of crack. The disparity in the law has lead to lengthy sentences for low-level crack sellers, who are almost exclusively African American.[34] Appeals to the federal judiciary and Congress have been futile. Even when the Sentencing Commission suggested changes to end the disparity, Congress, for the first time in history, rejected its recommendation.[35]

For a final contemporary example of the sacrifice of minority interests, consider a less serious but more controversial area, affirmative action, which I will discuss in more detail in chapter 13. The use of special racial consideration for minority applicants to college and graduate schools would be alleviated if admissions processes dropped their reliance on standardized tests such as the SAT and the LSAT. Studies show that such tests are notoriously poor predictors of performance either in school or after, but they measure quite accurately the incomes of the applicants' parents. Because many schools receive so many more applications than positions, and because our society is fascinated or intimidated by "hard figures," the standardized tests are retained for the convenience of the schools even though they privilege applicants from well-to-do families. Black, other minorities, and, indeed, all nonwealthy applicants' interest in fair admissions criteria are sacrificed.[36]

Any number of other examples can be found throughout almost every area of public life. Blacks with skills are hired by corporations, government, and other institutions, but usually in limited numbers so as not to arouse concern among white employees, customers, and suppliers. When this unacknowledged number is reached, blacks of equal or even higher qualifications are turned away. The same is true in the housing area. Where blacks are not systematically excluded, as is still the case in countless housing developments, all manner of procedures are in place to limit their numbers. That remains the unspoken policy in much of academia. Each black or Hispanic or Asian that is hired for a tenure-line position makes it that much harder for any subsequent minority applicant. Policies of involuntary racial sacrifice prevail, despite the obligatory "equal opportunity" statements on business stationery.

Decisions can turn on the sense of how customers or other employees will feel, as is evidently the case in better New York City restaurants, where a black waiter is seldom hired. Realtors agree to violate the Fair Housing Law rather than upset apartment buildings or communities that would rather not have black or Hispanic neighbors. When a customer is black, company policy in car dealerships may call for charging more simply because they feel, as several studies reveal, blacks should pay more.[37] There are no formal contracts involved in most of these situations. Rather, there is the reliance on silent covenants that those involved in them believe will increase profit, promote harmony, or eliminate discomfort for whites. They do not acknowledge the sacrifice of black interests in fair dealings, and, of course, when charged with racial discrimination, their denials are filled with outrage.

The unofficial understandings that sacrifice black interests and rights today are less dramatic but hardly less harmful than when the framers included protection for slave owners in the Constitution or, when in order to resolve friction between the North and the South, a special election commission adopted the Hayes-Tilden compromise in 1877. The compromise was public, but its foundation was a silent covenant that became a sentence of death by horrible means for untold thousands of blacks, conveying messages of life-threatening fear to those who survived.

That is the history. There are no assurances that contemporary unspoken covenants, negotiated to settle current problems, will not serve as precedent to doom all black people when destruction seems a means to gain real benefit for at least some whites. I imagine such a scenario in probably my most-read story, "The Space Traders."[38] Aliens land in the United States and entice the nation with wealth, asking in return that they be able to take all black Americans away to destinations unknown. Blacks are appalled, and the debate rages as many whites join blacks in condemning the trade as immoral and illegal. The obvious benefits to whites, however, lead government leaders and much of the citizenry to support the trade. The support is affirmed in a national referendum in which the trade garners 70 percent of the vote.

The trade is consummated on the last Martin Luther King, Jr., holiday the nation will ever observe.

In the night, the Space Traders had drawn their strange ships right up to the beaches and discharged their cargoes of gold, minerals, and machinery. They closed the doors. As the sun rose, they began to arrange in long lines some twenty million silent black men, women, and children, including babes in arms. First, the Traders directed the inductees to strip off all but a single undergarment. Then the doors swung open. Ahead, the traders' directed them toward the yawning holds where they would be swallowed by what Milton might have described as a "darkness visible." Behind them, the U.S. guards, guns in hand, stood watch. There was no escape, no alternative. Heads bowed, arms now linked by slender chains, black people left the new world as their forebears had arrived.[39]

Following publication of this story, I read portions of it to numerous audiences. When asked whether they could imagine such an event, blacks were overwhelmingly certain that it could happen. Whites were less certain. Then I indicated that I was not interested in how they would personally vote, but suggested they consider the whites in a community they knew well. I asked for a show of hands if they felt a majority of that community would, in the privacy of the voting booth, vote for the trade. Slowly and almost painfully, a majority of the whites would raise their hands. My audience polls were far from scientific, but together with both history and the current conditions reviewed above, I am convinced that the potential for silent racial covenants that would endanger all black people is real. Acknowledgment is not the needed assurance that it will not happen, but it is a necessary first step to assurance.

5

THE INTEREST-CONVERGENCE COVENANTS

GIVEN THEIR HISTORY OF RACIAL SUBORDINATION, how have black people gained any protection against the multifaceted forms of discrimination that threaten their well-being and undermine their rights? The answer can be stated simply: Black rights are recognized and protected when and only so long as policymakers perceive that such advances will further interests that are their primary concern.

Throughout the history of civil rights policies, even the most serious injustices suffered by blacks, including slavery, segregation, and patterns of murderous violence, have been insufficient, standing alone, to gain real relief from any branch of government. Rather, relief from racial discrimination has come only when policymakers recognize that such relief will provide a clear benefit for the nation or portions of the populace. While nowhere mentioned in the Supreme Court's *Brown* opinion, a major motivation for outlawing racial segregation in 1954, as opposed to the many failed opportunities in the past, was the major boost that this decision provided in our competition with communist governments abroad and the campaign to uproot subversive elements at home.[1] This fortuity continues a long history of similar coincidences motivating the advancement or sacrifice of black interests. Three major examples of what I call interest-convergence covenants involve the abolition of slavery in the northern states, the Emancipation Proclamation, and the Civil War amendments to the Constitution.

Abolition of Slavery in Northern States

Lincoln's issuance of the Emancipation Proclamation in 1863, and the divergent responses of blacks and whites to his action, were foreshadowed by abolition policies in the northern states a half-century earlier. In the northern states, slavery was abolished by constitutional provision in Vermont (1777), Ohio (1802), Illinois (1818), and Indiana (1816); by a judicial decision in Massachusetts (1783); by constitutional interpretation in New Hampshire (1857); and by gradual abolition acts in Pennsylvania (1780), Rhode Island (1784), Connecticut (1784 and 1797), New York (1799 and 1827), and New Jersey (1804).[2] In varying degrees, abolition in the North was the result of several factors: idealism stemming from the Revolution with its "rights of man" ideology; the lesser dependence of the northern economy on a large labor force; the North's relatively small investment in slaves combined with the great hostility of the white laboring class to the competition of slaves; the fear of slave revolts; and a general belief that there was no place for "inferior" blacks in the new societies.

Even so, abolition was not accomplished without a major effort in most states, and idealism usually was the makeweight for a decision firmly based on more pragmatic grounds of self-interest. As de Tocqueville observed, "In the United States people abolish slavery for the sake not of the Negroes but of the white men."[3] Vermont had only a few slaves, and its constitution explicitly outlawed slavery in 1777. Although New Hampshire also had but few slaves, a petition for freedom to the legislature in 1779 was considered "not ripe." Judicial interpretations of the state's 1783 constitution asserted the end of slavery, but confusion on the subject was not finally resolved until 1857, when a statute banned slavery.

Confusion best describes the status of slavery in post–Revolutionary War Massachusetts. Efforts to specifically ban slavery in the constitution of 1780 failed, but the state's high court interpreted that constitution to include such a provision in 1783, in one of a series of what became known as the *Quock Walker* cases.[4] Walker escaped from Nathaniel Jennison, who, on apprehending him, beat him severely. He then sued Jennison for assault and battery. An award for Walker was reversed in a later case, but in a third case, *Commonwealth v. Jennison*, Jennison was indicted for assault and battery, with the attorney general arguing that Jennison knew that in an earlier proceeding Walker had been granted his freedom. In his instructions to the jury, Chief Justice William Cushing said: "Although slavery had been tolerated in Massachusetts, it was incompatible to the new constitution and its spirit favorable to the natural rights of mankind." There is no opinion in the case, but it was widely discussed. While some slavery remained, it was understood that the law would not defend it.

Where slavery was more firmly entrenched, as in Pennsylvania, Rhode Island, Connecticut, New York, and New Jersey, the efforts of abolitionists met with more opposition. Slavery was wrong, many admitted, but who would compensate the slave owner for the loss of property if abolition laws were enacted? Each of these states adopted gradual abolition statutes designed to lessen the burden that abolition would place on the slave owner. In Pennsylvania, a 1780 act provided that no person born in the state after the date of enactment should be deemed a slave, but that such children would be considered as "indentured servants" of their parents' master until age 28.[5] The statutes of the other states were quite similar.[6]

The delayed effective date, according to some historians, was not the result of antiblack vindictiveness. Rather, it was the solution to the problem that plagued all abolition movements: who would pay the price of freedom? Under these gradual emancipation statutes, the slaves were forced to pay, through their labor, almost 100 percent of their market value during the long years as "indentured servants."[7] Commenting on this nineteenth-century precedent for the "all deliberate speed" principle in *Brown II*, one writer observed: "Freedom was thus conferred upon a future generation and the living were given merely the consolation of a free posterity."[8]

But freedom even for those blacks who were emancipated under these statutes left much to be desired. No longer slaves, they certainly were not yet citizens. Indeed, their intermediate status carried with it many of the obligations but few of the privileges of citizenship. The freedmen could not vote nor serve on juries, but they were taxed. They were excluded from the militia in peacetime, yet in Massachusetts, under a 1707 act, they were required to perform menial service on the parade ground or to labor on the roads in lieu of military service.[9]

From an economic standpoint, the freedmen were relegated to domestic work, while slaves, to maximize their value, performed every form of labor, including that of skilled craftsmen. Prejudice was strong; free blacks not only were excluded from jobs considered appropriate for white workmen, but were often the victims of insult and physical attack. Blacks were segregated in the worst areas of the towns where they lived, their children were often barred from the public schools, and on certain occasions they were even forbidden to appear in public places.

Obviously, northern states did not intend abolition of slavery to be equated with acceptance of blacks. As Leon Litwack points out, "Until the post-Civil War era, in fact, most northern whites would maintain a careful distinction between granting Negroes legal protection—a theoretical right to life, liberty, and property—and political and social equality."[10] Partial recognition of that character was no boon. Blacks know now and probably recognized then that the power to withhold political and social equality meant that legal protection could also be suspended or withdrawn whenever the grantors deemed it in their self-interest to do so.

The Emancipation Proclamation

As I will demonstrate, the *Brown* decision is the twentieth-century counterpart to the Emancipation Proclamation. Both may be the classic examples of the interest-convergence phenomenon. The earliest federal action on behalf of blacks, the Emancipation Proclamation, came in the only way that it could come, by executive action. It was generally assumed that the courts could not have ended slavery, which was condoned and protected in the Constitution. Congress feared the political consequences of abolishing the institution, and even Abraham Lincoln was far from enthusiastic about the executive order purporting to end slavery, which, with more than a little reluctance, he finally issued on January 1, 1863.[11]

Adequate evidence shows that Lincoln hated slavery. "If slavery is not wrong," he said, "nothing is wrong. I cannot remember when I did not so think and feel."[12] He had argued against slavery and denounced the Supreme Court's *Dred Scott* decision in his famous 1858 senatorial campaign debates with Stephen Douglas. As president, Lincoln both deplored slavery and urged the federal government to cooperate with states that moved toward gradual abolition through the establishment of a fund to compensate the loss slave owners would suffer if their slaves were freed.[13]

In his first inaugural speech, Lincoln had denied any purpose, legal right, or inclination "to interfere with the institution of slavery in the States where it exists." Lincoln's position that, whether for political or legal reasons, it was best not to interfere with slavery, quite probably reflected the prevailing view in the North. Abolitionists and blacks continued to press the matter, but the majority of whites were opposed to their position. The prevailing view in the North was that the Civil War was intended to preserve the Union, not to end slavery. But when, during the Civil War, field commanders issued orders on their own initiative freeing slaves in the areas of their military operations, Lincoln vetoed their actions. In his view, the question of emancipation was political and not military. Abolitionists, who had been urging Lincoln to end slavery, denounced his overruling of the field commanders. In a famous response to one of them, Horace Greeley, editor of the *New York Tribune*, Lincoln indicated that his primary goal was to win the war and preserve the Union. He wrote Greeley:

> I would save the Union. I would save it the shortest way under the Constitution. The sooner the national authority can be restored, the nearer the Union will be the Union as it was. If there be those who would not save the Union unless they could at the same time save slavery, I do not agree with them. If there be those who would not save the Union unless they could at the same time destroy slavery, I do not agree with them. My paramount object in this struggle is to save the Union, and is not either to save or to destroy slavery. If I could save the Union without freeing any slave, I would do it; and if I could save it by freeing all the slaves, I would do it; and if I could save it by freeing some and leaving others alone, I would also do that. What I do about slavery and the colored race, I do because I believe it helps to save the Union. I shall do less whenever I shall believe that what I am doing hurts the cause, and I shall do more whenever I shall believe doing more will help the cause. I shall try to correct errors when shown to be errors, and I shall adopt new views so fast as they shall appear to be true views. I have here stated my purpose according to my view of official duty; and I intend no modification of my oft-expressed personal wish that all men everywhere could be free.[14]

Lincoln's response to Greeley is significant for more than its candor. Here was, for perhaps the first and last time, a president of

the United States acknowledging that the civil rights of blacks, even
the basic right not to be a slave in a society dedicated to individual
liberty, must take a lower priority to the preservation of the Union.
The statement is important even considering the serious crisis posed
by the southern rebellion and the general belief of the time that
blacks were not the intellectual or moral equals of whites. But in this
instance, as in many others, the weight of events helped tilt the scales
of self-interest toward the black cause.

1862 was a difficult year for Lincoln. The war dragged on. Casualties and costs mounted. Military advisers urged emancipation as a
means of disrupting the southern economy, which, with its white
manpower in arms, relied on slaves to keep the farms and plantations
going. Rumor spread that foreign powers might both recognize the
Confederacy and supply it with financial aid and arms. Foreign abolitionists might oppose such plans if the North abolished slavery.[15] In
the North, where enlistments had flagged and much resistance broke
out to conscription, Lincoln was aware that a document purporting
to end slavery would open the way for enlisting thousands of blacks in
the Union army. Perhaps with all these matters in mind, Lincoln told
a delegation of church people who had come to plead for the outright,
uncompensated emancipation of all slaves, "I view the matter as a
practical war measure to be decided upon according to the advantages
or disadvantages it may offer to the suppression of the rebellion."[16]

In September 1862, Lincoln issued what he characterized as a
preliminary proclamation, warning that on January 1, 1863, he would
free the slaves in those areas in which the whites by that date had not
rejected the Confederacy "by simply again becoming good citizens of
the United States." On the first day of the new year, Lincoln issued
the Emancipation Proclamation.[17]

It was clear to Lincoln and other federal policymakers that the
proclamation served the best interests of the country, and was issued
primarily for that purpose. Blacks, though, were no less overjoyed
because the formal end to slavery was a fortuitous dividend of a policy
adopted for other reasons. One black preacher reflected the feelings
of the black community in an exuberant, if unrealistic, welter of
Biblical metaphor: "Sound the loud timbrel o'er Egypt's dark sea,
Jehovah hath triumphed, His people are free."[18]

Actually, as a legal matter, the proclamation freed no slaves, its terms having been carefully limited to those areas still under the control of the Confederacy and thus beyond the reach of federal law. Slaveholding territories which had sided with the Union were specifically excluded. But Lincoln's dramatic action had a symbolic effect that far exceeded its legal force. Blacks made no distinction between the areas covered by the proclamation and those excluded from its impact. Slaves did not revolt on a wholesale basis, but as word of the Emancipation Proclamation filtered down to them, increasing numbers simply slipped away or became disloyal, particularly when Union troops approached.[19]

On the political front, emancipation did open the way for the enlistment of blacks, and by war's end more than two hundred thousand blacks were serving in the Union army. As has so frequently been the case, the advantages to the nation of an action nominally taken to benefit blacks were lost on the mass of working-class whites. Even the September 1862 preliminary proclamation had sparked an adverse political reaction across the country. The political backlash cost Lincoln's Republican Party heavily in the midterm elections of 1862.

Less than a week after Lincoln signed the preliminary measure, the legislature in his home state of Illinois condemned the act as "unwarrantable in military as in civil law" and as "a gigantic usurpation, at once converting the war, professedly commenced by the administration for the vindication of the authority of the Constitution into the crusade for the sudden, unconditional and violent liberation" of the slaves.[20]

The Republicans slowly regained political support, but the adverse reaction of whites to the idea of fighting a war to free blacks remained a bitter and not-infrequently violent one. In July 1863, the drawing of the first names in New York under the new federal selective service law sparked several days of riots in which blacks were lynched and beaten. The rioters first sacked, then burned, the Colored Orphan Asylum, and committed many other atrocities.[21] The draft riots combined the bitterness of whites over being sent off to fight a war to free blacks with frustration over their economic situation. Just prior to the riots, three thousand longshoremen had gone on strike for higher wages. In keeping with the usual practice, employers replaced the strikers with blacks, who under ordinary circumstances would have been barred from these jobs. The government worsened matters by drafting the unemployed whites into a war to help win the freedom of slaves who the white workers feared would become strike breakers, and violent reaction followed.[22] This hostility to blacks persisted to the end of the war.

*　*　*

A number of points are suggested by the Emancipation Proclamation. First, blacks obtain relief even for acknowledged racial injustice only when that relief also serves, directly or indirectly, to further ends which policymakers perceive are in the best interests of the country.

Second, blacks, as well as their white allies, are likely to focus with gratitude on the relief obtained, usually after a long struggle. Little attention is paid to the self-interest factors without which no relief might have been gained. Moreover, the relief is viewed as proof that society is indeed just, and that eventually all racial injustices will be recognized and remedied.

Third, the remedy for blacks, appropriately viewed as a "good deal" by policy-making whites, often provides benefits for blacks that are more symbolic than substantive. But whether substantive or not, they are often perceived by working-class whites as both an unearned gift and a betrayal.

None of this is self-evident, nor is every advance in the status of blacks characterized by the three points set out above. The fact, though, is that so immense are the racial injustices visited upon blacks, and so great is the effort required to bring amelioration of the adverse conditions in education, employment, voting, public accommodations, and housing, that when a barrier is breached, the gain is eagerly accepted with too little question as proof of progress in the long, hard struggle to eliminate racial discrimination.

In summary, most Americans, black and white, view the gains in equality as a long, slow, but always-upward pull that must, given the basic precepts of the country and the commitment of its people to equality and liberty, eventually end in the full enjoyment by blacks of all rights and privileges of citizenship enjoyed by whites. But even a rather cursory look at American political history suggests that in the past, the most significant political advances for blacks resulted from policies which were intended to serve, and had the effect of serving, the interests and convenience of whites rather than remedying racial injustices against blacks. And all too often, from the draft riots that followed the issuance of the Emancipation Proclamation in 1863 to the white backlash that followed the civil rights gains made by blacks a century later, a great mass of whites have perceived civil rights for blacks not as a benefit for whites, as is often the case, but rather as a societal setback that must be opposed legally, politically, and, if necessary, violently.

The Civil War Amendments

The Republicans recognized that unless some action was taken to legitimate the freedmen's status and place barriers to the Democrats' return to political power, southerners would utilize violence to force blacks back into slavery, thereby renewing the economic dispute that had led to the Civil War. To avoid this "win the war but lose the peace" result, the post–Civil War Congress initiated the Fourteenth and Fifteenth Amendments and the civil rights acts of 1870–1875. They were the work of the radical reconstructionists, some of whom were deeply committed to securing the rights of citizenship for the freedmen. For most Republicans, however, a more general motivation was the desire to maintain Republican control of Congress and frustrate southerners from reasserting the political power they had wielded prior to the war.

The Fourteenth Amendment, unpassable as a specific protection for black rights, was enacted finally as a general guarantee of life, liberty, and property for all "persons." Corporations, following a period of ambivalence,[23] were deemed persons under the Fourteenth Amendment,[24] and for several generations business entities, corporations, trusts, and railroads received far more protection from the courts than did Negroes, much of it under a doctrine of "substantive due process" not clearly contained in the amendment's language.[25]

After lengthy debate, Congress enacted the Fifteenth Amendment in December 1868. Its stated purpose was to safeguard Negroes against a future white supremacy by guaranteeing that their right to vote could not be denied or abridged by the United States or any state. By enabling blacks to vote, supporters expected to ensure safe Republican majorities in elections for a dozen years, a fact far from lost on those who backed the amendment. Ratification of the Fifteenth Amendment was demanded as a condition of readmittance for those few southern states still out of the Union, and it was only with their votes that the amendment was passed. New York rescinded its adoption of the amendment, and the amendment was rejected by California, Delaware, Kentucky, Maryland, Oregon, and Tennessee.

With the political benefits to powerful political and corporate interests in maintaining Republican control in Congress secured, blacks over time became victims of judicial interpretations of the Fourteenth and Fifteenth Amendments and legislation based on them so narrow as to render the promised protection meaningless in virtually all situations.[26] For example, in the *Civil Rights Cases*,[27] the Supreme Court found the amendment inadequate to protect Negroes' entitlement to nondiscriminatory service in public facilities. The Reconstruction amendments, particularly the Fourteenth's guarantee of equal protection and due process, wrought a major reform of the Constitution with measurable benefits for every citizen. And yet, when policymakers' interests no longer aligned with those of the recently freed blacks, the protection was withdrawn from those blacks, who needed them more than ever.

It is easy and perhaps tempting to rationalize the history of self-interest motivation in determining the direction of racial policy-making as an interesting if troubling background, but hardly relevant in today's more enlightened world. There is, though, little indication that the favoring of white interests over black has changed. Indeed, the *Brown v. Board of Education* decision is the definitive example of interest-convergence as a motivation for racial policy-making.

6

BROWN AS AN ANTICOMMUNIST DECISION

THE COINCIDENCE OF LITIGATION aimed at eliminating the constitutional justification of state-sponsored racial segregation and the nation's need to strengthen its argument that democratic government was superior to its communist alternative was more than just a happy coincidence. It was, as indicated in the previous chapter, a helpful and necessary prerequisite to racial reform.

Early in my teaching career, I devised a sardonic formula for what I had come to understand as the basic social physics of racial progress and retrenchment. The formula went something like this:

Justice for blacks vs. racism = racism
Racism vs. obvious perceptions of white self-interest = justice for blacks

Students both black and white got the point, and the *Brown* decision provided a definitive example of it. Again and again, perceived self-interest by whites rather than the racial injustices suffered by blacks has been the major motivation in racial-remediation policies. We may regret but can hardly deny the pattern. This was certainly the case in the school desegregation cases. While blacks had been petitioning the courts for decades to find segregation unconstitutional, by 1954 a fortuitous symmetry existed between what blacks sought and what the nation needed.

I do not intend by this conclusion to belittle the NAACP lawyers' long years of hard work and their carefully planned strategies that brought the cases consolidated in *Brown v. Board of Education* to the Supreme Court. Indeed, the long crusade for racial justice has been marked by campaigns undertaken against great odds with the faith, as the old hymn puts it, that "the Lord will make a way somehow." I agree with the legal writers who maintain that post–World War II civil rights progress would have come without *Brown*. None of us can deny that the Court had the NAACP school litigation as a legal canvas on which to paint its views. The motivation for what became the *Brown* portrait, as well as other post–World War II government policies supporting civil rights, were Cold War concerns. My views on this are impressively substantiated by the historian Mary Dudziak's book, *Cold War Civil Rights*, based on her untiring searches through literally thousands of official government documents as well as international newspapers and news releases.[1]

Victorious in World War II, the United States emerged as one of two world leaders. Throughout the war, civil rights leaders pledged support to the effort, but urged that racial barriers in the military and in defense industries be removed. They urged federal action against the lynchings of blacks, some of them recently returned Army veterans of the war. This had been the pattern after World War I when returning soldiers had been the special targets of some southerners, determined that victory over oppression abroad would not alter traditional racial patterns at home.

Now, the continuation of segregation posed a contradiction for the self-proclaimed exemplar of freedom and democracy. Within a few years of the war's ending in 1945, the United States was deeply engrossed in what became a Cold War with the Soviet Union. Both nations were seeking to convert to their governmental systems the many peoples emerging from long years under colonial domination. Most of these peoples were not white and needed little prodding by communist adherents to feel the deepest concern as they heard about the continuing segregation and other racial injustices that flourished in the United States, with little or no redress provided to punish even those who committed the most brutal lynchings.

State Department officials tried to convey a positive message about American race relations. Democracy was a form of government in which social justice was achievable and, while slow and gradual, it was superior to dictatorial imposition. In addition to publications and the Voice of America broadcasts, the government encouraged and often sponsored black speakers willing to travel to foreign countries and convey positive reports about race relations. These programs, though, were undermined by the newspapers throughout the world carrying stories about discrimination practiced not only against American blacks, but against officials from Asia, Africa, and Latin America visiting here on official business.[2]

Murderous violence provoked international outrage. In July 1946, George Dorsey, having recently returned to Georgia after five years in the military, was gunned down with his wife and their friends, Roger and Dorothy Malcolm. Roger Malcolm, arrested after stabbing a white man in a fight, had been bailed out by a wealthy white farmer, J. Loy Harrison. Driving the four blacks to his fields where he wanted them to work, Harrison's car was halted at a bridge by a group of whites. Another car drove up from behind. The black couples were ordered out, whereupon they were tied up and killed, their bodies so riddled with bullets that they were unrecognizable. Harrison was asked whether he recognized anybody. He said no, the same answer he gave investigators later when asked could he identify those who took part in the crime.[3]

During the same summer, two other brutal acts gained international attention. Sergeant Isaac Woodard, on his way home after three years of service, was beaten with a nightstick by the chief of police in Aiken, South Carolina. Woodard lost the sight in both eyes. The police chief was indicted, but was acquitted "to the cheers of a crowded courtroom." Macio Snipes, the only black in his district in Georgia to vote in a state election, was killed at his home by four whites. The murders led to protest demonstrations and a committee against mob violence that met with President Truman in September 1946. Reportedly, Truman was moved by the committee's reports. Although a southerner, he wrote a friend: "I can't approve of such goings on and I shall never approve of it, as long as I am here. . . . I am going to try to remedy it and if that ends up in my failure to be reelected, that failure will be in a good cause."[4]

As is more often the case than most politicians seem to recognize, the morally right stance is often the politically correct one as well. Seeking to maximize his vote among blacks and white liberals in the 1948 elections, Truman took a strong civil rights stance. He wanted to deter blacks from giving their votes to the Progressive Party's Henry A. Wallace, or the popular Republican, Thomas E. Dewey.

He assumed he would hold on to the southern states, but, angered at the Democratic Party's civil rights platform, the southerners bolted and formed the States' Rights Party, nominating segregationist Strom Thurmond as their presidential candidate. And although the polls predicted his defeat, Truman won by a surprising margin of electoral votes, with black votes in urban areas an important key to his victory.

American policy was geared to fighting communism abroad and subversive activities at home. Truman, in 1947, had signed an executive order creating a program requiring a loyalty investigation for federal employment. Federal and state agencies enacted similar provisions. While seeking to insulate its organization from any hint of subversion, the NAACP cast its efforts for racial reform as part of the struggle against communism. Racism, of course, was at the heart of that struggle, but U.S. officials saw no advantage in acknowledging the obvious.

They were prodded to do so in October 1947, when the NAACP filed a petition with the United Nations, entitled "An Appeal to the World," condemning racial discrimination as "not only indefensible, but barbaric." W. E. B. Du Bois was the petition's principal author and proclaimed that it was not the Soviet Union that threatened the United States, but Mississippi's leaders. He sought the United Nations' help "to prepare this nation to be just to its own people."[5] The U.S. delegation refused to introduce the petition to the General Assembly. Even Eleanor Roosevelt, then a member of the NAACP's board and a member of the United Nation's delegation, did not support the petition, suggesting that she would resign from the United Nations delegation if any country took it up. No action was taken on the Soviet Union's proposal that the NAACP's charges be investigated, but the petition had accomplished its purpose of focusing attention on an issue that was already generating worldwide attention. And a continuing stream of racial conflicts served to intensify criticism.

When Senator Glen Taylor, Henry Wallace's vice presidential running mate, was arrested and roughed up as he tried to enter the colored entrance of a Birmingham, Alabama, church, the incident was criticized across the globe. A Shanghai newspaper said the matter was one of America's internal politics, but that it had international significance. In terms that have as much significance now as they had when written, the paper noted that the United States already led half the world and would probably continue to do so, adding: "If the United States merely wants to 'dominate' the world, the atomic bomb and the U.S. dollar will be sufficient to achieve this purpose. However, the world cannot be 'dominated' for a long period of time. If the United States wants to "lead" the world, it must have a kind of moral superiority in addition to military superiority.[6]

Sound advice, but somehow military power gives those who hold it the assumption that their own view is both right and moral. Thus, during the height of the antisubversion campaign, the government viewed criticism of racial discrimination, particularly by blacks, as unpatriotic. The FBI cracked down hard on black celebrities who criticized racial bigotry, particularly to overseas audiences. The famous singer and actor, Paul Robeson, gave continuing and fervent voice to criticizing the racial status quo. Government retaliation and the failure of black groups to come to their defense destroyed Robeson's career as well as many other outspoken blacks, including W. E. B. Du Bois and the singer Josephine Baker. Civil rights groups, deathly afraid of being charged as communist sympathizers, cut their ties with blacks who, despite government threats and retaliation, courageously spoke out against racism.

As it was, Robeson's well-publicized stand may have had an effect. If such talented and successful blacks as Paul Robeson could predict, in1949, that blacks would not fight for this country in a war with the Soviet Union, then it would do well for thoughtful men to consider the prudence of narrowing the gap between American ideals and their reality as experienced by blacks who had far more reason for disenchantment with their place in society than did Paul Robeson.

Before he left the Legal Defense Fund to accept a judicial appointment, I asked Thurgood Marshall why civil rights groups had not risen to defend Paul Robeson. Marshall's response was short and to the point. He told me it was a matter of survival. The NAACP and other black groups were deeply afraid of being charged with subversive affiliations. As Marshall put it, "Robeson had gotten out there too far and we had to cut him off." Civil rights groups felt, with reason, that standing behind Robeson, Du Bois, Baker, and other outspoken critics would be suicidal. In retrospect, though, I wonder whether active concurrence in the truths spoken by the most courageous would not have brought strengths that justified the risks.

Even after the *Brown* decision, the government continued to consider criticism by blacks as betrayal. During the Little Rock crisis in 1957, the great jazz musician, Louis Armstrong, cancelled a State Department–sponsored trip to the Soviet Union. Armstrong said: "[T]he way they are treating my people in the South, the government can go to hell." He added that if the people in the Soviet Union were to "ask me what's wrong with my country, what am I supposed to say?" The FBI recorded the episode and continued to collect information about Armstrong's activities. His offense was his "unpatriotic" unwillingness to close ranks against communist critics.[7]

The campaign to silence black criticism, of course, simply added to the stories of racial oppression that made headlines around the world. Chester Bowles, U.S. ambassador to India, spoke of the importance of race to foreign relations in a 1952 speech at Yale University:

A year, a month, or even a week in Asia is enough to convince any perceptive American that the colored peoples of Asia and Africa, who total two-thirds of the world's populations, seldom think about the United States without considering the limitation under which our 13 million Negroes are living.[8]

President Truman had been active in maintaining, via executive order, the Federal Employment Practices Commission (FEPC) established by President Roosevelt, and in July 1948, he introduced an executive order initiating the desegregation of the armed services. It was hardly accidental that he took these steps during the heat of the presidential campaign. Truman was genuinely concerned about morality and justice, but trying to improve the nation's foreign image was a key concern, as was retaining the black vote.

At least as valuable was a policy initiated by the Truman administration of filing *amicus curiae* (friend of the court) briefs in racial cases, mainly brought by the NAACP, that reached the Supreme Court. Each of these briefs stressed the international implications of racial discrimination, focusing both on the negative impact on U.S. foreign policy of a decision affirming segregation, and the positive value of a decision striking down segregation policies. The Court received several of these government briefs before those filed in the school desegregation cases.[9] In the graduate school cases of *McLaurin v.*

Oklahoma and *Sweatt v. Painter*,[10] they were increasingly pointed in their insistence that racial discrimination was "the greatest unresolved task for American democracy":

> The Court is here asked to place the seal of constitutional approval upon an undisguised species of racial discrimination. If the imprimatur of constitutionality should be put on such a denial of equality, one would expect the foes of democracy to exploit such an action for their own purposes. The ideals embodied in our Bill of Rights would be ridiculed as empty words, devoid of any real substance.[11]

By the time the school desegregation cases reached the Supreme Court, its members were quite familiar with the government's position that "freedom and equality must become living realities, if the democratic way of life is to survive[.] . . ."

The NAACP's briefs filed in the *Brown* cases argued that the "separate but equal" precedent of *Plessy* was not only unjust to blacks, but also bad for the country's image, a barrier to development in the South, and harmful to its foreign policy. It was the *amici* briefs filed by the Justice Department that hammered away at how important it was that the Court strike down public school segregation. To emphasize this point, the government quoted at some length Secretary of State Dean Acheson, who reported:

> [D]uring the past six years, the damage to our foreign relations attributable to [race discrimination] has become progressively greater. The United States is under constant attack in the foreign press, over the foreign radio, and in such international bodies as the United Nations because of various practices of discrimination against minority groups in this country. . . .[t]he undeniable existence of racial discrimination gives unfriendly governments the most effective kind of ammunition for their propaganda warfare.[12]

Acheson said that school segregation had been "singled out for hostile foreign comment in the United Nations and elsewhere," concluding that "racial discrimination in the United States remains a source of constant embarrassment to this government in the day-to-day conduct of its foreign relations; and it jeopardizes the effective maintenance of our moral leadership of the free and democratic nations of the world."[13]

The government's *amicus curiae* brief summed up its position that race discrimination "presents an unsolved problem for American democracy, an inescapable challenge to the sincerity of our espousal of the democratic faith." The brief closes with a quote from President Truman:

> If we wish to inspire the people of the world whose freedom is in jeopardy, if we wish to restore hope to those who have already lost their civil liberties, if we wish to fulfill the promise that is ours, we must correct the remaining imperfections in our practice of democracy.
>
> We know the way. We need only the will.[14]

There is no record that foreign policy concerns were debated by the justices in conference. Mary Dudziak, though, found that at least two justices, William Douglas and Earl Warren, had indicated in speeches or private correspondence their recognition that racial strife in the United States enabled our enemies to attack us with no ready response available.[15] In addition, the Supreme Court was acutely aware of the nation's need to protect its national security against those who would exploit our internal difficulties for the benefit of external forces. Justice Felix Frankfurter, a member of the *Brown* Court, concurring in one of the Senator Joseph McCarthy cases of that era,[16] observed that the Court "may take judicial notice that the communist doctrines which these defendants have conspired to advocate are in the ascendancy in powerful nations who cannot be acquitted of unfriendliness to the institutions of this country."

Frankfurter and other members of the Court were surely able to make a connection between the foreign policy difficulties abroad described by Dean Acheson, the fear of subversives at home exploited during the McCarthy era, and the adverse affect on blacks and the barriers to the freedom and equality so widely trumpeted as available to all during the war. In an implicit bargain for government support for civil rights programs, black individuals and organizations were expected to support the war and oppose communism. That support would be more forthcoming if the government took steps to alleviate the racial discrimination that so burdened their lives.

Looking back to that time, it is likely that not since the Civil War had the need to remedy racial injustice been so firmly aligned with the country's vital interests at home and abroad. The historic attraction to granting recognition and promising reform of racial injustice when such action converges with the nation's interests, provided an unacknowledged motivation for the Court's ringing statement in *Brown*. This statement provided a symbolic victory to petitioners and the class of blacks they represented while, in fact, giving a new, improved face to the nation's foreign policy and responding to charges of blatant racial bias at home.

The media were not slow in communicating the international significance of the *Brown* decision. The Voice of America carried the news around the world, reporting that hundreds of national and international leaders wired congratulations. Only Radio Moscow was silent. After summing up its effect on the children in the segregation states, *Time* magazine, in typical style, observed: "The international effect may be scarcely less important. In many countries, where U.S. prestige and leadership have been damaged by the fact of U.S. segregation, it will come as a timely reassertion of the basic American principle that 'all men are created equal.'"

Time's companion publication, *Life*, supported this position with the assertion that the Supreme Court "at one stroke immeasurably raised the respect of other nations for the U.S." And from *Newsweek* came these words: "the psychological effect will be tremendous . . . segregation in the public schools has become a symbol of inequality, not only to Negroes in the United States, but to colored peoples elsewhere in the world. It has also been a weapon of world Communism. Now that symbol lies shattered."[17]

W. E. B. Du Bois, then eighty-six years old, noted that "[n]o such decision would have been possible without the world pressure of communism" that rendered it "simply impossible for the United States to continue to lead a 'Free World' with race segregation kept legal over a third of its territory." He predicted, accurately, that the South would not comply with the decision for many years, "long enough to ruin the education of millions of black and white children."[18]

In 1954, most black people did not notice that the *Brown* decision represented a convergence of black and the nation's interests. The decision's black beneficiaries were too busy celebrating and too ready to hope that this victory might mark a turning point in the long struggle to provide effective schooling for black children. The priority now was implementation. Nor, although obvious, was the self-interest component of this or any other civil rights polices acknowledged by the Court or other body issuing the policy. Nonetheless, the phenomenon deserves far more attention than it generally receives.

7

THE ROLE OF FORTUITY
IN RACIAL POLICY-MAKING

Blacks as Fortuitous Beneficiaries of Racial Policies

THE INTEREST-CONVERGENCE PRINCIPLE discussed in the previous
chapter can be stated in two rules:

> *Rule 1.* The interest of blacks in achieving racial equality will be accom-
> modated only when that interest converges with the interests of whites in
> policy-making positions. This convergence is far more important for
> gaining relief than the degree of harm suffered by blacks or the character
> of proof offered to prove that harm.
>
> *Rule 2.* Even when interest-convergence results in an effective racial
> remedy, that remedy will be abrogated at the point that policymakers fear
> the remedial policy is threatening the superior societal status of whites,
> particularly those in the middle and upper classes.

As discussed in chapter 4, the involuntary sacrifice of black rights can
serve as catalysts enabling whites to settle serious policy differences. I
now see that these silent covenants that differ so much in result are two
sides of the same coin. The two-sided coin, with involuntary racial sacrifice on the one side and interest-convergent remedies on the other, can
be referred to as *racial fortuity*.

Racial fortuity resembles a contract law concept: the third-party beneficiary. In brief, two parties may contract to provide goods or services to
a third party. For example, a husband wishing to have flowers delivered

weekly to his wife contracts with a florist to provide this service. If the florist fails to do so, the husband can sue, but there is a large and complicated body of law as to whether the wife can sue the florist. Although she was the intended beneficiary, she was not a party to the contract and may not even have known about it.[1]

One aspect of this body of law is clear. The contracting parties must intend to confer a benefit on a third-party. As one court put it: "The test is whether the benefit to the third person is direct to him or is but an incidental benefit to him arising from the contract. If direct, the third party may sue on the contract."[2] Thus, in many states, the wife could sue the florist. If the benefit were incidental, however, the third party has no right of recovery.

Consider this hypothetical example. If Gotham Foods contracts with Ace Builder to build a new shopping center in the heart of Inner City, an all-black area, black residents may benefit from new job opportunities, better shopping at lower prices, and an upgrading of property values. Other businesses may be attracted to the area with similar benefits. Suppose, though, Ace Builder backs out of the contract. Gotham Foods can sue Ace Builder, but the residents of Inner City, as incidental beneficiaries, are simply out of luck. They will have no case that courts will recognize against either Gotham Foods or Ace Builder. This may be true even if some Inner City residents have taken actions and expended funds in the expectation that the shopping center would be built.

The law describes residents of Inner City as "incidental beneficiaries," those who a contract may have benefited even though the contracting parties did not have them in mind. This is precisely the condition in which black people find themselves in racial policy-making. Given that they have often worked hard in seeking remedies for varying forms of discrimination, they are certainly interested in the contracting or policy-making process, but as far as the law is concerned, they are only "incidental" or fortuitous beneficiaries. That is, white policymakers adopt racial policies that sacrifice black interests or recognize and provide relief for discrimination in accordance with their view of the fortuitous convergence of events.

Sometimes, as in my hypothetical example, the parties are identifiable entities. Often, though, there is no technical contract as such. Rather, policymakers weigh various options and come to agreements or silent covenants. The *Brown* decision reflects the Supreme Court justices' consensus that for reasons of foreign policy and domestic tranquility, constitutional protection for segregation must end. At the Constitutional Convention, agreements were reached that sacrificed black hopes for freedom because the framers concluded that they could not gain support for the Constitution unless it recognized slavery and protected slave owners' property in slaves.

As I have said, racial policy actions may be influenced, but are seldom determined, by the seriousness of the harm blacks are suffering, by the earnest petitions they have argued in courts, by the civil rights bills filed in legislative chambers, or even by impressive protests conducted in the streets. None of these change blacks' status as fortuitous beneficiaries. As with incidental beneficiaries in contract law, "[t]he test is whether the benefit to the third person is direct to him or is but an incidental benefit to him arising from the contract. If direct he may sue on the contract; if incidental he has no right of recovery thereon."[3]

But aren't racial policies often justified by claims that they are intended to remedy discrimination? Didn't Lincoln's Emancipation Proclamation, by its very terms, claim to abolish slavery? Didn't the post–Civil War amendments grant rights of citizenship to the former slaves? And didn't *Brown* grant the relief the NAACP lawyers sought by its finding that the Constitution cannot be read to countenance racial segregation in the public schools?

All true, but these commitments were made when those making them saw that they, those they represented, or the country could derive benefits that were at least as important as those blacks would receive. Blacks were not necessary parties to these commitments. Lincoln acted in an understanding with his generals and other supporters that if he abolished slavery, it would disrupt the Confederate work force, foreign governments would not enter the Civil War on the side of the Confederacy, and Union armies could enlist the freed slaves to fill their badly depleted ranks.

The post–Civil War amendments were adopted with the understanding that by doing so, Republicans would maintain control of the federal government for years to come. And the Supreme Court was motivated to decide *Brown* as it did because it agreed with the State Department that invalidating segregation in the public schools would benefit the nation's foreign policy. While blacks complained bitterly when each of these "civil rights" arrangements were not enforced because policymakers moved on to new concerns, blacks, as fortuitous beneficiaries, were unable to gain meaningful enforcement despite their good-faith expectation that commitments set out in the law, even in the Constitution, would be honored.

Thus when the crisis of 1876 prompted the Hayes-Tilden compromise, blacks who had built communities across the South presumably under the protection of constitutional and statutory commitments, found no relief for the destruction of their property or the wanton murder of their loved ones. And when the opposition to *Brown* gained far more strength than those who supported it, the Court backed away from the firm relief it had earlier promised. Despite the litigation of literally hundreds of school desegregation cases over decades, relatively few desegregated schools retained that status for very long. Both courts and the other branches of government, bowing to vigorous opposition, backed away from their initial commitments. As far as the law was concerned, blacks had been fortuitous beneficiaries.

Whites as Fortuitous Beneficiaries of Racial Policies

While the economic, political, and psychic benefits whites gained from slavery, segregation, and their mere status as whites are demonstrable, the real cost to whites is unacknowledged. As with blacks, most whites are not directly involved in racial policy-making. This is true even though the racial policymakers are usually white, and whites generally identify with these policymakers assuming their influence is pivotal—as, admittedly, it often is. But the policymakers' preferences, and often their insistence on laws that undermine black rights and provide legal standing to various forms of discrimination, do not ensure the maintenance of these discriminatory policies when conditions change. In this sense, whites too are fortuitous beneficiaries to the racial policies that they seek and hold dear.

Recall that the Jim Crow laws that would eventually segregate blacks in every aspect of public life began to emerge out of a series of unofficial racial agreements between white elites and poorer whites who demanded laws segregating public facilities to ensure official recognition of their superior status over blacks with whom, save for color, they shared a similar economic plight. For the most part, courts readily upheld these laws.

Then, in the late 1940s, policymakers and the Supreme Court

began to revoke support for segregation in its most blatant forms. President Truman, under pressure from civil rights groups, issued executive orders providing for "equal treatment and opportunity in the armed services, and abolishing racial discrimination in federal employment."[4] The Supreme Court began finding unconstitutional obvious infringements on basic rights to vote. The white primaries through which southern whites excluded blacks from the only mean- ingful participation in electoral politics were struck down.[5] Resisting whites saw these decisions as a peremptory revocation of policies they considered permanent. Yet while deeming themselves the prime moti- vations for policies of white preference, whites could no longer use the law to require continued enforcement of these preferences. Thus whites, too, became fortuitous beneficiaries of racial policies adopted and abandoned for reasons beyond race. As I will discuss in chapter 13, the up-and-down history of affirmative action in the courts is an excellent contemporary example of how this process works.

Racial Fortuity and Reparations Projects

In light of foreign and domestic concerns that probably influenced the Supreme Court's *Brown* decision, consider what interest-convergence factors might move policymakers to look favorably on the reparations for slavery claims. Racial reparations recently have been the subject of media attention and several law review articles.[6] After affirmative action, reparations could become the next area of major racial activism and controversy.

Randall Robinson in his book *The Debt: What America Owes to Blacks*,[7] ably sets out the arguments for reparations. Robinson and other commentators are aware of both the tremendous legal barriers they face in the courts and the overwhelming opposition of the public. Some writers suggest reparations can avoid increasing racially divisive outcome by avoiding attempts to compensate individual victims, a route filled with procedural land mines. Rather, the focus should be on repairing the past wrongs by building interracial trust, mutual respect, and a shared destiny. To this end, one quite-optimistic commentator suggests that reparations take the form of:

> subsidies to black-owned businesses, investment in education programs
> and scholarships for black youths, training programs for black workers,

affirmative action programs, resources for community-based organizations in predominantly black communities, and development and implementation of programs designed to educate the country about the legacy of slavery. Conceived and implemented in this manner, reparations can serve to bridge the color line, rather than to widen the divide.[8]

The reparations-for-slavery movement has a history that began even before the Civil War. Its proponents have been many and their arguments varied, but in general they assert: (1) slaves were not paid for their labor for over two hundred years, depriving their descendants of their inheritance; (2) the descendants of slave owners wrongfully inherited the profits derived from slave labor; (3) the U.S. government made and then broke its promise to provide former slaves with forty acres and a mule; (4) systematic and government-sanctioned economic and political racial oppression since the abolition of slavery impeded and interfered with the self-determination of African Americans and excluded them from sharing in the nation's growth and prosperity; (5) the reparations that Germany gave to Jews and the United States to Native Americans and Japanese Americans are precedents for the payment of reparations to African Americans.[9]

Opponents dismiss racial reparations as a pipe dream. None of those who were slaves or slave masters are still alive. Serious procedural barriers bar suits intended to require the descendants of slave owners to pay the descendants of slaves. Yale Law School professor Boris Bittker conducted a thorough review of the legal difficulties facing reparations litigation, concluding that it is highly unlikely that blacks living today will obtain direct payments in compensation for their forebears' subjugation as slaves before the Emancipation Proclamation.[10]

Hidden by the often-outraged opposition to reparations is the fact that this country compensates for generalized loss all the time: certainly large corporations through bankruptcy laws, restructuring, tax provisions, and—in the case of corporations such as Chrysler or Lockheed—outright government grants. There are differences between the Japanese reparations program and that sought by blacks, but even so, there are supportive reasons—the eligibility of heirs and the education fund—for feeling that the Japanese precedent might be helpful to black reparations' advocates.

In early 2003, Harvard Law School professor Charles Ogletree, along with Charles Gary, Johnnie Cochran, and a host of other lawyers, filed a reparations suit against the city of Tulsa and the state of Oklahoma on behalf of hundreds of survivors of the total destruction in 1921 of Greenwood, a prosperous black section of Tulsa.[11] Plaintiffs filed litigation following failure of negotiations for a reparations settlement. The history is clear. In 1921, a young black man who had accidentally stepped on the toe of a white female elevator operator was charged with molesting her. Fearing he might be lynched, armed black men volunteered to help the sheriff protect the youth. A scuffle with whites resulted, shooting started, and two blacks and ten whites were killed. When the outnumbered blacks retreated to the black community, whites looted hardware and sporting goods stores, arming themselves with rifles, revolvers, and ammunition. Large groups of whites and blacks fired on each other. Whites then decided to invade what they called "Niggertown" and systematically wipe it out.

To accomplish this end, more than ten thousand armed whites gathered, sixty to eighty automobiles filled with armed whites formed a circle around the black section, and airplanes were used to spy on the movements of blacks and—according to some reports—drop bombs on the blacks. Black men and women fought valiantly but vainly to defend their homes against the hordes of invaders who, after looting the homes, set them on fire. Blacks seeking to escape the flames were shot down.

Fifty or more blacks barricaded themselves in a church, where they resisted several massed attacks. Finally, a torch applied to the church set it ablaze, and the occupants began to pour out, shooting as they ran. Several blacks were killed. The entire black district became a smoldering heap of blackened ruins. Hardly a shanty, house, or building was left standing throughout the area. Domestic animals wandering among the wreckage gave the only signs of life in the desolation. Unofficial estimates put the death toll at 50 whites and from 150 to 200 blacks, many of whom were buried in graves without coffins. Other victims were incinerated in the burning houses and were never accounted for.[12]

In recent years, Tulsa raised a memorial to the victims of the massacre, but the city is actively defending against the litigation for reparations. The judge in the case granted the plaintiffs' request to take depositions of some of their clients, all of whom are in their eighties or older, in order to preserve critical testimony about the tragedy. The interest-convergence potential in this case is present, but city and state officials have not recognized that, if the reparations suit is successful, it could cost them many millions of dollars. Even if defendants prevail, the cost in prestige and lost business resulting from resurrecting these events could be very large. Reparations is an area of racial controversy in which there is even more white resistance than to affirmative action. The Tulsa litigation, though, by narrowing the usually broad coverage of reparations claims to a specific and undeniable racial attack that caused the deaths of countless blacks and the destruction of a whole community, quiets opponents and exerts pressure for relief.

According to Randall Robinson: "The issue here is not whether or not we can, or will, win reparations. The issue rather is whether we will fight for reparations, because we have decided for ourselves that they are our due."[13] Here is the activist strategy for responding to the restraints of racial fortuity. It is based on the conviction that a cause is worth pursuing despite the obstacles of law and public opinion. The pursuit can create conditions that convince policymakers, unmoved by appeals to simple justice, that relief is a prudent necessity. The Tulsa reparations litigation seeks to prime the pump of convergence by enabling city and state officials to recognize that the cause of black justice will serve their interests.

8

RACISM'S ECONOMIC FOUNDATION

I T IS ONE THING TO POINT OUT the ways in which racism manifests itself in this country: the involuntary sacrifices of black rights that often further settlement of differences among policymakers; the convergence of interests that almost always underlie progressive racial policies; the fortuity of circumstances that are seldom influenced either by the injustices blacks are suffering or by their petitions and protests. These approaches, these hidden covenants, offer perspectives on both historical and contemporary racial developments. They may not, though, answer the basic question.

What are the motivations, the invisible forces, that move both individuals and groups to function so predictably across time and a wide variety of conditions as to ensure a perpetually subordinate role for all but a fortunate few of those Americans who are not white? It is as though black people are trapped in a giant, unseen gyroscope. Even their most powerful exertions fail either to divert the gyroscopic prison from its preplanned equilibrium, or to alter its orientation toward dominance for whites over blacks. The symbols change and the society sometimes even accepts standards such as "equal opportunity" that civil rights advocates have urged on it, but somehow in practice such standards serve to strengthen not weaken the subordinate status of African Americans. And to our horror, that status is stabilized rather than alleviated by the movement up through the class ranks of the precious few blacks, including myself, who too quickly are cited as proof both that racism is dead and

that the indolence of blacks rather than the injustice of whites explains
the socioeconomic gaps separating the races.

For many years, I have been disturbing friends and critics by
expressing the view based on history and personal experience that
racism is permanent in this country.[1] My statement may seem more
provocative than instructive. Here I want to elaborate on it by
asserting that it is racism that underlies the paradox of a nation built
on the combination of free-market economy and popular democracy.
For support, I owe much to the work of Yale Law professor Amy
Chua,[2] who reminds us that political theorists and economists such as
Adam Smith, James Madison, and Thomas Babington Macaulay
warned that this combination simply could not work. Markets would
produce enormous concentrations of wealth in the hands of a few who
exploited the many. Meanwhile, democracy, by empowering the poor
majority, would inevitably lead to convulsive acts of expropriation and
confiscation.[3]

Professor Chua notes that this conflict has been more or less
successfully negotiated throughout the developed world. Defining
the terms broadly, markets and democracy have coexisted in the
United States for two hundred years, and at least a dozen other
developed countries, despite fears that the electoral power of
numbers would overwhelm the economic power of property, "have
remained continuously capitalist and democratic for the past half-
century," a phenomenon Chua calls "one of the great surprises of
modern history."[4]

She lists several factors that help explain how the exploitative oil
of capitalism has mixed with and polluted the potentially purifying
waters of democracy:

1. Market-generated material prosperity and government-support
   programs provide wages and benefits sufficient both to meet basic
   needs and to cause a number of working-class people to identify with
   conservative economic and political policies that, on even cursory
   examination, will not further their interests.
2. Powerful economic interests are able to exert disproportionate influence on the exercise of the vote, diluting its potential to challenge
   existing economic arrangements.
3. Americans believe deeply in upward mobility, that is, that anyone,
   high or low, can move up the economic ladder, as long as he or she

is talented, hard-working, entrepreneurial, and not too unlucky. This theme, explored in countless novels and films, is a key component of our secular religion and has, for many, quite sacred overtones. A part of this ideology is that each person should be able to meet his or her and the families' needs without reliance on the state or anyone else.

I would add to Chua's list consumerism that nourishes the upward-mobility belief system through credit card debt enabling individuals both to meet basic needs such as food and rent and to acquire material goods that are expected—yet ultimately fail—to satisfy deeper needs. Substituting the acquisition of material goods for real economic and political power literally consumes financial resources while simultaneously disempowering, through debt, any inclinations to protest.

Identifiably connected with these factors is the ideology of racism in the United States and some other developed countries that has been a powerful force fracturing the "lower classes" and inducing large numbers of them to think, vote, and act in defiance of what might be expected to be their rational economic self-interest.[5] In Chua's view, racism has probably operated in service of market capitalism. Racism (and the creation of a large racial underclass) has arguably made poor and working-class whites feel better about their relative plight, giving them a consoling sense of superiority and status vis-à-vis African Americans, Hispanic Americans, and other groups of color perceived (in many senses correctly) as "the sediment of the American stratificational order."[6]

The historic serves as a guide to understanding the present.[7] The ideology of whiteness continues to oppress whites as well as blacks. Now, as throughout the American experience, it is employed to make whites settle for despair in politics and anguish in the daily grind of life. Somehow, they link the fact that a majority of America's population is white and most power is held by whites with a sense that, as whites, they are privileged and entitled to preference over people of color. Over time, these views have solidified into a kind of property— a property—in whiteness. The law recognizes and protects this property right based on color, like any other property.

Professor Cheryl Harris suggests that, in a country that views property ownership as a measure of worth, a great many whites with relatively little property of a traditional kind—money, securities, land—come to view their whiteness as a property right.[8] "The wages of whiteness," Harris explains, "are available to all whites regardless of class position, even those whites who are without power, money, or influence. Whiteness, the characteristic that distinguishes them from blacks, serves as compensation even to those who lack material wealth."[9]

Racism hinders the formation of political alliances between poor and working-class whites on one hand, and poor and working-class minorities on the other. This, according to Chua, serves to explain the absence of a powerful working-class political party in the United States. In this regard, race was a major facilitator of the acculturation and assimilation of European immigrants during the late nineteenth and early twentieth centuries. Horribly exploited by the mine and factory owners for whom they tolled long hours under brutal conditions for subsistence wages, the shared feeling of superiority to blacks was one of the few things that united them. The blackface and racially derogatory minstrel shows of that period helped immigrants acculturate and assimilate by inculcating a nationalism whose common theme was the disparagement and disadvantaging of blacks, rather than uniting across racial lines to resist the exploitation and deprivation that, then as now, does not respect any color line.[10]

The writer and Nobel laureate Toni Morrison writes:

If there were no black people here in this country, it would have been Balkanized. The immigrants would have torn each other's throats out, as they have done everywhere else. But in becoming an American, from Europe, what one has in common with that other immigrant is contempt for *me*—it's nothing else but color. Wherever they were from, they would stand together. They could all say, "I am not *that*." So in that sense, becoming an American is based on an attitude: an exclusion of me.

It wasn't negative to them—it was unifying. When they got off the boat, the second word they learned was "nigger." Ask them—I grew up with them. I remember in the fifth grade a smart little boy who had just arrived and didn't speak any English. He sat next to me. I read well, and I taught him to read just by doing it. I remember the moment he found out that I was black—a nigger. It took him six months; he was told. And that's the moment when he belonged, that was his entrance.

Every immigrant knew he would not come at the very bottom. He had
to come above at least one group—and that was us.[11]

The significance of the Toni Morrison anecdote is its universality.
Indeed, it is difficult to think of another characteristic of societal functioning that has retained its viability and its value to social stability
from the very beginning of the American experience down to the
present day. Both the nation's history and current events give reason to
wonder, with Tilden W. LeMelle, "whether a society such as the
United States in which racism has been internalized and institutionalized to the point of being an essential and inherently functioning
component of the society—a culture from whose inception racial
discrimination has been a regulative force for maintaining stability and
growth and for maximizing other cultural values—can even legislate
(let alone enforce) public policy to combat racial discrimination.[12]

In ways so closely tied to an individual's sense of self that it may
not be apparent, the set of assumptions, privileges, and benefits that
accompany the status of being white can become a valuable asset that
whites seek to protect. In the post-Reconstruction era segregation in
virtually every aspect of public life became a physical manifestation
of this nebulous property right that evidently was insufficient to
provide whites with the sense of racial superiority they sought. Blacks
deprived of the law's protection were vulnerable to economic
exploitation and physical intimidation. Violence included literally
thousands of lynchings and pogroms by white mobs. It is likely that
such hate had its roots in an unconscious realization that the property right in whiteness had real meaning only as defenseless Negroes
were terrorized and murdered.

Du Bois reminds us that, to compensate their low wages, segregation gave whites a "public and psychological wage." As whites, they
were admitted freely to public functions and parks, the police were
drawn from their ranks, and they could elect local leaders who treated
them well. David Roediger adds that status and privileges "could be
used to make up for alienating and exploitative class relationships,
North and South. White workers could, and did, define and accept
their class positions by fashioning identities as 'not slaves' and as 'not
blacks.'"[13]

Here is a foundation for understanding today what was clear to
only a few fifty years earlier. Now we can see how the state-mandated

racial segregation that was the subject of the *Brown* litigation did not suddenly appear, as a former student, Nirej Sekhorn, put it, like a bad weed in an otherwise-beautiful racial garden, a weed the Court sought to eradicate with a single swing of its judicial hoe. It illustrates as well how segregation provided whites with a sense of belonging based on neither economic nor political well-being, but simply on an identification with the ruling class determined by race and a state-supported and subsidized belief that, as whites, they were superior to blacks.

Certainly, segregation was an obvious means for exerting racial dominance. Chief Justice Earl Warren had pondered the question, concluding, according to historian Richard Kluger, that the doctrine of separate-but-equal rested upon the concept of the inferiority of the colored race.[14] While concerned about overruling earlier decisions, and not wishing to inflame the situation by precipitous action, Warren set out his view when the Supreme Court met in conference in December 1953, following the second school segregation arguments.

What neither Warren nor most of the rest of us recognized was that segregation was not, as Nirej Sekhorn put it, simply a "taint" or "bias." It was the dominant interpretive framework for a social structure that organizes the American garden's very configuration. Segregation was not merely an oppressive legal regime, it consolidated the imaginative lens through which Americans would now conceive race. It also reaffirmed the binary system through which we Americans tend to think of race—i.e., "black" and "white."

Segregation unceremoniously erased intermediate categories through the biologically ridiculous but politically potent notion that "one drop" of black blood rendered an individual black. America has not recognized the concept of "mulatto," certainly not since post-Reconstruction. Homer Plessy, in his challenge to Louisiana's segregation law, asserted that he was seven-eighths Caucasian and had only one-eighth African blood. Based on that racial makeup, Plessy claimed entitlement to every right, privilege, and immunity secured to members of the white race. The Court ignored his racial configuration and simply applied the "one drop" rule. If Plessy was white and ejected from a white railroad coach, the Court said he would have suffered an offense for which the law would have provided a remedy, but if he was not white, that is, possessing even one drop of black blood, he had not been denied any property because he was not entitled to the reputation of being a white man.

The "one drop" concept applied by the *Plessy* Court highlights the rigidity of American racism, and, by virtue of the conceptual currency it quietly continues to enjoy, makes clear the extent to which Jim Crow segregation was not just a "bad weed." When racism is positioned as a firmly fixed political arrangement and, for many, a deeply held belief, the *Brown* Court's pronouncement that state-sponsored racial segregation was unconstitutional becomes more a racial provocation than a remedy.

While the Court in *Brown* viewed it as a legally imposed obstacle to the desegregation of the public schools, *Plessy* actually functioned as a confirmation of a long line of racist compromises. Reconstruction precipitated the vastest expansion of federal power since the nation's inception, an expansion for which there would be no match until the New Deal. And it did so in part by normalizing post-Reconstruction's racist retrenchment and, concomitantly, legitimating the rigid binary structure that had always been a key to racial separation.

By again confirming the historic status of Negroes as the hated and despised "other," *Plessy* marked a transformation in the politics of otherness: the genesis of a new imperative to rigidly fix black people as black ("one drop"). This renewed politics of otherness not only allowed entire categories of poor whites to develop a powerful sense of racial belonging, but also allowed entire categories of erstwhile nonwhite immigrants (the Irish are the most prominent example) to become white. The vociferous articulation of rigidly expansive notions of blackness created an entire range of racial opportunities for "would-be" whites.[15]

Thus, policies of racial segregation simultaneously subordinated Negroes while providing whites with a comforting sense of their position in society. Racism's stabilizing force was not limited to poorer whites. Even for wealthier whites, their identities were unstable because they were intrinsically dependent upon an "other." White racist antipathy belied the extent to which white people desperately needed and still need black people—or most blacks—in a subordinate status in order to sustain both the myriad fictions of white racial integrity and the real-world preferential treatment to which every white person is granted, whether or not they want it.

Ideologically, then, the statement "I am not black" has functioned as a kind of border—a psychic demarcation that allows "American" to be quickly (perhaps even thoughtlessly) distinguished from "not

American."[16] America has been able to define itself as a white country by marking blacks as those who do not constitute it. The law has served to rationalize racial boundaries with fictions that, in fact, conceal exploitation and marginalization that does not observe the color line. A prime example can be found by comparing how the Court-adopted fictions from *Plessy v. Ferguson* in 1896 and *Lochner v. New York* in 1905[17] served to disadvantage both blacks and whites.

In *Lochner*, the Court overturned state maximum-hour laws on the fiction that both employer, no matter how wealthy, and worker, no matter how poor, were each equally free to bargain on an employment contract. Both, parties, according to the Court's reasoning, were exercising a constitutional "right" that the state could not intrude on by enacting laws to protect workers from exploitation.

In *Plessy*, the fiction was that separate but equal, no matter the disparity in facilities, actually provided equality of treatment. Segregation was deemed a social arrangement to keep order and protect the public welfare, both well within the states' obligation to provide its citizens.

Note how both decisions protected existing property arrangements at the expense of powerless groups—exploited workers in *Lochner* and the degraded blacks in *Plessy*. Wage and race oppression were mutually reinforcing. Blacks recognized segregation as a means of their subordination. Whites applauded—even insisted on—the subordination of blacks. Their racism served as a self-distracting mechanism for a system that transformed them into wage slaves. *Plessy v. Ferguson*, far more than a conscionable departure from the visions of equality the radical Reconstruction sponsors of the Civil War amendments felt they were guaranteeing, provided legal confirmation of more than a century of political compromises. These compromises openly diminished the citizenship rights of blacks to the point of invisibility, while imprisoning most whites in an exploitative economic prison without bars.

Today, many whites oppose all social reform as "welfare programs for blacks." They ignore the fact that poor whites have employment, education, and social service needs that differ from the condition of poor blacks by a margin that, without a racial scorecard, becomes difficult to measure. In summary, the blatant involuntary sacrifice of black rights to further white interests, so obvious in early American history, remains viable and, while somewhat more subtle in its contemporary forms, is as potentially damaging as it ever was to black rights and the interests of all but wealthy whites.

For varying reasons, the major political parties have shown little serious interest in undertaking the challenging task of bringing together black and white voters by emphasizing the similarity of their interests and needs. As reflected in the earlier chapters, the racial obstacles would be difficult to overcome, but the politically potent coalition that could result would be formidable indeed. The late-nineteenth-century effort by the Populist Party failed, but it was moving in the right direction until appeals to racism brought it down.

In more recent times, the Rev. Jesse Jackson, seeking the presidential nomination for the Democratic Party first in 1983–1984 and then in 1987–1988, campaigned effectively to both blacks and whites by emphasizing the social needs of both. Jackson reached the working class across race lines when he spoke of those "who take the early bus, who change the beds and empty the bedpans, but who, when they become ill, can't afford a hospital bed." His success, culminating in his victory in the Wisconsin primary, evidently frightened the leaders of both parties, who used all manner of devious means to squelch his under funded but effective campaign.

In the last two decades, Republicans have been the dominant political force in the South, and increasingly across the country. They have achieved this position not by championing social reform, but by claiming that the Democratic Party was the party for "special interests," meaning, of course, the party for blacks. This position, along with attacking big government, has enabled Republicans to dominate southern politics at least since Ronald Reagan's election to the presidency in 1980. And like their Democratic predecessors, they have maintained control by making vague promises regarding needed social reform while emphasizing their determination to protect whites against "liberal" (read black) threats, from school integration to affirmative action. Sadly, much of the Democratic leadership, while absolutely dependent on black votes, particularly in national elections, goes to great lengths to avoid acknowledging this reliance. Indeed, Democrats also seek elusive white votes by claims that they are not catering to "special interests."

Is it too much to hope for another Harry Truman, who recognized and suffered the risks of forthright advocacy for civil rights? Certainly there were political motives beyond race that fueled Truman's policies; in his case, fighting communism abroad and subversion at home. Lincoln before Truman had issued the Emancipation Proclamation less to end slavery than to help the Union win the Civil War. Lyndon Johnson, after Truman, pushed for enactment of the 1960s civil rights acts in order to ease the racial tensions that had erupted in riots across major cities.

Yes, blacks were the fortuitous beneficiaries of measures undertaken to further other ends. Those leaders, though, acted in the face of criticism that they were altering the subordinate status of blacks. The search for such leadership should continue, but there are inspirational lessons we can learn from educators in both the nineteenth and twentieth centuries who determined that children's schooling must not wait for favorable policies or sensitive leaders.

9

SCHOOL LITIGATION
IN THE NINETEENTH CENTURY

A NCIENT HUMANS WERE AWARE OF THE TIDES, but did not know that the far-off moon influenced the ebb and flow of the earth's oceans. Similarly, the forces that over two hundred years caused black parents to oscillate between segregated and integrated education for their children were often hidden or disguised. What was obvious was the desire to provide their children with an education. Black children were taught in churches and community halls. Beginning in the nineteenth century, black parents in a few northern cities enrolled their children in public schools as soon as those schools were available,. When, as was often the case, the schooling proved disappointing, frustrated parents attributed the ineffective instruction at the schools to one of two assumptions that turned out to be faulty:

1. If the schools were all black, failure was attributed to the racially segregated character of those schools. "If whites were attending these schools," black parents concluded, "conditions would be better." This has been the predominant diagnosis both in the nineteenth and, as I shall describe in chapter 10, in the twentieth century.
2. If their children were attending predominantly white schools, blacks assumed that these schools were demonstrably better in physical resources and, thus, the quality of education would be better. In fact, however, school officials provided better schools for middle- and upper-class white students than for the children of the working class.

And whatever a white school's quality, it might not be available to black children or, if it were, it might not be appropriate to meet their needs. Because school officials favor whites, black parents often conclude, our children don't stand a chance in the integrated schools.

The experience of black parents in Boston, Massachusetts, with separate and integrated school policies, is both instructive and representative. When public schools opened in Boston in the late eighteenth century, black children were neither barred nor segregated. But by 1790, racial insults and mistreatment had driven out all but three or four black children. In this regard, the Boston children's experience was no different from those of other "free" black children in northern schools. Racial hostility rendered educational equality for black children impossible even though they were attending the same schools as whites.

In 1787, Prince Hall, the black Revolutionary War veteran and community leader, petitioned the Massachusetts legislature for an "African" school. He urged the school board "to provide separate schools so that black children would not be raised in ignorance in this land of gospel light." The board rejected the petition. Blacks and liberal whites later opened a black school in the home of Primus Hall, Prince Hall's son. For what was to prove the first but not the last time, educational equality seemed to lie with the separate rather than the integrated school. Established in 1806, and initially financed by blacks with the help of whites, the school later received support from the Boston School Committee. The committee began exercising ever-greater control over the school as its contributions increased. By 1835, complaints about the poor quality of instruction and poor conditions in the black schools led to the construction of a new school, but the heavy-handed policy-making remained.

Many black parents, unaware of or forgetting the mistreatment of black children in white schools fifty years earlier, became convinced that they had a new and better idea: integrated schools. Thus motivated, a suit to desegregate Boston's public schools was filed in state court. Using arguments in 1850 remarkably similar to those the Supreme Court would hear and accept a century later, Charles Sumner, abolitionist lawyer and later U.S. senator, aided by

Robert Morris, one of the nation's first black lawyers, maintained that the black schools were inferior in equipment and staffing; that they were inconvenient for those black children living closer to white schools; and that neither state nor federal law supported segregated schools.

The court rejected all these arguments in *Roberts v. City of Boston*.[1] The Massachusetts court, speaking through its highly regarded Chief Justice, Lemuel Shaw, found that the School Committee's segregation policy was reasonable. Sumner and Morris had argued that under the constitution and laws of Massachusetts, all persons, without distinction of age, sex, birth, color, origin, or condition, were equal before the law. The court responded that the broad general principle did not guarantee the same treatment for all, but only that the law would equally protect the rights of all as those rights are determined and regulated.

Having defined their rights as not including entitlement to attend white schools, Shaw had little difficulty with the plaintiffs' claims that "[t]he separation of the schools, so far from being for the benefit of both races, is an injury to both . . . tend[ing] to create a feeling of degradation in the blacks and of prejudice and uncharitableness in the whites." He brushed aside plaintiffs' argument regarding the psychological damage of segregated schooling. It is urged, he wrote,

> that this maintenance of separate schools tends to deepen and perpetuate the odious distinction of caste, founded in a deep-rooted prejudice in public opinion. This prejudice, if it exists, is not created by law, and probably cannot be changed by law. Whether this distinction and prejudice, existing in the opinion and feelings of the community, would not be as effectually fostered by compelling colored and white children to associate together in the same schools, may well be doubted. . . .[2]

Shaw's view is harsh, but the rationale almost certainly reflected the views of most white people of that time. At least some blacks of the period felt his prediction of white hostility was accurate. One of them, Thomas P. Smith, in a speech delivered before "the colored citizens of Boston" in December 1849, noted that the black "school is now in a better state than it ever was before. The interior, finish and conveniences of the building, the management and systems of instruction, the order and discipline of the scholars, their cheerfulness and spirit, are unsurpassed by any school in the city." He predicted:

> Were the [black] school abolished, of course the whole mass of colored children of various ages and conditions, with very few exceptions, would be precipitated into one or two schools at the West end, where the great body of our people live. Suppose those schools to be full, as they are; in that case the colored ones could not be admitted, unless some of the present ones are excluded. That would not be done. Then other school houses would have to be built, of course, for the accommodation of these very children, and when finished they would enter, and there be alone in their glory, as at present; having made much trouble and expense, and really accomplished nothing.[3]

Paradoxically, five years later, the pulls of politics proved for a short time stronger than the court's ruling. The Massachusetts legislature, for political reasons having little to do with the black parents' arguments to *Shaw*, enacted a law barring the exclusion of any child from the public schools on account of race.[4] As Thomas Smith had predicted, victory was short-lived. As would happen a century later, when *Brown* was implemented, school officials feared that white parents would not send their children to black schools or allow them to be instructed by black teachers. Within a short time, black schools were closed and black teachers dismissed. Textbook aid provided to black children under segregation also ended, and after a decade or so, state officials conceded that Boston's public schools had again become identifiable by race.

The *Roberts* decision, rather than its subsequent legislative repeal, became a major precedent in nineteenth-century school litigation. Many state courts, even after the nation adopted the Civil War amendments, found that classification based on race was not an abridgement of rights protected by the Thirteenth and Fourteenth Amendments. Most courts also held, though, that racial classification was only reasonable where separate schools were in fact provided for blacks. Where only one public school was maintained in a district, several courts in the north held that blacks could not be excluded. Where separate schools were provided for blacks, courts were not influenced by the fact that white schools were located closer to the plaintiffs' homes, and upheld assignments to separate schools even when these were located a considerable distance away.

Sometimes the disparities between schools for blacks and those for whites became too much even for nineteenth-century courts. A federal court used the equal protection clause to strike down a Kentucky statute which directed that school taxes collected from whites be used to maintain white schools, and taxes from blacks to operate black schools. In operation, this scheme required duplication of facilities, which, given the great disparities in taxable resources, resulted in a greatly inferior education for black children. Other courts reached similar conclusions. Courts refused to follow the *Roberts* decisions, and held that where local officials segregated their schools without legislative authority, they would order the admission of black children to white schools.

It is worthy of note that in 1881, in a radical departure from most authorities, the Kansas Supreme Court stated:

At the common schools, where both sexes and all kinds of children mingle together, we have the great world in miniature; there they may learn human nature in all its phases, with all its emotions, passions, and feelings, its loves and hates, its hopes and fears, its impulses and sensibilities; there they may learn the secret springs of human actions, and the attractions and repulsions, which lend with irresistible force to particular lines of conduct. But on the other hand, persons by isolation may become strangers even in their own country, and by being strangers, will be of but little benefit either to themselves or to society. As a rule, people cannot afford to be ignorant of the society which surrounds them; and as all kinds of people must live together in the same society, it would seem to be better that all should be taught in the same schools.[5]

Few courts in the North shared the Kansas Supreme Court's egalitarian view, and in the South, when public schools slowly began during the Reconstruction period, they were generally operated on a segregated basis. After political control was returned to the South, racial hostility led to the closing of many black schools and the firing of black teachers, and this despite the fact that black leadership during Reconstruction had initiated public education in many southern states.

Legal efforts to attack separate schools directly in the early decades of the twentieth century were foreclosed by the Supreme Court's *Plessy v. Ferguson* decision. It is of some interest that Justice Brown, in writing the opinion in *Plessy v. Ferguson*, relied heavily on *Roberts v. City of Boston*, arguing (erroneously, as we know from the legislative overturning of the *Roberts* result) that if school segregation was permissible in one of the states "where the political rights of the colored race have been longest and most earnestly enforced," then the segregation of public streetcars challenged in *Plessy* should be deemed reasonable under the Fourteenth Amendment, the enactment of which, of course, took place long after the *Roberts* decision.[6]

Even given the times and the racial temperament of the era, it is amazing how insensitive both the public and most courts were to the great yearning of black people for effective schooling. The rationale of *Roberts v. City of Boston* ignored the fact that schools for Negroes were woefully inadequate. Even had *Roberts* remained good law in that state, it was certainly not a controlling precedent for other states and certainly not for the U.S. Supreme Court.

The *Roberts* decision was not based on law or logic, but on public sentiment and the unacknowledged concern that the fear and distaste for blacks who were unlearned would increase if they became educated. How else can one explain, to say nothing of justify, the stark disparities of funding, buildings, equipment, teacher salaries, and every other measure of educational resources provided white and black schools? These patterns of inequality began with the provision of public schooling in the nineteenth century and continued throughout the twentieth. And despite the *Brown* decision in mid-century, the gross disparities continue and, in the largest urban and many of the most rural districts, have grown worse.

The vision of school articulated by the Kansas Supreme Court in 1881, as a place "where both sexes and all kinds of children mingle together," remains the schooling goal of integration advocates today. The *Brown* decision seemed to provide legal weight to that ideal schooling goal, but the opposition, fiercely and openly waged for many years, remains staunch, if less rabid. Indeed, I find it stunning that the arguments for and against segregated schools that determined cases in the nineteenth century foreshadow those that have become all too familiar both before and after the *Brown* decision.

Regrettably, in our time neither side seems to benefit or even recognize that their positions, stated with so much passion, are neither new nor likely to influence actions based less on logic or rights than on deeply held beliefs of entitlement. The resolution of those debates are usually based on power relationships rather than on either schooling needs or simple justice.

10

THE SCHOOL DESEGREGATION ERA

> This is not to detract from the nobility of the Warren Court's aspiration in Brown, nor from the contribution to American life of the rule that the state may not coerce or enforce the separation of the races. But it is to say that *Brown v. Board of Education*, with emphasis on the education part of the title, may be headed for—dread word—irrelevance.
>
> —Alexander Bickel, *The Supreme Court and the Idea of Progress*

YALE LAW SCHOOL PROFESSOR ALEXANDER BICKEL was a major constitutional scholar of his time. When, in 1970, he questioned the long-term viability of the Brown decision in a highly praised book, civil rights lawyers and liberal scholars were annoyed. Few of us at that time had any doubts that we would eventually prevail in eradicating segregation "root and branch" from the public schools. Now, more than three decades later, Professor Bickel's prediction, heavily criticized at the time, has become an unhappy but all too accurate reality. In this chapter I will examine the resistance by whites and the rigidity by civil rights lawyers and leaders that combined to transform Bickel's prediction into prophesy.

The "All Deliberate Speed" Standard

Even the optimists among us had continuing reasons to regret the "all deliberate speed" standard for implementing *Brown I*. The Supreme

Court insisted in *Brown II* that its unique-compliance formula was intended to do no more than allow time for the necessary administrative changes that transformation to a desegregated school system required. After a decade of experience with the standard, Judge Robert L. Carter, former NAACP General Counsel, surmised that the formula actually permitted movement toward compliance on terms that the white South could accept.[1] Until *Brown II*, Carter said, constitutional rights had been defined as personal and present, but under the guise of judicial statesmanship, "the Warren Court sacrificed individual and immediate vindication of the newly discovered right of blacks to a desegregated education in favor of a remedy more palatable to whites."

Carter suggests that the Court failed to realize the depth or nature of the problem, and by attempting to regulate the pace of desegregation so as to convey a show of compassion and understanding for the white South, it not only failed to develop a willingness to comply, but instead aroused the hope that resistance to the constitutional imperative would succeed. As had happened so frequently before, southern politicians began waving the Confederate flag and equating the *Brown* decision with a Supreme Court-led attack on states' rights. Highway billboards called for the impeachment of Chief Justice Earl Warren, and candidates were elected to office on campaigns based on little more than shouting "Never."

In a major challenge to federal authority, Arkansas Governor Orval Faubus asserted the doctrine of states' rights as he barred with national guard troops the entry of black students into Little Rock High School. Defending its judicial authority in an unprecedented opinion signed by all nine justices, the Supreme Court responded by unanimously reaffirming the *Brown* holding and, notwithstanding its recognition of the chaotic, tense, and violent conditions that had existed during the 1957–1958 school year in the area, denied the delay requested by the Little Rock, Arkansas, school board.[2] The Court stated that "law and order are not here to be preserved by depriving the Negro children of their rights." Moreover, the Court cited Article VI of the Constitution and *Marbury v. Madison*[3] to say: "The federal judiciary is supreme in the exposition of the law of the Constitution. . . . No state legislator or executive or judicial officer can war against the Constitution without violating his undertaking to support it. . . ."

But when the states' response was not flagrant and violent, the Court went along with clearly obstructive procedural requirements, including pupil-placement laws and one-grade-a-year plans that it knew were designed to delay or evade substantial compliance with the principles enunciated in *Brown*.[4] Even so, Carter reasoned that as a legal matter, "*Brown* altered the status of blacks before the law. No longer supplicants, seeking, pleading, begging to be treated as full-fledged members of the human race. . . . Now they were entitled to equal treatment as a right under the law."[5]

In an effort to understand the sources of resistance, Carter and a few others began to recognize the true depths of racism. Carter wrote:

> Brown's indirect consequences have been awesome. It has completely altered the style, the spirit, and the stance of race relations. Yet the pre-existing pattern of white superiority and black subordination remains unchanged; . . . Few in the country, black or white, understood in 1954 that racial segregation was merely a symptom, not the disease; that the real sickness is that our society in all of *its* manifestations is geared to the maintenance of white superiority."[6]

Several years passed before the Court began manifesting its impatience with school-board delay and obstruction. Finally, in 1964, the Court stated that the time for mere deliberate speed had run out. The occasion for the statement was a decision in *Griffin v. Prince Edward County Board of Education*, one of the initial cases considered in *Brown*, where the school board had closed all schools rather than comply with the *Brown* edict. In *Griffin*, the Court held that the county–school-board closure of the public schools, while contributing to the support of private, segregated schools, denied black children equal protection of the laws. If necessary, the Court held, the lower courts could require the county supervisors to exercise the power to levy taxes for school funds adequate to operate and maintain the public school system without racial discrimination.[7]

In spite of these belated efforts, very little school desegregation took place. The eleven states of the former Confederacy had a mere 1.17 percent of their black students attending school with white students by the 1963–1964 school year. In the following year, the percentage had risen to 2.25 percent, and with the help of the Civil Rights Act of 1964 and guidelines for desegregation devised by the

United States Department of Health, Education and Welfare, the percentage reached 6.01 percent. Most school desegregation suits were brought on behalf of blacks, but Mexican Americans also suffered various forms of school segregation throughout the southwestern states, particularly in California and Texas. It was not until 1970 that Mexican Americans were held to be "an identifiable ethnic minority group" for the purpose of school desegregation.[8]

The fear of losing federal funds became a motivating factor inducing school authorities to effectuate some small measure of desegregation. Some judges welcomed the assistance provided by Congress and the Executive in Title VI of the Civil Rights Act of 1964.[9] The enforcement leverage of Title VI increased greatly by the passage in 1965 of the Elementary and Secondary Education Act, authorizing the direct payment of billions of dollars in federal funds to local school systems. In the early 1970s, it still seemed possible that school desegregation might eventually prove the fact as well as the law of the land.

The School Desegregation Lawyer

For civil rights lawyers, school desegregation litigation became our case-by-case equivalent of the Christian Crusades. Those of us who represented black parents and their children were encouraged by our knowledge of the law and the faith of our clients that we would eventually prevail in the courts. They and theirs, we were determined, would someday be deemed equal in law and society. In the years-long process, our clients faced lengthy delays and continuing economic threats and physical harassment in their communities.

Before signing them on as plaintiffs, we carefully explained to parents the risks in challenging segregation. We knew that some whites, trying to curb the new militancy among blacks, were making physical threats and exerting economic pressures. In that climate we urged parents to carefully consider the risks before making a final commitment to join in the litigation. Very few decided not to go forward. Many of the parents accepted our view that integration was the only means for improving their children's educations. Others joined the school suits as a means of combating through law the segregation that had diminished their lives in ways beyond their ability to define or their willingness to discuss.

During the early 1960s, I doubt that I was the only civil rights lawyer who saw him- or herself as the briefcase-carrying counterpart of the Lone Ranger. We flew into town from New York, prepared for court hearings with local counsel. At the hearings, we spoke out fearlessly in courtrooms often filled with hostile whites on one side, and admiring blacks on the other. Whatever the outcome, we were the heroes to our black clients and their friends and supporters. "Lawyer," they would tell us admiringly, "you sure did stand up to those crackers." They offered congratulations both when we won and when they and we knew that we should have won. Expecting rejection of our petitions in trial courts, we prepared our complaints with all the proof that trial courts might not let us introduce at trial, in order to hasten the appeals. Certainly it was hard, but we were, we thought, breaking down the legal barriers of racial segregation and opening a broad new road toward freedom and justice.

I spent so much time in Mississippi during the early 1960s that state officials—as unneeded proof that they were aware of our comings and goings—assessed (and, after consultation with New York tax lawyers, I paid) state income taxes for two or three years based on the percentage of my income earned while in the state. Those were exciting and sometimes frightening times. But when northern friends asked me whether I was afraid, I responded with a question of my own. How could I be afraid to go down and spend several days representing black people who had quite literally put their livelihoods, their homes, and even their lives on the line seeking no more than the rights guaranteed by the Constitution and the simple decency they deserved as citizens, as human beings? Following that answer, those who asked seldom inquired further, but of course I was often afraid for our clients and myself.

I will never forget spending nights at Dr. Aaron Henry's home in Clarksdale, Mississippi. Dr. Henry, a pharmacist who owned a drugstore, was also a most outspoken state NAACP president whose determination to fight racial bias, usually on several fronts at once, kept him and his family in danger.[10] I represented his wife, Noelle. She had been teaching in the local schools for eleven years, but we felt that the school board refused to renew her contract in order to retaliate against her husband. I argued, without success, that even with year-to-year contracts, the board could not terminate her without reason. The school board denied it, but it was quite obvious that the reason was her husband's civil rights activity.

The Henrys' modest home did not have a guest room so I slept on the couch in the living room. Each evening around dusk, a man would knock and be admitted. He carried a shotgun and sat in a chair beside the large window in the living room and stayed on guard duty until dawn. His presence was both reassuring and a visible reminder that in the Mississippi Delta, civil rights activism involved dangers that were more than rhetorical. When I awakened in the morning, the volunteer guard had already departed.

Even a dozen years after the Supreme Court's decision holding racial segregation in state-run facilities unconstitutional, legions of whites in the deep South determined, often violently, that the Court's desegregation orders would never be enforced. For them, separate-and-unequal was more than a racial policy, it was a self-defeating narcotic under the influence of which even the lowliest white person could feel superior. The deep South had become a closed society, with the media in lockstep with segregationist politicians. With very few exceptions, whites adhered actively to the prosegregationist line or kept a discreet silence.

In Jackson, Mississippi, for instance, a young judicial clerk to a very conservative federal judge whispered to me in the courthouse hall that he wanted to discuss civil rights in private, suggesting he had information that would be helpful to our cause. He was understandably nervous, and we arranged to meet rather late at night in the home of the people with whom I was staying. The clerk insisted on secrecy, and I recall he came around the house and knocked quietly on the back door. He did not seem to notice the racial role reversal involved. I don't remember much about our conversation except his stammered indication that segregation was wrong and his fear of what might happen to him if any white person learned of his views on the subject. If he ever offered the promised information, it was of such slight value that I have forgotten it.

The year was 1961. Attorney (and now senior federal judge) Constance Baker Motley and I were in Jackson on what must have been one of a dozen trips seeking court injunctions barring the University of Mississippi from denying admission to James Meredith, who was seeking to become the first black admitted to the state's flagship school. While in Jackson, we met with a small delegation of people from rural Leake County. Their spokespersons were Winson and Dovie Hudson, two sisters with purpose in their eyes. Pillars of the all-black Harmony community, they had come seeking our help in getting their beloved Harmony School reopened. The white school board had closed it as a means of intimidating the Harmony community activists who used the school, which had been built by themselves in the 1920s with financial help from the Rosenwald Fund. The school also served as a community meeting place.

Sadly unaware of the value of a black school in a small community, I told them that our crusade was not to save segregated schools but to eliminate them. If they decided to desegregate the schools in Leake County, the NAACP Legal Defense Fund (LDF) would surely represent them. It was an offer they decided to accept, and one both they and I had reason to regret. Indeed, when back in New York I told the LDF staff about the meeting and my willingness to pursue the case on their behalf, they were speechless—and understandably so, given the fierce resistance we faced trying to desegregate the state's premier university. One staffer told me in jest, "Bell, you go on down there and try to desegregate some public schools in Mississippi, and when they shoot your black ass, we will be able to raise a shit-pot of money at your memorial service." Everyone laughed, but I was serious. Wrong, but serious.

The Hudson sisters and their neighbors gathered some fifty-two signatures of black parents on a desegregation petition, and I filed the suit against the Leake County school board. At about the same time, I also filed similar suits against the school districts in Jackson and Biloxi, Mississippi. The always-hostile white opposition in Leake County turned ugly. Nightriders came through Harmony firing guns into homes. Many of the signers lost their jobs, or had their credit cut off by merchants. Before long, only thirteen names were left on the petition.

Counsel and clients found they were the special objects of hate by whites, and persons to be avoided at all costs by many but, thank goodness, not all blacks. Jean Fairfax of the American Friends Service Committee provided welcome financial and social support to the Harmony community and their leaders. We often traveled together the fifty miles from Jackson to Harmony. Jean did the driving. She understood that her sense of direction was far better than mine. When I acknowledged as much, she would respond, "Oh, Derrick, that's no compliment. Anyone's sense of direction is better than yours." She was right, but it was more than a joke. Those trips were not without their risks, and making a wrong turn and getting lost could put us in areas where whites did not want us and where we certainly did not wish to be. Jean drove the dusty roads swiftly, surely, and seemingly without fear. "No," she said when I asked her whether she was afraid, "that's what God is for." The litigation resulted eventually in an order to desegregate the first grade in the fall of 1964. And, as luck would have it, the Leake County schools were scheduled to open before those in the large cities of Jackson and Biloxi.

By that point, tensions ran high in Leake County. The day before schools were scheduled to open, Jean and I drove to Leake County and spent the evening visiting parents with children ready to enter the first grade. None were willing to send their children to white schools. We continued our search very early the next morning. By then, the Justice Department had responded to our calls for support. John Doar, then the Justice Department's Assistant Attorney General for Civil Rights, joined us as we visited parents. One family had left their home and we could not find them. We found one father working in the cotton field. His voice breaking, he wept as he told us that he was afraid for his children and family. It was already quite warm, but I could distinguish the perspiration from the tears flowing down Jean's and John Doar's cheeks and tasted the salt of my own tears.

It appeared that no school desegregation would take place in Leake County that day. The Hudsons, though, found one set of parents— A. J. Lewis and his wife, Minnie—whose daughter, Debra, was about to start elementary school. We drove to their home, and Jean talked to the parents and to Little Debra, who said she was ready to go.

John Doar organized a group of federal marshals who would escort us to the school. Jean and I would drive with Debra and her mother, with marshals' cars leading and following us. Preparing for the trip, the marshals opened their car trunks and took out shotguns and other gear. I was more than nervous. The first car started and then I got the signal to go. I stepped on the accelerator hard and the car lurched backward. I was in reverse.

I corrected that embarrassing error and we drove to the elementary school without incident. A large crowd stood across from the school and jeered our arrival. Debra and her mother got out of the car and the marshals escorted her to the school where they went in to register. While waiting, I decided to show I was not afraid of the hooting onlookers. I got out of the car, took off my jacket, opened the trunk, put my jacket inside, and then closed the trunk. I then stood there until Debra and her mother came out of the school and the marshals said, "Let's get out of here."

Easier said then done. We got in our car and I then realized that the car keys were in my jacket pocket that I had locked in the trunk. The marshals looked at me as though I were the most stupid person in the world, a look that mirrored how I felt. Finally, they ordered us into one of their cars and we quickly left the scene. The marshals were local people who did not relish protecting us and certainly did not want to give the appearance that they were doing other than their jobs.

The headline in the local newspaper that week read: "LONE NEGRO GIRL ENTERS PREVIOUS WHITE SCHOOL." Debra's father, A. J. Lewis, was fired from his job that very day, and whites attempted to burn down his house. Jean Fairfax was able to get the family financial support from the American Friends Service Committee. Even so, there were tough times ahead for the family and eventually the Lewises divorced. Debra, though, completed high school in Leake County, left the area, and held several interesting positions. When she died of pneumonia in 2001, the Harmony community erected a memorial in her memory. And so, as it did in so many districts, school desegregation came to Leake County with symbolism and courage and hope for change. Along with voting rights and challenges to segregated facilities, it was a small, perhaps important, but certainly costly step that both blacks and whites recognized would irreparably alter their future relationships.

On one trip to Harmony in the summer before the desegregation order was scheduled to take effect, Jean Fairfax had driven over to visit with parents in a nearby community. I was staying with one of the Harmony leaders, Mrs. Behonor McDonald. I remember it was a quiet, heat-hushed evening. Walking with Mrs. McDonald up a dusty, unpaved road toward her modest home, I asked, "Where do you and the other black families find the courage to continue working for civil rights in the face of so much intimidation? Black folks active in the civil rights movement are losing their jobs, facing all manner of pressure and intimidation, and you told me shots were fired through your windows just last week."

Mrs. McDonald looked at me and said slowly and seriously, "I can't speak for everyone, Derrick, but as for me, I am an old woman. I lives to harass white folks."

I have often included that story in my lectures and writings. The reaction is always the same. Blacks first laugh than applaud her courage. Some whites in the audience, though, seem confused, unnerved. "Isn't she practicing the same harassment that blacks have been suffering at the hands of whites?" one of them will ask.

The question shows they missed the significance of her response. As blacks recognize immediately, Mrs. McDonald didn't say she would or could respond in kind to the violence aimed at her. She was not even saying that she risked everything because she hoped or expected to win out over the whites. She knew from harsh experience that they held all the economic and political power, and most of the guns as well. Rather, she recognized that—powerless as she was—she had and intended to use courage and determination as a weapon; in her words, "to harass white folks."

While disavowing that she was the spokesperson for those in Harmony working for racial justice, it seemed to me that her words accurately reflected their commitment. The goal was organized resistance to racial subjugation, and its harassing effect was probably more potent precisely because they risked so much without either economic or political power and with no certainty that they could change a system that they had known and hated all of their lives. Those who stood together with the Hudsons avoided discouragement and defeat because, at the point that they determined to resist their oppression, they were triumphant. Mrs. McDonald's answer to my question reflected the value of that triumph to their spirits, and explained the source of courage that fueled their dangerous challenge to the white power structure of that rural Mississippi county. Nothing the all-powerful whites could do would diminish that triumph.

Years later, I was talking to the Hudson sisters at a conference. By that time, they had fought and won battles to vote, to integrate public facilities, to get their fair share of government loans and subsidies—most of it without litigation. I reminded them of the counsel I had offered when they came to Jackson in 1961, seeking legal help in reopening Harmony School. "Looking back," I said, "I wonder whether I gave you the right advice when I refused to help reopen your school, and urged desegregating the school system." I may have been seeking sympathy, but I didn't get it. "Well, Derrick," Winson responded, "I also wondered whether that was the best way to go about it." Then she added, "It's done now. We made it and we are still moving."

Without a commitment from individuals like the Hudsons and their neighbors in Harmony, who were able to overcome fear, discouragement, and defeat after defeat, we civil rights lawyers and our organizations, who take most of the credit for change and reform, could have accomplished nothing. And yet, fixated as we are on current problems, there is too little interest in battles past and won. Those who labored without concern for credit have not, with few exceptions, been credited.

Even with their strength and commitment, it was hard not to see just how difficult it would be to alter racial patterns that were so deeply set, so strongly believed. I was thinking about these things—undergoing an epiphany, really—during a school desegregation hearing in a southern courtroom. Lost in thought and stunned by what I had seen in that courtroom, I did not notice that the judge had recessed for lunch. The local attorney touched me on the shoulder: "Lawyer Bell. You goin' to lunch with us?"

I heard him speaking, but what he was saying did not register. "Yes, yes," I muttered. "What did you say?"

"Are you O.K.? The judge recessed for an early lunch. You goin' with us?"

"I guess so. Give me a few minutes to get my papers together."

"We'll wait for you out front. The Negro restaurant is clear across town, you know."

I just sat there still not believing what I had seen that morning. The hearing on our school desegregation case was delayed because the judge wanted to administer the oath to a group of new citizens. This member of the federal judiciary had been particularly resistant to our suit, allowing the school board all manner of delays and expressing his disdain for us and our clients in most obnoxious ways, including turning away from us to face the wall when we spoke, overruling our objections while allowing the school board lawyer to introduce all sorts of totally irrelevant testimony and materials. As I recall, they included all the old pseudoscientific studies asserting that black people were genetically inferior, and that therefore the contrary conclusions in *Brown* were wrong and the case should be overruled.

But this morning, the judge underwent a total change of demeanor. He asked the new citizens to gather around the bench to be sworn in, and then welcomed them to the country in tones of sweetness and warmth that were the total opposite of how he had treated my clients seeking the relief the Supreme Court had said they were entitled to several years earlier.

I was surprised at this Jekyll-Hyde transformation, but what held me in my seat was the realization that in the moment when these white people became citizens, their skin color made them more acceptable to this country, more a part of it, than my black clients would probably ever be. The presumptions based on their whiteness would make it far easier for them to find employment, lease or purchase homes, obtain bank loans. They were immediately able to enroll their children in the schools as a matter of right that my clients were fighting to be included in based on a law very difficult to enforce.

What did it mean? Why was I trying to get these children admitted to schools where they were not wanted, where, unless they were exceptional, they would fare poorly, probably dropping out without a diploma, perhaps responding to their hostile treatment and getting into difficulties that would result in their expulsion? It did not seem that the unwillingness to treat blacks as full citizens, despite *Brown*, had really changed in the more than one hundred years since Chief Justice Shaw's prediction in the 1850 *Roberts v. City of Boston* case that the prejudice in segregated schools, "if it exists, is not created by law, and probably cannot be changed by law. Whether this distinction and prejudice, existing in the opinion and feelings of the community, would not be as effectually fostered by compelling colored and white children to associate together in the same schools, may well be doubted. . . ."[11]

This was my fourth year at the NAACP Legal Defense Fund. I was now supervising three hundred school desegregation cases all across the South. I felt I was doing God's work and yet, at that moment, I was filled with doubt. I knew the sacrifices the parents of these children were making, the economic and even physical risks involved in becoming plaintiffs in these suits. Many had joined the cases at our urging. They were willing to risk a lot to give meaning to what the Supreme Court had said was their right back in 1954. And now it was 1964, yet segregation in the schools remained the rule, not only here but across the South and, without the express requirements of law, in much of the country.

The local attorney returned. "Derrick, we have to get started if we are to get back here when the judge reconvenes court." He sensed what I was feeling. "Don't let that cracker judge get to you. He's just trying to hold back progress. And he can't do it. Ready?"

Even the need to drive across town to find lunch in a black-owned diner served to fuel my doubts about progress, but I nodded, got up and followed him out the courthouse door.

Progress, we civil rights adherents believed, was inevitable, and we grasped at even small indications that we would eventually prevail. On more than one occasion, during my years of litigating school deseg-regation cases, I would watch in wonder as school officials reported under oath that they were complying with the *Brown* decision while everyone knew that they were administering policies designed to maintain segregation in their schools. Then, during a recess, the same officials would sidle up to me in the hall and whisper that while for "political reasons" they had to testify as they did on the stand, they were quietly pleased that we NAACP people had filed suit because they could not afford to maintain two sets of schools. Naively, I thought their whispered concessions connoted agreement with our integration petitions. In fact, those same officials, probably also for "political reasons," were already preparing plans that, when the courts finally ordered them to desegregate, would ensure their white patrons—parents and children—continued to enjoy priority in all matters of school policy.

It's true I was often more committed than wise. The belief that I was doing the Lord's work did not relieve me of the obligation to consider carefully—and often—exactly what I was doing. In those days, of course, there was little time for reflection. As reason rather than excuse, my case load was heavy and the lawyers representing the school boards, with few exceptions, ignored all the relevant rules of professional behavior in defending school boards against what should have been the indefensible.

Yale Law professor Burke Marshall examined the actions of the legal profession and the bar.[12] He concluded that in the history of massive legal and political resistance to the *Brown* decision in the South, "the bar played an enormously important role."[13] Members of the legal profession defending segregation practices behaved in ways that violated ethical rules of conduct.

Under the 1970 Code of Professional Responsibility, it was incumbent on members of the American Bar Association that they not make claims or defenses not warranted under existing law, including the presentation of fraudulent, false, or perjured testimony. This code was repeatedly violated in the South. Marshall explains that *Brown* made it necessary in litigation to attempt to portray state action that everyone knew was based on race as if it were color-blind. As a result, the judicial process had to contend with a myth—a myth that many courts accepted without question. Assertion of myth, as Burke Marshall makes clear, was essential in order to prevent the racial structure of the society from collapsing overnight. So for years, "the legal system was forced to imagine a world that did not exist, and state officials and their lawyers, including prosecutors, as well as the courts themselves in many instances, became a part of an effort to base legal conclusions on the presumption of the existence of the imagined world."[14]

A Time of Limited Progress

Accepting arguments not unlike those they told their children about the tooth fairy, federal district judges, with few exceptions for reasons of either politics or belief, were willing to give school boards as much time as they needed to comply with the *Brown* decision. They gave every indication that they would never enter an effective desegregation order unless forced to do so. Specific instructions toward that end did not come from the Supreme Court until 1971, after more than a decade and a half of slogging through what civil rights lawyers described as "trench warfare."

Seeking to clarify what techniques federal courts could employ to carry through the affirmative duties of desegregation, the Court chose as its vehicle *Swann v. Charlotte-Mecklenburg Board of Education*.[15] Chief Justice Burger noted that the case arose in a state with a long history of maintaining racially segregated schools. In such school districts, lower courts had the authority to order that each school be racially balanced to eliminate invidious racial distinctions with regard to transportation, supporting personnel, school abandonment and new school location, extracurricular activities, and other administrative practices. Reasonable busing to achieve these goals was permissible. As to faculty assignments, the Court approved the setting of ratios designed to result in roughly the same ratio of black to white teachers in each school throughout the system.

Chief Justice Burger admonished the lower courts to approach these equitable questions in a manner that would convey the sense of basic fairness inherent in equity. This way, it was hoped, school authorities would at some point achieve full compliance with *Brown I*. He cautioned that it did not follow that the communities served by such systems would remain demographically stable, for in a growing, mobile society, few would do so. Neither school authorities nor district courts were constitutionally required to make year-by-year adjustments of the racial composition of student bodies once the affirmative duty to desegregate had been accomplished and racial discrimination, through official action, eliminated from the system.

Following the decision in *Swann v. Charlotte-Mecklenburg*, the question remained as to whether the school desegregation standards imposed on a southern school district with its history of de jure segregation would be applied in northern school litigation. In *Keyes v. School District No. I, Denver, Colo.*,[16] the Supreme Court responded to this question with a strongly affirmative answer. Justice Brennan noted that the maintenance of segregation in a substantial portion of the district would have "a profound reciprocal effect on the racial composition of residential neighborhoods within a metropolitan area, thereby causing further concentration within the schools. . . ." Thus, when a school board has intentionally segregated a meaningful portion of a school system, a prima facie case of unlawful segregative design is established. The burden then shifts to the school authorities to prove that the makeup of other schools within the system is not also the result of intentionally segregative actions.

In a separate opinion, Justice Lewis Powell expressed concern about school desegregation plans that require extensive student transportation solely to achieve integration. Citing the value of the neighborhood school, he felt the Court should be wary of compelling, in the name of constitutional law, what might seem to many a dissolution in the traditional, more personal fabric of their public schools.

This, he predicted (accurately, as it turned out), could hasten the dismantling of neighborhood education, as parents left the public school system for the suburbs or private schools. Furthermore, a divisive debate over who is to be transported where would divert attention from the paramount goal of quality in education.

School desegregation advocates hailed both decisions. Now we had the tools to really move school systems to comply finally with the *Brown* mandate. We paid little heed to the cautionary language of Burger in *Swann*, or the concerns expressed by Powell in *Keyes*. Few recognized that the long-sought orders requiring meaningful desegregation, while limiting the barrier of delaying tactics by school boards, would move white parents to manifest their continued opposition to busing and racial balance by leaving school districts where orders for such relief took effect.

Busing and White Flight

In response to departures that, in some districts, resembled an exodus, the Court began rejecting desegregation plans it viewed as too far-reaching or too disruptive of communities. If one read between the lines of these actions, it appeared that, while discussing the standard of liability that lower courts should require, the Court actually was expressing concern about the cost and disruptiveness of the remedies lower courts had entered.

Dissenting in two school cases a few years later, Powell reflected what would be a growing concern for members of the Court. He urged that it was unlikely that school boards and lower courts would be able to implement the remedies it had imposed in the two cases, suggesting several probable undesirable consequences of the adopted approaches. Students, teachers, and other personnel would be reassigned; neighborhood schools would be eliminated; parents would lose the power to decide how their children were to be educated; white as well as black parents who stressed education as a means of upward mobility would withdraw their children from public schools in large numbers; and public schools would lose community support as they "increasingly . . . become limited to children from families that either lack the resources to choose alternatives or are indifferent to the quality of education."

Powell's ominous warnings proved prescient. Outside the court-

room, white children, the prospective objects of the school desegregation orders, were leaving the public schools or moving to the
suburbs at a rapid rate. By the late 1970s, roughly half of all nonwhite
children in the nation resided in the twenty to thirty largest school
districts. The minority children averaged 60 percent of the school
population in these districts, only a few of which contained a majority
of white students. In the ten largest districts, the minority percentage
averaged 68.2 percent. In Los Angeles, for example, civil rights officials agreed to drop a twenty-five-year-old desegregation suit because
the proportion of white students in the district had dropped to
17 percent from more than 65 percent when the lawsuit was initiated
in 1963.

Some argued that the white exodus was a demographic phenomenon with little or no connection to school desegregation orders,
while others have attacked the Court for doing more harm than good.
Busing, in particular, met with intense and well-publicized hostility
for encouraging white families to flee to the suburbs to avoid its
reach, resulting in urban schools that are even more racially isolated
than before busing. In the first years of the Reagan administration,
the President placed strict limits on the use of busing; Congress
debated measures to limit the scope of busing remedies; and the Justice
Department affirmatively fought busing plans in Seattle and Tacoma,
Washington; Norfolk, Virginia; Nashville, Tennessee; and several
other school districts.

White flight, however, may be attributed to a number of factors
quite separate from busing, such as urban crime and overcrowding (to
name only two). The depth of the emotions aroused by the issue of
busing, even in the face of countervailing data, points to the real basis
of controversy. Busing arouses such resentment because it deprives
whites and many black parents of their "freedom" to choose their
children's schools.

These concerns, combined with white fear of racial mixing, led to
racially separate housing patterns within cities. Whites, running from
the blacks in the inner cities, have hidden in the suburbs behind an
impressive array of economic, social, and legal barriers. Local governments were active accomplices through mortgaging practices, the
location of public housing and urban renewal projects, and zoning
regulations. Racial isolation in housing has both created single-race
schools and insulated these schools from court challenges. Eventually,

school boards were able to explain away single-race schools as the result of "natural" separation rather than official discrimination, and through such arguments were able to avoid desegregation decrees.

Racial-balance advocates argued that if whites migrated to the suburbs to avoid compelled integration, then the answer was to include the suburbs in an intersystem desegregation plan that would remove the reason whites leave urban neighborhoods. They reasoned there is no reason to run if there is no place to hide. The courts, busing advocates claimed, had handcuffed themselves when they ignored residential housing patterns in determining whether a constitutional violation had occurred, thus excluding suburbs from desegregation decrees. In their view, courts, out of a fear of excessive judicial intervention, actually feed resegregation by driving whites out of the urban public schools. It is not busing but the courts' willingness to honor the private choices of whites who retreat to the suburbs that link white flight to greater segregation in urban schools.

The Court cut short these arguments in 1974. In *Milliken v. Bradley*, the Court allayed middle-class fears that the school bus would become the Trojan horse of their suburban Troys.[17] In a 5 to 4 decision, Chief Justice Burger held that the district court was in error when it ordered fifty-three suburban school districts to participate in the desegregation of the predominantly black Detroit school system. *Milliken* held that a court could not impose a multidistrict remedy for a single district's de jure segregation problem without a finding that the other school districts included somehow participated in a segregation scheme, and without those districts having the opportunity to be heard. Reflecting the majority's reluctance to embroil itself in a remedial situation with such predictable difficulties, Justice Burger feared that absent a complete restructuring of the laws of Michigan relating to school districts, the district court would become, first, a de facto "legislative authority" to resolve these complex questions, and, second, the "school superintendent" for the entire area, a task which few, if any, judges are qualified to perform, and one which would deprive the people of schools controlled through their elected representatives.

The *Milliken* decision did not entirely close the door on metropolitan relief. But the initial hope that metropolitan plans could be forced on resisting suburban, mainly white, school districts evaporated for all save the most committed civil rights proponents of integrated schools. In their view, the most substantial impediment to school desegregation was the court's short-sighted acquiescence to patterns of residential segregation.

Courts were generally unwilling to consider the incidence of housing discrimination as relevant to school desegregation, or to hold school boards responsible for remedying segregation caused by housing segregation. They also failed to consider or to counteract the role of other government agencies in perpetuating segregation. Whites had every incentive to flee the inner city while racism and the perceived (and usually actual) inferiority of black schools kept white families from moving into predominantly black neighborhoods. Thus courts' tolerance of residual school segregation created an inescapable cycle of racial separation. White suburbs have been insulated from real integration and urban centers have been denied it.

Black Students in Mainly White Schools

As a result of judicial reluctance to push court-ordered desegregation, schools remained predominantly white, and pressure mounted on all sides against the integration effort. In the 1980s it was the disillusionment of black parents with a remedy that disproportionately burdened blacks that most dramatically shifted the political landscape regarding busing. According to a Gallup poll conducted in 1981, half the black population in the United States believed that busing to achieve school integration had "caused more difficulties than it is worth."[18] Black children were shuffled in and out of predominantly white schools to take the places vacated by whites fleeing to outlying suburbs. In these white schools, black children all too often met naked race-hatred and a curriculum blind to their needs. Black parents, who often lived far from the schools where their children were sent, had no input into the school policies and little opportunity to involve themselves in school life.

One of the most disturbing and frustrating aspects of the integration experience for young black children was "tracking." Under such policies, white students are admitted to accelerated schools and programs, and black children are relegated to inferior ones.[19] Tracking internalizes the bias and stigma of segregation, nullifying the benefits of intraschool integration. Even when school desegregation orders were carried out, the notion that placing black children in

mainly white schools would ensure that blacks would get the education offered whites was frustrated by school policies designed to serve
the needs and interests of the white children while treating the black
children as barely tolerated guests in matters of curriculum, teacher
selection, and even social activities.

In addition to tracking, desegregation plans requiring that they
send their children far from home could be as coercive and potentially
harmful as the freedom-of-choice plans rejected by the Court two
decades earlier. The reservations of many black parents were understandable, given the less-than-impressive evidence gathered as to the
educational benefits black children could expect to find at the end of
the bus ride. The 1980s saw a growing disenchantment with mandatory integration as the linchpin of an educational policy for black
children. Many parents, advocates, scholars, and judges came to see a
singular focus on racial balance in public schools as actually counter-
productive. Zealous faith in integration blinded us to the actual goal
of equalizing educational opportunities for black children, and led us
to pursue integration without regard to, and often despite, its ultimate impact on the well-being of students.

None of these obstacles prevented large numbers of black students
from attending mainly white schools. Those who graduated from these
schools feel that they overcame the difficulties in obtaining a good
education that so concerned W. E. B. Du Bois, who warned in 1933:
"A mixed school with poor and unsympathetic teachers, with hostile
public opinion, and no teaching of truth concerning black folk is bad."
They stand as illustrations of Du Bois's concession that, "[o]ther
things being equal, the mixed school is the broader, more natural basis
for the education of all youth. It gives wider contacts; it inspires
greater self-confidence; and suppresses the inferiority complex."[20]

11

THE END OF THE *BROWN* ERA

THE EMANCIPATION PROCLAMATION remains a positive moment in American history despite its mainly symbolic character. *Brown v. Board of Education* has achieved and will probably retain similar status. The three decades of campaigning to desegregate school systems, though, came to a less-than-exultant end. Black parents recognized long before their civil rights lawyers that the effort to racially balance the schools was not working. Desegregation plans were designed to provide a semblance of compliance with court orders while minimizing the burden on whites. Judges, many more conservative than their predecessors, found ways to declare the schools desegregated even in districts where the percentage of black children rose in the wake of white flight. Finally, the statistics on resegregation of once-nominally desegregated schools painfully underscores the fact that many black and Hispanic children are enrolled in schools as separate and probably more unequal than those their parents and grandparents attended under the era of "separate but equal."

Black Parents Revolt

Because the value of integrated schooling proved elusive, black parents and educators began looking for a more viable vehicle for their educational goals. The search was opposed by those civil rights leaders who maintained that *Brown* could only be read to require an end to intentional discrimination against black children through their assignment to integrated schools.

With an advocate's hindsight, Robert Carter suggested that while *Brown* was fashioned on the theory that equal education and integrated education were one and the same thing, the goal was not integration but equal educational opportunity. If equal educational opportunity can be achieved without integration, Carter reasoned, *Brown* has been satisfied. In this, he parted company with those claiming that the inescapable conclusion of the Court's decision in *Brown* is that racial separation is itself an injury, regardless of parity in the facilities.[1]

By the time of his article, Carter had been out of the civil rights movement for a dozen years, but he now supported those who focused on quality of education and challenged proponents of racial-balance remedies in the courts. When groups not committed to racial balance obtained a court order for educationally oriented forms of relief, they were often opposed by civil rights organizations committed to integration, who intervened with more expertise and resources. This sometimes resulted in open confrontations between the NAACP and local blacks who favored plans oriented toward improving educational quality.

In *Calhoun v. Cook*, a group of plaintiffs became discouraged by the difficulty of achieving meaningful desegregation in a district that had gone from 32 percent black in 1952 to 82 percent in 1974. The local NAACP branch worked out a compromise plan, in which there would be full faculty and employee desegregation as well as the hiring of a number of blacks in top administrative positions, including a black superintendent of schools, but with only limited pupil desegregation. In approving the plan, the federal court was apparently influenced by petitions favoring the plan signed by several thousand members of the plaintiffs' class.[2] Defending the plan, Dr. Benjamin E. Mays, one of the most respected black educators in the country, stated:

> Black people must not resign themselves to the pessimistic view that a nonintegrated school cannot provide Black children with an excellent educational setting. Instead, Black people, while working to implement *Brown*, should recognize that integration alone does not provide a quality education, and that much of the substance of quality education can be provided to Black children in the interim.[3]

The national NAACP office was not impressed by support of the compromise by local leaders, black school board members, and the thousands who signed the petitions. Horrified by the compromise it deemed a sellout, the NAACP ousted the Atlanta branch's black president who had supported it. Then, acting on behalf of some local blacks who shared their views, LDF lawyers filed an appeal in the Atlanta case attacking the plan for failing to require busing of whites into the predominantly black schools. The appellate court upheld the district court's finding that the system had done all that *Brown* required. In a brief opinion denying the LDF petitions for rehearing, the court stated: "It would blink reality and authority . . . to hold the Atlanta School System to be nonunitary because further racial integration is theoretically possible and we expressly decline to do so."[4]

A similar revolt broke out in Detroit. After failing to achieve an interdistrict metropolitan remedy in Detroit in the *Milliken v. Bradley* case, the NAACP sought a unitary system in a school district that was more than 70 percent black. The district court rejected the NAACP plan designed to require every school to reflect (within a range of 15 percent in either direction) the ratio of whites to blacks in the school district as a whole, and approved a desegregation plan that emphasized educational reform rather than racial balance. The court stated that "rigid and inflexible desegregation plans too often neglect to treat school children as individuals, instead treating them as pigmented pawns to be shuffled about and counted solely to achieve an abstraction called 'racial mix.'"

At the time, the mayor of Detroit, Coleman Young, and the president of its school board, C. L. Golightly, both black, praised the court's opinion for rejecting the idea that busing is a magic formula and for addressing itself to the improvement of Detroit's school system. Not surprisingly, the then–NAACP General Counsel Nathaniel R. Jones disagreed. He reportedly called the decision "an abomination" and "a rape of the constitutional rights of black children," and indicated his intention to appeal immediately. A local NAACP official referred to the decision as a "calamity [that] takes us back to the days of *Dred Scott*."

On appeal, the Sixth Circuit approved the district court's order requiring the school board to provide school improvements designed to improve educational effectiveness in the mainly black schools. The costs of these educational components would be shared by the board and the state of Michigan based on the latter's participation in the segregatory policies. The Supreme Court granted review and affirmed. Justice Burger acknowledged that the Court had not previously addressed directly the question whether a federal court can order remedial education programs as part of a school desegregation decree. He explained:

> These specific educational remedies, although normally left to the discretion of the elected school board and the professional educators, were deemed necessary to restore the victims of discriminatory conduct to the position they would have enjoyed in terms of education had these educational components been provided in a nondiscriminatory manner in a school system free from pervasive de jure racial segregation.[5]

Altering its original cries of outrage at the district judge's opinion in the *Detroit* case, the NAACP decided to support the "educational component" plan on appeal. That plan, while rejecting racial-balance proposals made by both plaintiffs and the school board, did provide that no school should have a black student population of less than 30 percent, a standard easily met as whites continued to flee the Detroit schools.

School desegregation litigation, where alternatives to racial-balance remedies were placed in issue, often sparked major battles at the procedural level. The entitlement of one group of minority parents or another to intervene in the case was a matter that courts had to resolve. In St. Louis, for example, black parents brought suit in 1972 to desegregate the St. Louis public schools and in 1975 entered into an agreement with the school board approved by the district court.[6]

The NAACP in St. Louis sought to intervene on behalf of another group of black pupils claiming that the consent agreement did not provide for a full desegregation plan. When their motion was denied, they appealed, and the Eighth Circuit reversed and remanded the case. On remand, the district court held a trial to determine whether the St. Louis school board had intentionally caused segregation of students under standards set by the Supreme Court in *Milliken I* and *Dayton*. In a lengthy opinion, the district court found that the St. Louis schools were de jure segregated prior to *Brown* but that, in compliance with that decision, they had fully desegregated the school system in late 1954. In the years that followed, however, the system became increasingly black, as did the city, because of the "exodus of whites and affluent blacks from the City to St. Louis County. . . ."

The court listed the factors that contributed to this exodus and traced the corresponding increase of blacks in the city's schools. Experience in St. Louis showed that a particular school could retain stable integration as long as the percentage of blacks remained below 50 percent, but when it exceeded this level, the integrated enrollment soon became an all-black or a virtually all-black enrollment. The court rejected an NAACP desegregation plan "which require[d] massive busing of pupils within the city of St. Louis," because it found that the school board was not responsible for the resegregated schools in any constitutional sense. The court therefore instructed the board that, in drawing up a plan for further integration of the schools, "the criteria shall be quality education, which includes integration of the races, where practicable and feasible."

Courts at this point were approving and many black parents and community leaders were urging enforceable educationally oriented settlement decrees. These agreements reflected the understanding that Thomas P. Smith in 1849 had advocated in a speech to the black community in Boston.[7] Smith, as mentioned earlier, urged the retention of separate schools because the integration effort would create great upset and eventuate in more separate schools. His views, rejected by the leadership, proved as accurate in the twentieth century as they were in the nineteenth.

A similar debate raged during the 1930s as the NAACP contemplated the massive litigation campaign that was to culminate in the *Brown* decision. At that time, W. E. B. Du Bois urged that the NAACP not commit itself to either separate or integrated schools. Du Bois lost that debate, but his views did not change. Du Bois urged a distinction between segregation, which should not reflect an unwillingness of blacks and whites to work, live, and cooperate with one another, and discrimination, which was inferior treatment based on race. But the NAACP and many blacks could see no distinction in the two terms. They rejected his contention that "oppression and insult [had] become so intense and unremitting that until the world's attitude changes . . . volunteer union for self-expression and self-defense was essential."[8]

Du Bois did not hold views simply for ideology's sake, and his earlier beliefs had fluctuated on the integration–separation issue. During his early years at the NAACP, which he helped found and in which he served as editor of the organization's official publication, *The Crisis*, from 1910 until 1934, Du Bois attacked Jim Crow laws and generally inveighed against the establishment of black schools. But later, discouraged by the federal government's failure to aid blacks during the Depression, Du Bois concluded that survival would require black self-help. Thereafter, he de-emphasized integration, explaining, "No idea is perfect and forever valid. Always to be living and apposite and timely, it must be modified and adapted to changing facts."[9]

As reviewed here, the NAACP and other major civil rights groups did not change their views as to the value of integration policies throughout the 1970s, despite growing resistance and the increased difficulty of effectively integrating large urban school systems with their steadily decreasing percentages of white students. In a controversial law review article, I suggested that civil rights lawyers had become more committed to their belief in integration than they were to the educational interests of their clients.[10] A reassessment of school desegregation strategies was appropriate because the great crusade to desegregate the public schools had faltered. I wrote that desegregation now faced increasing opposition at both local and national levels (not all of which could now be simply condemned as "racist"). While the once vigorous support of federal courts was on the decline, new barriers had arisen: inflation made the attainment of racial balance more expensive, the growth of black populations in urban areas rendered it more difficult, and increasing numbers of social science studies questioned the validity of its educational assumptions.

Civil rights lawyers dismissed the new obstacles as legally irrelevant. Having achieved so much by courageous persistence, they did not waver in their determination to implement *Brown* using racial-balance measures developed in the hard-fought legal battles of the 1960s and 1970s. This stance presented great risk for our clients and the class they represented. For many, their educational interests were no longer in accord with the integration ideals of their attorneys. I suggested that, now that traditional racial-balance remedies were becoming increasingly difficult to achieve or maintain, we should recognize that racial balance might not be the relief actually desired by the victims of segregated schools.[11]

My article incensed more civil rights advocates than it convinced. For many civil rights workers, success in obtaining racially balanced schools became a symbol of the nation's commitment to equal opportunity, not only in education, but in housing, employment, and other fields where the effects of racial discrimination were still present. One commentator, Dean Earnest Campbell, observed, "[T]he busing issue has acquired meanings that seem to have little relevance for the education of children in any direct sense." I think Dean Campbell was correct in viewing proponents of racial balance as fearful that the loss of busing as a major tool for desegregation would signify the end of an era of expanding civil rights.

For adherents, the busing debate symbolized a major test of the country's continued commitment to civil rights progress. Any retreat was deemed an abandonment of this commitment and a return to segregation. Indeed, some leaders saw busing as a major test of black political strength. Under a kind of domestic domino theory, civil rights leaders feared that failure on the busing issue would trigger a string of defeats, ending a long line of major judicial and administrative decisions that substantially expanded the civil rights and personal opportunities of blacks in the post–World War II period.[12]

Looking back, it is apparent that rigidity on the racial-balance and busing issue helped bring about the very resegregation that these leaders and lawyers most feared. As I will discuss in Chapter 13, quite similar arguments are being made in support of affirmative action. It is, advocates claim, a test of the country's continued commitment to civil rights. Any retreat will evidence an abandonment of this commitment and will return us to the days of "separate but equal" or even *Dred Scott*.

In school desegregation, the goal of equal educational opportunity became merged with racial balance and busing as the means of its attainment. The rejection of the means was viewed as the defeat of the goal. In affirmative action, the goal of getting black and other nonwhite students into college is merged with the tactic of utilizing race in admissions standards. I can only hope that the loss of the tactic will not lead to abandonment of this still-worthwhile goal.

The Risks of Court-Ordered Desegregation

We were aware that using court orders to send black students into white schools where they were not wanted could be dangerous and was always traumatic. For a long time, I pointed to the strong kids who survived and even prospered under the pressures. Birdie Mae Davis, the lead student plaintiff in the Mobile, Alabama, desegregation case, was a favorite example. She testified in court that she had ignored the name-calling and was doing well in her classes. When another student said Dr. Martin Luther King, Jr., was a communist, she out-argued him with the facts about King's life. We were proud of Birdie Mae. Regrettably, I paid far less attention to all those students less able to overcome the hostility and the sense of alienation they faced in mainly white schools. They faired poorly or dropped out of school. Truly, these were the real victims of the great school desegregation campaign.

Even when a school's administration was not overtly hostile, black children did not always fare well. Ray Rist, an educational reporter, published a book, *The Invisible Children*, based on a year-long observation of a voluntary desegregation program in an upper income, all-white elementary school in Portland, Oregon.[13] The book recounts in detail the systematic, mostly unthinking devastation of two dozen six-to-ten-year-old black children.

As with most voluntary school integration programs, dispersal of the black children was the norm. In Portland, no more than forty-five black children were bused to any single elementary school, and white schools of four-hundred to five-hundred pupils received as few as four and in most instances only ten to fifteen black students. Brush Elementary, the all-white school Rist selected for daily observation, received about thirty black children.

The principal, along with most of his all-white teaching staff, had never taught a black child. He hired a black school aide because he felt that most of the white students had never spoken to a black person. His lack of racial sensitivity was illustrated in a staff discussion about the collection of milk money, when he said, "I guess we had better not call it chocolate milk any longer. It would probably now be more appropriate to refer to it as black milk."

The Portland school board's policy equated integration and racial assimilation. This policy, Rist explains, is a "means of socializing nonwhite students to act, speak, and believe very much like white students." It leaves dominant group values intact, does no damage to notions of white superiority, and helps to gain the support of those whites who view it as a means of helping "nonwhite peoples to become fully human by instilling in them 'white' ways of thinking and feeling."

In keeping with the assimilationist tone of the program, the principal assigned one or two black children to each classroom, and scheduled only a few special teacher-training sessions, which were poorly handled. The principal's desire was to treat the black students just like the whites. This approach was undermined by his failure to recognize and address fears and misconceptions of teachers about the black children's academic ability and behavior problems, the adequacy of their home backgrounds, and their moral turpitude.

Nervous and apprehensive about the new arrivals, the teachers, lacking proper training and skills, and with all their racial stereotypes intact, welcomed the black children to a totally new environment. Soon, they were exchanging "horror stories" at lunch about what their black students had done in the classroom. There apparently was no discussion of the older white students who cursed and taunted the black children on the playground and going to and from their special bus.

Almost from the start, the black children from poor backgrounds experienced difficulty in keeping up with the high-achieving, upper-class white children. No special help was provided. When the principal noted that one black student had an IQ score of 81, he went immediately to the child's teacher and told her not to put any pressure on the child to perform. With an IQ of 81, he explained, "there [wasn't] much she could expect." Peer relations were also a problem for the black youngsters. A few white children were friendly, but others were hostile or simply distant. Teachers unthinkingly added to both problems by physically separating black students in the classroom either for special instruction or in response to the black students' requests. Acceptable behavior from the black children was the teachers' primary goal.

Almost miraculously, some black youngsters adjusted and completed the year satisfactorily. Others dropped out. When Lou, a fourth grader, left the school before Christmas to transfer back to a school near his home, a teacher reported that on his last day "he went around telling everyone how he hated them and hoped they would all die." Most of the black children maintained that they liked Brush and hoped to return. Some, of course, had known no other school. Their parents also seemed to think the Brush experience was positive and a clear improvement over the black schools. But few black parents had any substantial contact with the school. Rist doubts their assessment would have been so positive had they been "really aware" of what was happening to their children. He concludes that the parents had volunteered their children not because of where they were going, but because of what they were leaving.

The Invisible Children contains what must be the definitive formula for how not to treat black children in mainly white schools. Yet what Rist observed in 1964 has been replicated in many school integration efforts across the country. Rist points out that "[w]hite dominance of Brush School was so strong that the presence and contributions of black people were discounted. The black children confronted a school milieu that either rejected or ignored their existence." He searched for weeks before finding a picture containing blacks posted in a classroom. But how could it have been otherwise? The school board rejected school desegregation plans requiring whites to give up their home schools. White parents at Brush met during the year and concurred in the suggestion that the program was acceptable as long as the number of black students did not exceed thirty. In short, as Rist summarized integration policy at the Brush school, "[d]ay after day, . . . the . . . black students came off the bus to a setting where the goal was to render them invisible. And the more invisible they became, the greater the satisfaction of the school personnel that the integration program was succeeding!"

Integration advocates will dismiss the Ray Rist stories as "growing pains," but the pattern of black and Hispanic children's educational experience being undermined by uncaring teachers whose approach is geared to racial stereotypes is far more widespread than any of us want to contemplate. School policies aimed at assisting white children and placating their often-anxious parents lead to high failure and drop-out rates among children of color, human casualties that cannot be dismissed because some children of color fare well.

Faced with the necessity of complying with school desegregation plans, school officials adopted plans that merged interest-convergence components with the willingness to sacrifice the interests of black parents and children by, in effect, maintaining important aspects of segregation within racially balanced schools. In 1985, Daniel Monti, in his book *A Semblance of Justice*, detailed the working of these silent covenants in the St. Louis school desegregation process.[14]

Professor Monti reported that for many years, St. Louis school officials staunchly resisted any liability for segregation in their schools. Then, after court orders were finally entered, the same individuals used school desegregation mandates to achieve educational reforms, including magnet schools, increased funding for training, teacher salaries, research and development, and new school construction. According to Monti, school officials accomplished all these gains for the system without giving more than secondary priority to redressing the grievances of blacks. They told him candidly that they used desegregation to create a metropolitan school system, the only sensible way to deliver educational resources across the St. Louis area.

Had he wished to do so, Monti could have reached similar conclusions about how school desegregation benefits the system rather than black children in many other school districts. In St. Louis and elsewhere, school officials used the school desegregation controversy to increase their legitimacy as the proper policy-making body for public education—an accomplishment furthered by the fact that civil rights lawyers like myself did not include orders calling for the replacement of school board members in our petitions for relief, even though they and their predecessors in office were responsible for the discriminatory policies and the delaying tactics we attacked in the courts. We knew they were responsible, but felt both that they would obey court orders and that relief seeking their removal would be impossible to obtain.

When districts finally admitted more than a token number of black students to previously white schools, the action usually resulted in closing black schools, dismissing black teachers, and demoting (and often degrading) black principals. I heard too often of respected principals of black schools who, in order to keep their pensions, had to accept janitorial positions in mainly white schools. There they could be seen by all picking up paper on school lawns. Civil rights attorneys made some effort to stem the loss of black teachers and principals through litigation, but I am afraid our main emphasis was on desegregating the schools. In all too many cases, black faculty and administrators, along with the children they served, were secondary to our priority: desegregate the schools.

Forgotten as well were the outstanding black high schools, some dating back to the 1890s, such as Dunbar and Armstrong in Washington, D.C., Frederick Douglass in Baltimore and St. Louis, Booker T. Washington in Atlanta, and Crispus Attucks in Indianapolis. Staffed with talented teachers, some of whom possessed doctoral degrees, these schools turned out black graduates who went on to impressive careers.

Writer Jill Nelson interviewed Benjamin J. Henley, Jr., and Charles S. Lofton, two retired Dunbar High School teachers.[15] Native Washingtonians, between them they had worked in the D.C. public schools for nearly a century. Each came from families in which memories of slavery were very much alive and a sense of history and education was viewed as essential to upward mobility. They were schoolmates at Dunbar High School in the 1920s, during the school's long heyday as an elite public institution that trained some of black America's finest minds. Teachers at Dunbar inspired them to join their profession. Lofton told Nelson: "[I]ntegration, with all the good it brought, was also the beginning of the end of Dunbar, and Negro education as I'd known it. I wouldn't want it to go out that I'm not for integration—I am. I'm not for what it did to Dunbar and to students."

This story is perhaps apocryphal, but no less accurate. An old black woman was asked what she thought about the decades-long effort to desegregate the nation's public schools. Shaking her head, she responded with sadness in her voice, "We got what we fought for, but we lost what we had."

Judicial Retrenchment

Two considerations probably influenced the Court's full retreat from its earlier commitment to school desegregation. First, as discussed earlier, was the serious and steadily growing opposition to busing in general as a means of effecting school desegregation, particularly the overwhelming opposition to busing children between the inner city and the suburbs. Second was the studies of the educational effects of school desegregation, which had been inconclusive as to the value either in education or in socialization for black or white children.

Unable to see any resolution of these obstacles, courts began considering the process by which school cases could be removed from their dockets on findings that the school district had achieved unitary status. Court hearings debated whether the district made good-faith efforts toward desegregation, the number of remaining schools identifiable by race, and the feasibility of additional desegregation. Despite civil rights lawyers' objections, courts decided that school districts could at some point be relieved of their obligation to integrate their public schools even though substantial racial separation continued or might emerge in the absence of continued judicial oversight.

In the thirty-year-old *Board of Education of Oklahoma City Public Schools v. Dowell*, the Supreme Court held that formerly segregated school districts might be released from court-ordered busing even if some segregation persists, so long as all "practicable" steps to eliminate the vestiges of discrimination had been taken.[16] The Oklahoma City case decision reflected the fatigue and disillusionment on the majority of the Court with the protracted litigation and seemingly interminable supervision required in school desegregation cases.

The futility of the fight compounded the frustration. Consequently, the courts have taken almost every opportunity to release school districts from court-ordered desegregation, even where a substantial number of racially identifiable schools remain or might emerge. Once a desegregation decree is dissolved, plaintiffs must make a showing of intentional discrimination to merit renewed judicial supervision. That is a nearly impossible showing to make because residential segregation leading to substantial resegregation of schools will emerge from "natural" causes, without evidence of a segregative intent by the school board and thus without remedy.

In a twist of bitter irony, white flight has been used as a free-wheeling argument to block desegregation in almost every context. Courts have refused to consider even intentional residential segregation in finding liability or fashioning appropriate relief. Yet in other cases, courts have taken judicial notice of this form of resistance and dissolved desegregation orders to prevent further white flight. Allowing white flight to justify avoiding desegregation created a perverse incentive: it placed the least pressure on areas in which whites were extremely hostile to busing and, consequently, which were the least likely to desegregate voluntarily. In effect, as was true so often in the past, the viability of constitutional guarantees of equal protection was dependent upon popular opinion.

Measuring the Gains and Losses

Advocates of school desegregation can, of course, seek solace in the thousands of children—white as well as black—who attended racially desegregated schools and felt they were advantaged by their experiences. Many researchers have found that desegregation increases the academic achievement of black students. Black children attending desegregated schools perform better on standardized achievement and IQ tests, and are more likely to complete high school and to enroll in and graduate from college, than black students in single-race schools. This means, of course, that desegregation may substantially improve the opportunities available for black adults in every arena.[17]

The pride and sense of accomplishment that should come with this outcome are counteracted by the racial hostility as well as the economic and housing barriers that limit integrated schooling to those black and Latino families able to live in mainly white, middle-class areas. As a result, there is a steady decline in the number of children able to obtain a racially integrated education in American schools. A study issued in early 2003 by the strongly pro-integration Harvard Civil Rights Project[18] reported that, as of the 2000–2001 school year, white students, on average, attended schools where 80 percent of the student body was white. Minority students were increasingly attending schools that were virtually nonwhite. Quite often, devastating poverty, limited resources, and various social and health problems are concentrated in these schools. The nation's largest city schools are, almost without exception, overwhelmingly nonwhite. In suburban districts that were virtually all-white three decades ago, serious patterns of segregation have emerged as more and more nonwhites move into suburban areas.

The findings of Jonathan Kozol are more striking than nationwide statistics. He focuses on the schools in the Mott Haven section of the Bronx in New York, and reports that, in the elementary schools serving the neighborhood, only twenty-six out of eleven thousand children are white. This segregation rate of 99.2 percent leaves two-tenths of one percentage point as the distinction between legally enforced segregation in the South of fifty years ago and the socially and economically enforced apartheid in this New York school district today.[19]

The racial isolation in the Mott Haven schools is a dramatic reflection of most school systems serving inner-city or mainly black or Latino areas across the country. And most of these systems are not only segregated but systematically under funded. They contain dedicated teachers, to be sure, but most teaching staffs are filled with young and inexperienced teachers and those who have been beaten down by the array of difficulties in teaching students who come to school from poverty-stricken areas. The classical educational triangle of student-teacher-parent is difficult to establish and maintain, and it is often nonexistent. With some exceptions, school boards are reduced to providing excuses rather than solutions to the array of challenges posed by schools that are as segregated and unequal in fact as, in the *Plessy v. Ferguson* era, they were under law.

The academic status of all black children, including those attending integrated schools, is not encouraging. Despite evidence that integration has improved the performance of minority students, shocking disparities still mark the educational attainments of black students and white students. Black students are twice as likely to drop out of high school as white students.[20] On standardized achievement tests in reading, black nine-year-olds scored an average of ten points lower than white nine-year-olds. As many as 40 percent of minority youths are functionally illiterate.[21]

Conditions for Latino children are even more dreary. Segregated both by race and poverty, and with a developing pattern of linguistic segregation, Latinos have by far the highest school dropout rates. The Supreme Court did not recognize the entitlement of Latino children to desegregation until 1973.[22] Latinos often asked for bilingual education as part of the segregation remedy as a means of gaining equal access to the curriculum and eventually full integration.[23] While the federal government provided support for this movement, it probably prompted a strong antibilingual movement among many whites that— even as the segregation of Latino children increased—succeeded in outlawing bilingual education through voter referenda in California, Arizona, and Massachusetts.

The unhappy fact is that the quality of education is shockingly bad in many—perhaps most—schools attended by poorer black and Spanish-speaking children in what are nominally desegregated schools. Facilities often range from inadequate to awful and because of many factors, including seniority and teacher-union rules, and invalidated and often-irrelevant job requirements, whites make up the majority of the faculty and administrators. Many of the white teachers are as dedicated and hard-working as their black and Hispanic colleagues. The barriers in their way are many, and some otherwise-productive teachers, no matter their race, simply give up. Some leave teaching, others remain but limit their efforts to trying to maintain order, assuming that, since their students don't want to learn, there is no need to even try to teach them. Such attitudes, of course, soon become self-fulfilling.

12

BROWN AS LANDMARK
An Assessment

PLANNING FOR THE FUTURE requires an accurate assessment of what *Brown* accomplished either directly and indirectly, and what it failed to do. Such a critique is difficult because *Brown* has become a legal landmark, an American icon embraced as a symbol of the nation's ability to condemn racial segregation and put the unhappy past behind us.

Indeed, the *Brown* decision has become so sacrosanct in law and in the beliefs of most Americans that any critic is deemed wrongheaded, even a traitor to the cause. Certainly, few veterans of the efforts to implement *Brown* through the racial-balance model are objective about the obstacles they faced. A typical response when confronted with their meager progress might be: "Sure, school integration has not worked because real integration has not been tried." And despite its short-lived effectiveness in desegregating public schools, no one will deny the statistics of improved performance by some of the minority students who attended desegregated schools and their often-positive anecdotes of achievements under fire.

The general view remains that *Brown* was the primary force and provided a vital inspirational spark in the post–World War II civil rights movement. Defenders maintain that *Brown* served as an important encouragement for the Montgomery bus boycotters, and that it served as a key symbol of cultural advancement for the nation. Even my progressive law students accept the view that *Brown* achieved more than it did.

When I shared my alternative *Brown* decision (see chapter 3) with my constitutional law class, most students resisted the notion that affirming and enforcing "separate but equal" would have led to more progress than occurred under *Brown*.

Nonetheless, my New York University colleague Paulette Caldwell and I both teach against the view of *Brown* as the icon of equality. At a dinner honoring Professor Caldwell, one of her students, Stacie Hendrix, told the gathering that she had viewed *Brown v. Board of Education* as a symbolic victory intended to change the state of race relations in America. Then she said:

> Professor Caldwell taught me to think critically about whether *Brown* was ever intended to improve the status of people of color in the United States. She taught me that law isn't always an engine of justice no matter how well intentioned the parties might be. She taught me that laws are products of the societies that promulgate them and of the elites that govern those societies, containing all their fears, hatred, and insecurities as well as their hopes and ideals. In order to change a society, we must change more than its laws.[1]

Over the decades, the *Brown* decision has spawned at least as much debate and scholarly articles among scholars in law and across the academic spectrum as any other issue. In the early years, much of the writing either claimed that *Brown* was wrongly decided or heatedly responded to those charges.[2] The debate continues, but for better or worse, the *Brown* decision is a key part of our law even if its current relevance is in doubt. Given my contrary assessment, it is appropriate to provide a sampling of contemporary views held by constitutional law scholars whose views at least partially support mine. I doubt they are ready to accept my proposition that a decision based on a more thorough knowledge of race and its societal role might have more effectively moved the country in the direction the Warren Court wished it to go. They do, though, hold a less deferential assessment of *Brown*'s value than is now the consensus view.

University of Virginia law professor Michael Klarman published an in-depth study that goes against the tide of *Brown* approval.[3] He finds that, in the long run, racial reform was inevitable because of a variety of deep-seated social, political, and economic forces that would have undermined racial segregation whether or not the Supreme Court had

intervened. Klarman acknowledges that while *Brown* acted as a catalyst for the civil rights legislation in the 1960s, it did so not for the
reasons commonly cited.

In addition to the Cold War motivations I discussed in chapter 6,
Klarman notes several nonlegal events that also served as catalysts,
such as Jackie Robinson's and Branch Rickey's breaking the color bar
in professional baseball, and the impact of Emmett Till's 1955 murder
in the Mississippi Delta and the subsequent acquittal of his killers. In
different but highly significant ways, these events served notice that
long-accepted racial practices would not continue unchallenged. In
short, Klarman contends that a multitude of social, political, and
economic forces were responsible for both *Brown* and overall racial
change among them, including World War II, the Cold War,
Democratic Party recruitment of black voters, and changing demo-
graphics.

As to the importance of World War II, Klarman notes that because
war is a cooperative endeavor, constituents of society join together to
face a common enemy, while differences such as race tend to be
submerged. Black soldiers, remembering that their support for World
War I was followed by no significant change in racial practices, determined that in return for their participation in WWII, they would have
to fight battles against the Axis and against Jim Crow. The singer,
actor, and activist Harry Belafonte explained:

> [T]he Second World War happened, and my mother told me that the
> fight against Hitler was our fight, and I went off, just like that. We were
> fighting against tyranny, fighting for freedom. But when we—the Black
> soldiers—came home, we found it was business as usual. There were no
> changes in the segregation laws. There was no right to vote. And yet
> being part of that war changed something in us—we'd had a peek at
> freedom. I knew if I could fight for it over there, I could fight for it in
> America.[4]

Military service had a great impact on black aspirations for full citizenship. Wartime exigencies created a setting conducive to extracting
political concessions from an administration anxious to avoid disunity
and disorder that civil rights demonstrations threatened to produce.
Recognizing leverage not usually available, civil rights leaders were
able to obtain wartime concessions, including the establishment of the

temporary Fair Employment Practices Committee, which monitored race discrimination in war-related industries, and the war Labor Board, which outlawed racial wage differentials.

The conscription of white males into military service produced a tightening labor market that caused employers to hire blacks for positions previously denied to them. As a result, the black middle class burgeoned, but when opportunities for blacks dissipated with the end of hostilities, blacks were left frustrated and resentful. White southerners who left their region for the first time during the war were exposed to racial norms never experienced. For the first time, they were forced to live, work, and serve with blacks. Also, industrialization began to erode the original agricultural basis for the Jim Crow social system. It is said, only partly in jest, that the Sun Belt is the result of desegregation and air conditioning.

Clearly, World War II laid the groundwork for the destruction of Third World colonialism, and U.S. foreign policy had to address the force of such global concessions. And finally, the war against fascism forced white Americans to contemplate the content of their own values and to emphasize distinctions between themselves and the enemy.

On the political front, the Democratic Party's new electoral competitiveness in the industrial Northeast and upper Midwest had two effects. It diminished the party's dependence on the southern electorate and left it freer to compete for the black vote despite the risk of alienating the South. Also, black voters, having shown their willingness to vote for either party, began to make their votes available to the highest bidder.

As southern prosperity became dependent on northern investment, the nation's leaders focused on creating a social environment that would favor such investment. The South was also dependent on federal funds, and as the New Deal policies reoriented the Democratic Party from its southern base toward a broader geographic and demographic coalition of ethnic and racial minorities, the threat to cut off federal funds to stubborn southern states grew teeth. To some extent, regional urbanization and industrialization, rising education levels for both whites and blacks, demographic shifts in the southern population, and the gradual transformation of social scientific and popular attitudes toward racial difference in the South all began to temper the harshness and rigidity of southern racial practices.

As suggested at the outset of his discussion, Professor Klarman believes that racial change was inevitable, and that while the *Brown* decision did play a role in that change, it did so in a perverse way. Where previously, southern resistance to racial change had been scattered, *Brown* crystallized that resistance. It unified southern racial intransigence, propelling politics in virtually every southern state to the far right on racial issues, and catapulting into office southern politicians who were forcefully committed to the preservation of the racial status quo. Nationally televised scenes of southern law enforcement using police dogs, high-pressure fire hoses, tear gas, and truncheons against peaceful, prayerful black demonstrators converted millions of previously indifferent northern whites into enthusiastic proponents of civil rights legislation that the Kennedy and Johnson administrations no longer deemed it wise to resist.

Klarman's position is consistent with my interest-convergence thesis. Even before the enactment of the Civil Rights Act of 1964 barred racial discrimination in places of public accommodation, business leaders in several southern towns, facing serious economic loss in the wake of protests that caused customers of both races to stay away from shopping areas in droves, met quietly and decided on the specific dates after which they would remove Jim Crow signs and stop denying admission or segregating black customers. Hotels, restaurants, and stores were pleased to learn that desegregation increased profits when they welcomed rather than shunned black customers. When it was enacted, the 1964 Civil Rights Act served as justification for policy changes that, out of economic considerations, most, but not all, were quite ready to make without legal coercion.

In his book, *The Hollow Hope: Can Courts Bring About Social Change?*, Gerald Rosenberg examines the civil rights movement and its ability to effectuate change in education, voting, transportation, accommodations, public places and housing. In the realm of education, Rosenberg agrees with Professor Klarman that *Brown v. Board of Education* is a symbol, but not for the reasons previously thought. Close examination reveals that before Congress and the executive branch acted to enforce *Brown* under the Civil Rights Act of 1964 and the 1965 Elementary and Secondary Education Act, the Supreme Court's decision had virtually no direct effect on ending discrimination in America's public schools.[5] Indeed, in Rosenberg's view, the evidence suggests that *Brown*'s major positive impact is "limited to reinforcing the belief in a legal strategy for change of those already committed to it."[6]

Acknowledging that we can never know what would have happened without *Brown*—or, as I imagined, if there had been a decision that enforced Plessy's "separate but equal" rule—Rosenberg believes that the existence and proliferation of the civil rights movement suggest that change may have occurred regardless. For instance, the economic development following World War II and the international pressure to remedy the situation promoted the government to support efforts to end segregation:

> The combination of all of these factors—growing civil rights pressure from the 1930s, economic changes, the Cold War, population shifts, electoral concerns, the increase in mass communication—created the pressure that led to civil rights. The Court reflected that pressure; it did not create it.[7]

Jack Boger, a longtime civil rights lawyer and now a law professor at the University of North Carolina, Professor Boger provides a perspective that seeks to acknowledge the value of *Brown* without ignoring its shortcomings. Speaking at a spring 2002 conference held at American University, Boger suggested that what sets *Brown* apart from earlier great cases on race is less the object of the Court's attention, namely, public education, important as that function is to modern citizens. Instead, it was the implicit affirmation by the nation's highest court in this crucial case of the full equal status of African Americans as persons and citizens. This intellectual and rhetorical reconceptualization flew in the face of a political culture still firmly wed, at state and national levels, to Jim Crow apartheid and black subordination in public and private life.

Unlike the more grudging graduate school cases in which African Americans were treated as the objects of benevolent quasi-contractual relations that could be altered at will by whites, Boger asserts, in language quite like that Judge Robert Carter used,[8] that *Brown* assumed from the outset that blacks are first-class "fee simple" citizens whose rights must be respected and whose liberties cannot be unilaterally readjusted, either by white legislatures or by white courts.

In that sense, then, Boger says, many of us felt that in *Brown* lay the new constitutional, legal, and even moral foundation for all that came after it: the civil rights movement, the sit-ins of the early 1960s, and the reaffirmation of civil rights by Congress in the 1964 and 1965 acts. In Boger's view, Gerald Rosenberg's *The Hollow Hope* thus misses the point. It is not the number of references to the *Brown* opinion, or the immediate effectiveness of the *Brown* decree, that determine its value. *Brown* imposed a new normative statement of American polity, and in that sense, like the Declaration of Independence, the Emancipation Proclamation, and the Gettysburg Address, purported to clarify for Americans normatively who they were or should be, and thereby allowed all who were willing the chance to work, with implicit legal support, toward the fulfillment of this normative vision.

This surely was the hope and expectation, but the promise of *Brown* proved a mirage. Seidman, who I quoted earlier, called it equality by proclamation. The statement that separate facilities were inherently unequal served to legitimate current arrangements. Thereafter, those blacks who remained poor and disempowered were viewed as having failed to take advantage of their definitionally equal status.[9]

Having reminded us of *Brown's* potential, Boger does not ignore the limits of its vision that are pertinent today. Its historical account failed to acknowledge the full magnitude and duration of white supremacy and the extent of black subordination after *Plessy*. As a consequence, the Court permitted the development of a "specific intent" or tort theory of equal-protection-clause violations announced fully in later civil rights cases. It implicitly assumed an otherwise unblemished world of racial equality marred only by discrete, individual, redressable incidents of violation, rather than a near-seamless national web of constitutional injury. Here, Boger's critique is in line with that of Seidman's.[10]

Reflecting back on his experience in an all-white school, Boger had written in an earlier article that separating children by race "worked a terrible evil" on white children. It was a "psychologically damaging and educationally destructive experience for my white friends and myself, and I venture, for millions of other children." He feels that it has taken "literally decades for my generation to begin to shed the unconscious, but pernicious, grip of the segregated environments in which we were brought up, with all of the fears, suspicions, and misunderstandings that they created."[11]

University of Pennsylvania political science professor Rogers Smith builds on Boger's "terrible evil" theme. Speaking at the New York

University Law School from a draft of an unpublished paper, Smith faulted the Court for basing its findings—perhaps unavoidably in order to find a constitutional harm—on the evidence that segregation had rendered blacks a "damaged race," while making no mention of any harm to whites. The opinion's oft-cited language about the inferior status generated by segregation and its probably irreparable damage to the hearts and minds of black children can be read as a scathing derogation of American blacks.

Professor Kevin Brown recognizes that "to have avoided replicating the message about the inferiority of African Americans in desegregation," the opinion would have had to articulate "how de jure segregation harmed Caucasians as well."[12] Smith prefers to read *Brown* as assuming harm to both races, noting the false sense of superiority and all its cultural deficiencies that afflict whites assigned to segregated schools.

The modern views of *Brown* should, at the least, cause today's civil rights advocates to pause before seeking judicial help in the resolution of serious racial issues. Further reason for caution is provided by the far-from-satisfactory outcome in the University of Michigan affirmative action cases that I will discuss in the next chapter.

This suggestion is easier to make than for litigation-oriented lawyers to follow. I recognize, of course, that the other options for governmental relief, the executive and legislative branches—save for a brief period in the 1960s when procivil rights policies were politically advantageous—have taken stances on racial issues that have swung from unresponsive to hostile. And so we continue to rely on courts, even though the federal courts, now filled with conservatives appointed by Republican administrations, are not much concerned about racial and other social issues. Like the gambler who enters the card game knowing that it is fixed, we are drawn to the courts because they are the only game in town.

13

AFFIRMATIVE ACTION AND RACIAL FORTUITY IN ACTION

THE CONCLUSIONS OF LEGAL COMMENTATORS about the less than critical role of *Brown* in post–World War II racial reform are not well known and would probably not be accepted by much of the public. It thus should not be surprising that the mostly unrecognized racial fortuity that so influenced the outcomes in school desegregation campaigns are also central to the decades-long controversy over the legality and fundamental fairness of affirmative action in general, and minority admissions to colleges and professional schools in particular. Once again, the rhetoric obscures the issues, allowing the argument to focus on the cost to whites of racial remedies rather than their necessity or appropriateness. As a result, few persons have recognized why, without the pressure of law, white-dominated institutions began opening schooling and employment areas to minorities long excluded both by outright bias and by discrimination's debilitating effect on their qualifications. The major cases I will review in this chapter reflect the pressures of interest-convergence and the resistance to any reform that threatened alteration of the racial status quo.

Affirmative Action Policies: The Controversy

As we have seen, an implicit stumbling block impedes society's approach to racial remedies. The issues of cost and cost assessment crucial to earlier racial remedies, though, were not closely examined during the tumult of the late 1960s. Then, urban rebellions, sparked by the 1968 murder of Dr. Martin Luther King, Jr., served as scary reminders that, more than a dozen years after *Brown* and a half-dozen years after enactment of federal civil rights laws, most corporations, government agencies, and institutions of higher learning remained virtually all-white and mostly male. At these organizations, managers chose to establish "racial and gender preferences" to accomplish the admission, hiring, and upgrading of a moderate number of white women and people of color. They did so rather than overhaul the policies and practices that, beyond blatant racial and sexual discrimination, were responsible for their institutions' all-white and all-male culture. The affirmative action approach served the immediate need of breaking down this culture, and as a bonus it brought in competent individuals able and willing to advance the institutions' goals.

This was certainly the case with minority admissions programs. Faced with social and political pressures to increase the minuscule number of minority students, colleges and professional schools typically opted to use minority racial status as a positive admissions factor. The alternative route, the reformulation of admission standards, although certainly possible, was generally rejected as "drastic and academically injurious." Certainly, racially neutral admissions programs would pose administrative difficulties. But the chosen solution, utilizing race and recognizing minority exceptions to traditional admissions standards based on grades and test scores, has served to validate and reinforce traditional policies while enveloping minority applicants in a cloud of suspected incompetence. Law school officials, claiming commitment to grades and test scores, have done little to dispel the cloud. In one way or another, they have contended that, unless they were permitted to retain criteria that provided extra points or special consideration to minority applicants, either virtually no minorities would be admitted or overall qualifications would have to be lowered.

Lost in this heads-we-win-tails-you-lose debate is the fact that both colleges and professional schools regularly admit students whose parents or close relatives are alumni or major contributors. At the college level, applicants with superior athletic potential leap-frog over hundreds, perhaps thousands, of students with better grade-point averages and test scores. In 1978, Justice Harry Blackmun pointed out the obvious:

It is somewhat ironic to have us so deeply disturbed over a program where race is an element of consciousness, and yet to be aware of the fact, as we are, that institutions of higher learning, albeit more on the undergraduate than the graduate level, have given conceded preferences up to a point to those possessed of athletic skills, to the children of alumni, to the affluent who may bestow their largess on the institutions, and to those having connections with celebrities, the famous, and the powerful.[1]

Also mostly lost in the turmoil over whether minority admissions violate traditional standards of merit is the impressive evidence that grades and test scores do not predict success in the practice of law or medicine. A great many minority students admitted with relatively low grades and scores "do satisfactory work and a number of them outperform regular admissions students whose records appear much better."[2] Many schools, though, insist on retaining admissions standards so unpredictive of performance that, if used for hiring, might well be held to violate fair employment practices.

Minority students admitted under a dual admissions policy can achieve success, but to do so they must carry a heavy and undeserved burden of inferior status. Critics of preferential admissions maintain that these programs must be abandoned because of the stigma of inferiority that attaches to minorities in these programs. Somehow, though, the stigma does not attach to those specially admitted because of parental wealth or influence, and critics do not urge that they be dropped. The so-called stigma is really a not-so-subtle form of racism. Maintaining qualifications that privilege wealth and position and disadvantage minorities, and then admitting a certain number of those minorities, is as much affirmative discrimination as affirmative action. As it is, the term "affirmative action" connotes remedial activity beyond what normally would be provided. It implies *noblesse oblige*, not legal duty, and suggests the dispensation of charity rather than the granting of much-deserved relief.

The presence of racism in policies intended to remedy racism is not generally recognized and is usually submerged in complex and ultimately confusing legal discussion about the appropriate equal protection standard to apply to remedial measures embodying racial classifications. Admissions requirements based on grades and standardized test scores, of course, posed a serious barrier to many whites as well as to minorities. But as history would enable us to predict, the attacks from upwardly striving whites focused neither on the exclusionary effect of the general admissions process nor on the most-favored-status it provided well-to-do applicants. Rather, these whites directed their challenge at the relatively minuscule number of seats that institutions set aside for minorities to ameliorate the harmful effects of past discrimination.

The open use of racial classifications to identify the socially and economically disadvantaged provided a legal argument to opponents of minority admissions. But the fact that special treatment for minority applicants upset working and middle-class whites so much more than preferences for applicants whose parents are faculty members, alumni, or major contributors cannot be explained solely by recent Supreme Court decisions holding that any racial classifications must be reviewed with utmost suspicion. Even if affirmative action opponents succeed in their effort to invalidate any consideration of race in the college admissions process, they will have done so without in any way affecting the white, upper-class bias that permeates the admissions decisions of almost all colleges and professional schools.

The self-defeating nature of opposition by so many whites to affirmative action programs should be evident. One would imagine that only a perverse form of racial paranoia could explain white opposition to racial remedies that historically benefit whites more than blacks. White women have been the major beneficiaries of affirmative action. And to the extent that affirmative action rules often require advertising jobs rather than simply filling them via existing "old-boy" networks, white men have had access to positions they would have never learned of without the policies so many of them abhor.

Paradoxically, we cannot expect that opposition to minority admissions will disappear as colleges and professional schools expand their admission criteria to include whites whose promise, like their black counterparts, is not reflected in grades and test scores. Working-class and upwardly striving middle-class whites perceive incorrectly but no less fervently that the share of educational opportunities available to their children is endangered by minority admissions programs. Their belief is strengthened by the conviction that blacks are not supposed to get ahead of whites, and by the realization that poor whites are powerless to alter the plain advantages in educational opportunity available to the upper classes. Losses to the white privileged are accepted and attributed to "just the breaks."

The *Bakke* Court Challenge to Affirmative Action

Legal challenges to college and professional school affirmative action policies led to the Supreme Court's 1978 decision in *Regents of the University of California v. Bakke*.[3] When Allan Bakke, a white man, applied for and had been denied twice admission to the University of California's Davis Medical School, he claimed that the reason was that the school had set aside sixteen out of one hundred admission slots for minority candidates. His lawsuit to gain admission to the medical school ignited a national controversy that had been building for years.

The litigation, compulsively covered in the media, resulted in a confusing, multifaceted decision. Four members of the Court would have approved the Davis policy as an appropriate corrective for past discrimination. Four members found that the Davis program established a quota that violated Title VI of the Civil Rights Act of 1964, prohibiting racial discrimination by institutions receiving federal funds. Justice Lewis Powell, writing for himself, found that the set-aside was unconstitutional, but felt that to further interests of diversity, the Constitution permitted some consideration of race in the evaluation of applicants. In effect, Justice Powell's opinion became the ruling of the Court.

The *Bakke* decision, far from resolving the minority admissions controversy, increased the determination of those arguing that any use of race was invalid. Efforts to increase the number of minority college and professional students through race-sensitive admission policies prompted a series of legal attacks during a period when the Court appeared enthralled by the notion that a color-blind nation would be achieved tomorrow if it refused to accept any consideration of race today. As a result, the Court became increasingly reluctant to validate preferences based on considerations of race or sex, and has regularly found programs constitutionally insufficient in set-aside programs, employment, and voting.

A vibrant cottage industry developed around the issue. According to one survey, the last half of the 1990s alone produced at least eight major books on affirmative action, more than fifty articles in popular magazines, another thirty articles in law reviews, including three major symposia, and numerous articles in a range of surprising places, from engineering publications to medical journals.[4] In the area of race-sensitive admissions, proponents maintained that consideration of race was both a fair and a necessary balance given the continued exclusion and marginalization of blacks in the society.[5] Opponents, ignoring history as well as contemporary reality but keenly sensitive to the growing fears among many whites that preferences for blacks displaced more deserving whites, hammered away with their message that racial preferences are unfair, unneeded, a deviant departure from prevailing methods of selection, and a threat to the American way of life.[6] Opponents have carried the day in the legislatures and the media.[7]

Minority Admissions and White Paranoia

In a society in which the essence of whiteness is an entitlement to priority over blacks for things of value, affirmative action programs were certain to lead to major opposition expressed in what Professors Susan Sturm and Lani Guinier refer to as the "Stock Affirmative Action Narratives":[8] "If I didn't get in, racial preference must have been the cause." This easily reached assumption provides psychic comfort at the cost of common sense to even impressively qualified applicants. It is a painful proof that the essence of racism, the sense of priority of place over the "other," still is both present and pervasive.

In 1986, while teaching as a visitor at Stanford Law School, on at least a half-dozen occasions I was stopped in the hall by white first-year students who learned I had been on the Harvard Law School faculty. These students would ask whether Harvard had an extensive minority admissions program. When I asked why they thought it was more extensive than Stanford's, their responses were always: "Well, I applied at Harvard, but I didn't get in." I would point out that the Harvard Law School received up to ten thousand applications from students, at least a third of whom presented records indicating they could do the work, but the law school's first-year class was limited to about 550 students. The Stanford students thanked me for my explanation, but seemed to feel that an unfair preference for less qualified minorities had kept them from gaining admission to their first-choice school.

If students able to gain admission to a top school like Stanford are vulnerable to such obviously outlandish beliefs, imagine how many whites, facing rejection for a job or a seat at the college of their choice, are told, dishonestly: "I am sorry. We really liked your credentials. Government regulations, though, mandate we give the job or the seat for which you are clearly qualified to a minority person." How easy it is to transfer the disappointment of rejection from the company doing the rejection to an unnamed candidate assumed to have inferior qualifications.

As an example, there is the case of Ben Jackson, a journalism professor writing under a pseudonym, who ruminated for a full page in a national publication about not getting a much-wanted job at another school and learning that the job had gone to "a black guy." Checking this individual out on the Internet, Jackson found the black's qualifications less good than his own. He recognized that many schools are under pressure to hire minority faculty as their minority student population increases, and that it was probably wrong to assume that the African American was less qualified. He acknowledged, though, that "I am a white male dealing with diversity issues in a very personal way." He recalled a black teacher confronting her mainly white classes with the admonition "that white people can't say they're not racist until they compete against a black person in the job market. I thought it was an odd statement. Now, I understood what she meant."[9]

Being rejected for a position for which one has applied is upsetting regardless of the reasons, but I wonder whether Jackson would have been as upset if the job had gone to a faculty member's child or someone else with "old boy" connections he found unimpressive. And whatever his feelings, without the racial-paranoia angle, it is unlikely that a national newspaper would have published his essay. Frankly, all the moaning about the pressure to hire black and other nonwhite professors is belied by the paucity of their numbers on most faculties.

The *Hopwood v. Texas* Challenge to *Bakke*

It is the sense of racial wrongness that captures the attention of readers and some courts. Cheryl Hopwood, the white plaintiff who in 1996 successfully challenged the University of Texas Law School admissions process in a federal court of appeals,[10] complained that she was rejected even though she had a higher Texas Index (TI) score (a composite of the student's undergraduate grade-point average and LSAT score) than some black and Mexican-American applicants who were admitted. She was thus, she argued, more deserving of admission than they. She also scored higher than more than one hundred white applicants who were admitted, a fact evidently of little concern to either Hopwood or the courts. In fact, Hopwood's rejection was probably more socioeconomic than racial. In accordance with a practice followed by many graduate schools, her application was downgraded because she attended a community college and a state school rather than an elite undergraduate college, the primary feeder schools for postgraduate and professional institutions.

Despite this evidence, in *Hopwood v. Texas*,[11] a panel of the Fifth Circuit found that considering race or ethnicity in admissions decisions is always unconstitutional, even when intended to combat perceived effects of a hostile environment, to remedy past discrimination, or to promote diversity. While the court of appeals recognized that the Supreme Court's *Bakke* decision permitted the limited use of race, it concluded that the Court's hostility to subsequent affirmative action cases in the set-aside and employment areas indicated that it had, in effect, overruled *Bakke*.

Minority Admissions Through Nonracial Criteria

In response to the *Hopwood* ban on using race in the admissions process, the Texas legislature ordered each of the state's public undergraduate institutions to admit all applicants whose grade-point averages were in the top 10 percent of their high school's graduating class.[12] This approach, strongly supported by black parents and the NAACP, is thought to encourage minority enrollment from high schools that have an overwhelmingly minority student body. David Orentlicher believes that the 10-percent approach may do much to improve the public primary and secondary schools by altering incentives for school quality. Under the current system, politically influential parents of school-age children prefer that their children attend the stronger schools, while the children of politically weak parents attend the poorer schools. Under the Texas approach, parents have less to gain by concentrating their children at stronger schools and more to gain by dispersing their children over a larger number of schools. Accordingly, Texas's 10-percent policy may lead to a public-school system with smaller disparities in quality from school to school.[13] As Orentlicher concedes, legal, political, and educational hurdles remain to be overcome in order for the 10-percent approach to have the diversity results hoped for it.

Reportedly, some white parents who moved to the suburbs to ensure superior schools for their children are making varying arrangements to have their high school-age children live within the districts served by mainly black schools to improve their chances of landing in the top 10 percent of their graduating classes. If true, it is another indication that even with individuals, self-interest can trump racial beliefs when those interests become sufficiently clear. Even so, the percentage plans may face court challenges from those who claim the plans are no different than overt racial preferences. In addition, colleges where gaining admission is only one barrier to a college education will have to improve recruitment and financial aid policies to actually enroll minority students from mainly minority schools.[14]

Rice University in Texas adopted another approach to the *Hopwood* ban. The university feared that, although it was a private institution not covered by the *Hopwood* decision, it could lose $45 million annually in federal aid, about 15 percent of its budget, if it failed to conform its admissions policies to the court decision.[15] Almost overnight, the admissions officers at Rice stopped saying aloud the words "black," "African American," "Latino," "Hispanic," or even "minority" in their deliberations. The next year, the proportion of black students admitted in the freshman class fell by half; the proportion of Hispanics, by nearly a third.

Unhappy with this outcome, Rice officials said that the school was committed to having a diverse student body. In the years since, according to a *New York Times* reporter, it has

developed creative, even sly ways to meet that goal and still obey the court. Thus the admissions committee, with an undisguised wink, has encouraged applicants to discuss "cultural traditions" in their essays, asked if they spoke English as a second language and taken note, albeit silently, of those identified as presidents of their black student associations.[16]

Rice also increased recruiting at high schools with traditionally high minority populations; in 2001, these efforts resulted in a freshman class with a near-record composition of blacks and Hispanics. Of the seven-hundred freshmen, 7 percent are black, 11 percent Hispanic. The Rice University experience provides a guideline for other colleges, not that other colleges needed added incentive to avoid becoming a target of the affirmative action foes. By the late 1990s, the College of William and Mary stopped rating its applicants on a nine-point scale. The University of Virginia dropped a rating system somewhat similar to that used by the University of Michigan, and Georgetown University dropped a committee that gave a second reading to applications from minority candidates. Other colleges are taking similar steps.[17] In the wake of the Michigan decisions, though, the presidents of the University of Texas at Austin and Rice University reported that it was likely they would again consider race in admission decisions.[18]

The nonracial admissions measures adopted even prior to the Michigan decisions reflect the fact that college policymakers recognize and want to retain the many values provided by a racially diverse student body. Although this is impressive, the ability and willingness of other schools to rely on racially neutral criteria has led opponents of affirmative action on the Supreme Court to contend that race-sensitive admissions practices at Michigan and elsewhere are not necessary either to achieve a diverse class or to help overcome the disadvantages of past and current discriminatory policies. And if this argument serves in a future case to gain a majority to invalidate any use of race in the admissions process, opponents will then probably challenge the "proxies" for race that Rice University and many other schools have been using.

New Landmarks: The University of Michigan Minority Admissions Cases

In 2003, opponents felt in position to topple affirmative action in the only area where it retained some validity, thanks to Justice Powell's vote for diversity in the *Bakke* case. They had filed two suits, one challenging the admissions practices of the University of Michigan Law School, and the other Michigan's undergraduate admissions policies. In interviews, the three white plaintiffs repeated the charge that any use of race rendered them victims of reverse discrimination. Unde-terred by either the thousands of applicants seeking admission to the university, or the great many white as well as minority students admitted with poorer scores than they presented, they maintained that Michigan's minority admissions programs were the reason their applications were rejected.[19]

In its defense, the University of Michigan, supported by civil rights groups, made an all-out effort to defend the challenged minority admis-sions programs. Affirmative action advocates, encouraged by favorable rulings in the court of appeals[20] and convinced that they had as strong a record as they were likely to get, organized a massive effort to break the Court's usual five-person majority that, over the previous decade, had invalidated race-sensitive programs in a number of areas.[21] While affirmative action defenders are committed to admissions criteria that provide special consideration to race, their lawyers shifted the focus from remediation for past discrimination to the value of diversity to the schools and to the society. In support, they lined up sixty-four *amici* briefs representing more than three hundred organizations, including academics, labor unions, scores of Fortune 500 companies, and nearly thirty retired military and civilian defense officials. The *amici* briefs all maintained that a racially diverse, well-educated work force is essential to the success of their operations.[22]

The build-up to the decisions was dramatic. The results were a relief to some and a disappointment to others. In the undergraduate case, *Gratz v. Bollinger*, the Court majority found that the under-graduate admissions policy, "which automatically grants 20 points, or one-fifth of the points needed to guarantee admission to every single underrepresented minority applicant solely because of race, is not narrowly tailored to achieve the interest in educational diversity that respondents claim justifies their program."[23]

In the law school case, *Grutter v. Bollinger*, the Court ruled 5 to 4 to approve its admissions policy. To the surprise of many, Justice Sandra Day O'Connor, who generally votes with the four conserva-tive justices to defeat affirmative action policies, provided the swing vote and wrote the majority opinion. She described the law school's admission process as a "highly individualized, holistic review of each applicant's file, giving serious consideration to all the ways an appli-cant might contribute to a diverse educational environment." She found that while race counts as a factor, it is not used in a "mechanical way."[24] She affirmed that the strict standards the Court applies when determining the validity of racial classifications still apply, but in their application, she took "into account complex educational judgments in an area that lies primarily within the expertise of the university. Our holding today is in keeping with our tradition of giving a degree of deference to a university's academic decisions, within constitutionally prescribed limits."[25]

O'Connor noted that the law school's focus on diversity is reflected by the weight it gives to factors besides race; that is, it accepts nonminority applicants with grades and test scores lower than underrepresented minority applicants (and other nonminority applicants) whom it rejects. By weighing many other diversity factors besides race, O'Connor felt that the law school could make a real and dispositive difference for nonminority applicants as well. She accepted the university's contention that diversity "promotes learning outcomes," "better prepares students for an increasingly diverse workforce and society, and better prepares them as professionals." She found these arguments echoed by the *amici* briefs filed by major corporations and military officials maintaining that the skills needed in today's increasingly global marketplace can only be developed through exposure to widely diverse people, cultures, ideas, and viewpoints.

O'Connor asserted that race-conscious admissions policies, even those utilized to ensure diversity, must be limited in time. She took the law school at its word that it would like nothing better than to find a race-neutral admissions formula and would terminate its use of racial preferences as soon as practicable. The Court, she said, expects that twenty-five years from now, the use of racial preferences will no longer be necessary to further the interest approved today. This optimistic estimate ignores both the fact that it comes twenty-five years after the *Bakke* decision initiated heated controversy over the meaning of diversity. The *Grutter* decision will probably continue rather than settle that debate.

Justice O'Connor and Interest-Convergence

The law school decision, in particular Justice O'Connor's opinion, is a prime example of interest-convergence in action. As indicated earlier, O'Connor has usually been an opponent of affirmative action, a posture that has prompted severe criticism from legal commentators.[26] Duke Law School professor Jerome Culp reports that she has approved some forms of affirmative action and spoken eloquently about the nature of racial oppression.[27] Culp adds that: "Unfortunately, for black Americans, she has also been a linchpin in the creation of an effective majority on the Court that would limit the ability of any level of governmental or private entity to change the racial status quo."[28] Although Justice O'Connor does not explicitly declare racial classifications to be unconstitutional, she supports an extremely limited view of the use of race. In her view, such policies should be presumed invalid,[29] demanding strict scrutiny in judicial review of all uses of race,[30] and suggesting that their use and application be limited.[31] She wrote the opinions in two major cases that virtually shut the door on set-aside programs intended to get long-excluded minorities into government construction contracts. In one case, *City of Richmond v. J. A. Croson Co.*,[32] she found that a city council that had an African-American majority in a city approximately 50 percent black, constituted a political majority from which the minority needed to be protected—referring here to whites as the minority—and thus justified heightened judicial scrutiny of the affirmative action plan.

Also, in *Adarand Constructors v. Pena*,[33] a 5 to 4 decision, O'Connor held that all racial classifications, imposed by whatever federal, state, or local governmental actor, must be analyzed by a reviewing court under strict scrutiny. In another close decision invalidating a collective bargaining agreement calling for the retention of a percentage of minority teachers in the case of lay-offs, O'Connor voted with the majority[34] and, in a concurring opinion, suggested that an affirmative action program might be valid, but only if it furthers a legitimate remedial purpose and "implements that purpose by means that do not impose disproportionate harm on the interests, or unnecessarily trammel the rights, of innocent individuals directly and adversely affected by a plan's racial preference."[35]

O'Connor's affirmative action jurisprudence illustrates her negative attitude to racial preferences and racial classifications. She has repeatedly pronounced her concern about how affirmative action plans may affect whites. She is worried about "trammel[ing] on the interests of nonminority employees."[36] Given these concerns, it is surprising that she supported the law school's diversity-oriented admissions policy. She evidently viewed it as a benefit and not a burden to nonminorities. In addition, it was a boost to a wide range of corporate and institutional entities with which she identifies.

According to Professor Joan Tarpley, "Justice O'Connor's decisions in this area reflect her commitment as a protector of the institution-alized 'rights of whites.'" When she perceived in the Michigan Law School's admissions program an affirmative action plan that minimizes the importance of race while offering maximum protection to whites and those aspects of society with which she identifies, she supported it. Diversity in the classroom, the work floor, and the military, not the need to address past and continuing racial barriers, gained her vote. Once again, blacks and Hispanics are the fortuitous beneficiaries of a ruling that can and probably will change when other priorities assert themselves.

This benefit in minority admissions, as conferred by O'Connor, is more than overshadowed by her rejection of affirmative action programs in the business and employment fields. The affirmative action plan in *Croson*, the monetary incentive in *Adarand*, and the minority ownership policies in *a* positive affirmative action decision, *Metro Broadcasting, Inc.*, overturned by *Adarand*, had a common intent. As Tarpley describes them: "Each was designed to offer a helping hand to black, small-business owners who were self-employed." For support, Tarpley quotes from a major study on racial wealth dispari-ties that finds: "Severe economic restrictions have historically prevented many African Americans from establishing successful busi-nesses. These include segregation, legal prohibition, acts of violence, discrimination, and general access only to so-called black markets."[37] The challenged affirmative action plans that were held unconstitu-tional would have helped many families see their small businesses succeed, and struggles to lessen a deeply rooted poverty could have produced the beginnings of generational asset building.

*   *   *

The dissents in the University of Michigan Law School decision reflect the narrowness of this "victory" for affirmative action and its vulnerability in future litigation. Chief Justice Rehnquist, writing for himself and the three dissenters, denied that the diversity position met the Court's tough standards for racial classifications set in earlier cases. He contended that the majority had departed from the close scrutiny given other affirmative action cases and that its review of the Michigan Law School's admission policies was "unprecedented in its deference."[38] Rejecting the school's contention that it sought a "critical mass" of minority students so that they would not feel isolated or that they would have to serve as spokespersons for their race, he noted that, year after year, a percentage of African-American students far larger than that of either Hispanics or Native Americans was admitted. He concluded that:

> the Law School has managed its admissions program, not to achieve a 'critical mass,' but to extend offers of admission to members of selected minority groups in proportion to their statistical representation in the applicant pool. But this is precisely the type of racial balancing that the Court itself calls "patently unconstitutional."[39]

In a lengthy opinion in the law school case, Justice Clarence Thomas, concurring in part and dissenting in part, expressed his opposition to affirmative action in all its forms, covering every argument in great detail. His certainty on the constitutionality of the issue of when race can be validly utilized seems based on his personal belief that:

> blacks can achieve in every avenue of American life without the meddling of university administrators. Because I wish to see all students succeed whatever their color, I share, in some respect, the sympathies of those who sponsor the type of discrimination advanced by the University of Michigan Law School (Law School). The Constitution does not, however, tolerate institutional devotion to the status quo in admissions policies when such devotion ripens into racial discrimination. Nor does the Constitution countenance the unprecedented deference the Court gives to the Law School, an approach inconsistent with the very concept of "strict scrutiny."[40]

Thomas called diversity a "faddish slogan of the cognoscenti." His criticism, like that of many affirmative action opponents, ignores the continuing viability of racism. They would strike down all racial classifications in the admissions process and not permit schools to use the diversity and critical-mass approaches to maintain some minority presence in their classes. At the same time, they give only passing mention and no weight to the barriers of racial discrimination that are at the heart of the opinions of the justices who would have approved the undergraduate program.

One of the dissenters in the undergraduate case, Justice Ruth Bader Ginsburg, reminded the Court that the effects of centuries of law-sanctioned inequality remain painfully evident in both our communities and our schools. The system of racial caste, ended only recently, created large racial disparities that endure in unemployment, poverty, and health care. Job applicants with equal credentials receive different receptions depending on their race, and prejudice still occurs in real estate markets and consumer transactions. Given the continuing vitality of bias, both conscious and unconscious, Ginsburg found it appropriate to use race in Michigan's admissions processes. She added that even if the Court found any use of race invalid, schools anxious to maintain their minority enrollments would resort to the use of qualifications that could serve as proxies for race. "If honesty is the best policy," she concluded, "surely Michigan's accurately described, fully disclosed College affirmative action program is preferable to achieving similar numbers through winks, nods, and disguises."[41]

While her position is supported by reams of statistics and the personal experience of most people of color whatever their economic status, Ginsburg could not garner five votes to justify considerations of race as a means of remedying past and continuing racial discrimination. Indeed, the results in the two Michigan cases, with their multiple opinions, concurrences and dissents, will further confuse rather than clarify Justice Powell's opinion in *Bakke*. It will probably encourage affirmative action opponents to mount more litigation challenges as well as exert pressure for the appointment of judges opposed to affirmative action in any form.

Justice Antonin Scalia, dissenting in the law school case, predicted that the two decisions he derided as a "split double header seem perversely designed to prolong the controversy and the litigation." Reviewing some of the possible litigation, Scalia said, "I do not look forward to any of these cases. The Constitution proscribes government discrimination on the basis of race, and state provided education is no exception.[42]

Justice David Souter, dissenting in the undergraduate case, highlighted the confusion between the two decisions that will probably
lead to the future litigation Scalia fears. Souter points out that, with
the exception of granting minority applicants twenty points, each
application is viewed holistically, as is the case in the law school
admissions policy that a majority of the Court approved. Souter noted
that nonminority students may receive twenty points for athletic
ability, socioeconomic disadvantage, or attendance at a socio-
economically disadvantaged or predominantly minority high school.
At the provost's discretion, they may also receive ten points for being
residents of Michigan, six points for being residents of an underrepresented Michigan county, and, among other matters, five for
leadership and service.

The Court majority in the undergraduate case expressed a preference for percentage plans like those in Texas, California, and Florida,
where a top percentage of each high school graduating class is guaranteed enrollment in a state college. Souter, though, saw little
difference between the percentage plans and the Michigan points
scheme the Court disallowed. The percentage plans get their racially
diverse results without saying directly what they are doing or why. In
contrast, Souter said, "Michigan states its purpose directly and, . . . I
would be tempted to give Michigan an extra point of its own for its
frankness. Equal protection cannot become an exercise in which the
winners are the ones who hide the ball."[43] Rather than try to steer a
course between the law school decision approving a holistic review of
each application and the granting of points on an admissions scale
struck down in the undergraduate case, many schools will opt to
abandon any overt mention of race and move toward maintaining
their minority student enrollments through the "winks, nods, and
disguises" that Ginsburg deplores.

The Court's approval of holistic reviews of each application will
certainly not dissipate the opposition to minority admissions. In addition to further litigation, we can expect that the Republican Congress
and the president will exploit popular opposition by introducing anti-
affirmative action legislation. It may well take the tack of the *amicus*
brief the Bush administration filed in the Michigan cases, maintaining
that the Michigan program unfairly penalizes white students and is
therefore unconstitutional. Only a few weeks after the Court decided

the Michigan cases, Ward Connelly, who led successful campaigns to ban racial and ethnic preferences in California and Washington State, announced that he and other affirmative action foes would launch a similar campaign in Michigan and other states.[44]

Challenging Traditional Admissions Criteria

As suggested earlier, the uproar over the validity and fairness of affirmative action policies has served to provide an undeserved legitimacy to traditional admissions criteria, grades, and standardized tests. Since they are supposedly neutral as to race, and have played a prominent role in hiring and admissions criteria, an effective challenge will be difficult but not impossible. And whatever the outcome, the conventional assessment and predictive criteria on which most colleges and graduate programs have heavily relied will continue to influence admissions decisions. A mountain of studies reveals that they are no more fair, democratic, or meritocratic for many whites than they are for members of racial or gender minorities. The tests clearly privilege those who come from higher economic backgrounds who can afford the expensive preparatory coaching that virtually guarantees enhanced scores.

This is the thrust of the study by Professors Susan Sturm and Lani Guinier of the Scholastic Assessment Test (SAT), the Law School Admissions Test (LSAT), and civil service tests, all of which are used to predict future performance based on existing capacity or ability. Their research has led them to conclude that these tests do not correlate with future performance for most applicants, at least not as a method of ranking those "most qualified." Instead, these tests, which constitute the foundation of our "meritocracy," tell us more about past opportunity than about future accomplishments on the job or in the classroom.[45]

According to the data reviewed by Sturm and Guinier, those wishing to challenge traditional admissions processes either in court or through protests will have the following eye-opening information available:

1. Aptitude tests such as the SAT do not predict performance as measured by first-year grades. The correlation of about .32 to .36 is lower than the correlation between weight and height; that is, one

would have a better chance of predicting a person's height by looking only at his or her weight than of predicting freshman grades by looking only at SAT scores. LSAT scores are no better predictors of law school grades.

2. High school grades are more predictive of college freshman grades than is the SAT. Using the SAT in conjunction with grades provides only a small increase in predictiveness of college completion.

3. Standardized tests not only assume a single, uniform way to complete a job, thus excluding those who might perform just as competently in another way; but they give an advantage to candidates from higher socioeconomical backgrounds and disproportionately screen out women and people of color, as well as those in lower-income brackets. Based on raw data provided by the College Entrance Examination Board, the linkage between test performance and parental income is consistent and striking. Within each racial and ethnic group, SAT scores increase with income.

4. Children of high-income parents can afford coaching in test-taking strategies (often costing $1,000 or more) and in packaging their accomplishments to show themselves at their best in their applications. Some test-preparation schools charge as much as $175 to $415 per hour. Parents can spend up to $25,000 for a year of weekly private coaching sessions that prepare their children for the SAT. Preparatory schools claim they can improve scores by four hundred points.[46]

Justice Thomas, while he would strike down as unconstitutional all admissions practices that utilize race either directly or indirectly, acknowledges the unfairness of legacy admits and standardized test results that play so important a role in the admissions process. Dissenting in the law school case, he wrote:

Putting aside the absence of any legal support for the majority's reflexive deference, there is much to be said for the view that the use of tests and other measures to "predict" academic performance is a poor substitute for a system that gives every applicant a chance to prove he can succeed in the study of law. The rallying cry that in the absence of racial discrimination in admissions there would be a true meritocracy ignores the fact that the entire process is poisoned by numerous excep-

tions to "merit." For example, in the national debate on racial discrimination in higher education admissions, much has been made of the fact
that elite institutions utilize a so-called "legacy" preference to give the
children of alumni an advantage in admissions. This, and other, exceptions to a "true" meritocracy give the lie to protestations that merit
admissions are in fact the order of the day at the Nation's universities.[47]

Nonetheless, Thomas does not believe the equal protection clause
prohibits "the use of unseemly legacy preferences or many other kinds
of arbitrary admissions procedures." What the equal protection clause
does prohibit, he repeated, "are classifications made on the basis of
race. So while legacy preferences can stand under the Constitution,
racial discrimination cannot." Here, stated with rigid forthrightness,
is the strongly held argument facing those who would challenge
admissions standards that many in addition to Thomas admit are
unfair but not invalid because they do not directly discriminate on the
basis of race.

In the highly competitive college and graduate admissions process,
the open and obvious departures from the standards of fairness and
merit are accepted, even defended, by many working-class whites for
whom they pose unrecognized but very real barriers. And yet policies
of racial preference, by any objective terms perhaps the most justifi-
able departure of all, are bitterly opposed in the courts, in the
legislatures, and in the polls. It may be that legal challenges by civil
rights and community groups calling attention to the inaccuracies and
unfairness of standardized tests, even in losing cases, will place them
under public scrutiny that could lead to their revision or even abandonment. If so, then it will not be the first time that civil rights
campaigns, initiated to remedy racial barriers, resulted in reforms that
worked to the benefit of all—usually, however, providing more
advances for whites than for blacks.

In a footnote to his dissent, Thomas suggested that if the Court
had the courage to forbid the use of racial discrimination in admissions, "legacy preferences (and similar practices) might quickly
become less popular—a challenge not lost, I am certain, on the elites
(both individual and institutional) supporting the Law School in this
case." The longtime affirmative action critic Carol Swain makes a
similar point. She finds the diversity approach attractive for elites

looking to avoid controversy. "Racial preferences are a low cost means to avoid identifying and adopting new and fairer practices that could improve America by reducing sources of racial friction and changing the incentive structure for all Americans."[48]

A *Wall Street Journal* article on legacy preferences found that colleges like them because they keep alumni happy and more inclined to donate. Overwhelmingly, legacy policies benefit whites, and according to Gary Orfield, professor of education and social policy at Harvard: "If the Supreme Court were to end affirmative action, colleges would be under tremendous pressure to reconsider whether to continue preferences to alumni children, of whom the vast majority are white and privileged."[49]

In summary, affirmative action, meaning any form of directly advantaging blacks and other nonwhite minorities as compensation for past discrimination, has support from only a minority on the Supreme Court. It is probably opposed by a substantial majority of the population, and it is a politically hot issue that liberal office holders want to ignore and their conservative counterparts are anxious to exploit.

For now, the two Michigan decisions continue *Bakke*'s window of opportunity for policies ostensibly designed for diversity even when motivated by affirmative action. They are likely to be challenged in the courts and in the political arena. As Sturm and Guinier predict, the affirmative action turmoil will continue to obscure the fact that standardized tests and special preferences advantage upper-class whites to the disadvantage of all those not in that category.

More importantly, here as with school desegregation, racial controversy obscures economic issues that will adversely affect far more minority students than the headline-grabbing affirmative action issue. Many colleges are now suffering deep budget cuts that mean higher tuition and less money available for financial aid. A Century Foundation study estimates that if the nation's most selective colleges abandoned affirmative action and looked only at grades and test scores, about five thousand fewer black and Hispanic students would be admitted to these schools each year. Officials estimate that, because of budget cuts, at least twenty thousand black and Hispanic students will be shut out of California's 108 community colleges in 2004.[50]

There are no easy answers here. Civil rights policymakers and the rest of us must look at all aspects of an issue and not focus on a case or cause that catches our eye and the public's attention. A speaker at a conference I attended declared that if we lost the Michigan cases, it would set us back to the *Dred Scott* era. Even a decision striking down all racial classifications in college admissions would not have done that. Indeed, a defeat for affirmative action advocates might have motivated a challenge now to the use of standardized tests and preferential nonrace policies that will eventually be needed. There was little discussion at that conference of how many minority students would have their college hopes endangered because of the economic downturn. In our strategies, we should address our energies and resources to budget reductions and the other economic issues that, as the *Chronicle of Higher Education* article pointed out, are the real killers of minority admissions.

I commend the lawyers who moved the issue in the Michigan cases from affirmative action to diversity. Recognizing the attraction of interest-converging arguments can extract a measure of victory from what otherwise would be almost-certain defeat. Affirmative action advocates, though, should not fool themselves. The Michigan Law School victory primarily aided the corporate entities and colleges who find diversity, as they earlier found affirmative action, a less disruptive means of gaining a minority presence without abandoning comfortable policies of hiring and admission that benefit themselves. Again, we are the fortuitous beneficiaries of decisions in which we were not really parties. History teaches that such victories are not permanent and are subject to change with only that recognition that we should have at their adoption.

14

SEARCHING FOR EFFECTIVE SCHOOLS
IN THE POST-*BROWN* ERA

IN 1980 I HAD RESIGNED MY FACULTY POSITION at the Harvard University Law School in order to accept the deanship at the University of Oregon's law school. Following the public announcement, I received an urgent request from Ron Herndon, a militant black leader in Portland, Oregon. Herndon explained that the school board there was resisting the black community's efforts to interpret *Brown* as requiring improvements in the mainly black schools rather than integrating them under a plan blacks feared would close many of them and reassign their children to white schools where they did not wish them to go. Herndon urged me to speak for the black community's position at an upcoming school board meeting.

I wondered about the propriety of myself—the new and, probably of some significance, the first black dean of the state's only public law school—appearing on one side of a heated racial debate. I decided that, appropriate or not, I would appear, and did so. My defense of the black communities' position gave pause to the school board's members and much satisfaction to the black community. It was a reprise of my hearings in southern courtrooms years before, more theater than substance, but perhaps of some value.

While the school board's meeting was covered on television and in the local papers, I don't recall that anyone at the law school ever mentioned my appearance. The more telling point is that as a veteran of the efforts to implement the *Brown* decision, I found myself opposing the school board's efforts to use *Brown* precisely as I had urged before dozens of courts several years earlier. Now, tardily, having abandoned my integrationist idealism, I recognized my obligation to support black parents' efforts to provide effective schooling for their children. Where, I wondered, had *Brown* or our understanding and expectations for *Brown* gotten derailed?

Disenchantment with desegregation as a means of solving educational inequalities led to alternative means of achieving effective schooling for those not able to escape to the suburbs or enroll in expensive private schools. Two major directions are worth examining. One is the effort, now three decades old, to eliminate or reduce the serious disparities in funding school districts within a particular state. The other is the resurgence of inner-city educational efforts including some public schools, independent black schools, Catholic schools, charter schools, tuition vouchers, and privately funded supplemental school programs.

School-Funding Suits

For years, advocates assumed that integration, on its own, would improve the educational prospects of black children, but time proved that the persistent educational gap between black and white students was only indirectly traceable to segregation. Instead, the root of the problem appeared to be the substantial disparities in the resources provided to black students relative to white students. Many, including myself, decided that given the difficulty of integrating black and Latino students with their swiftly fleeing white counterparts, we should concentrate on desegregating the money.

With this shift in consciousness in the early 1970s, the serious disparities in how states funded public schools in wealthy districts became an important legal issue. Given the judicial and political willingness to abandon desegregation decrees, even the NAACP, while stalwart defenders of mandatory desegregation as the linchpin of school strategies, began to look to funding challenges as an essential element in obtaining equal educational opportunities for disadvantaged children of all races.

In the first major school finance case, the California Supreme Court struck down the state system for funding public education as unconstitutional.[1] The California finance scheme relied on local property taxes as a major source of school revenue, with the balance drawn from a state foundation program which provided a minimum amount of guaranteed support for all districts. Despite state aid, disparities between school districts were still enormous. At one end of the spectrum, one district spent $577.49 per pupil in 1968–1969, while another was able to spend $1,231.72 per student. The assessed valuation or property per pupil in the first district was only $3,706, versus $50,885 per child in the second district.

The California Supreme Court found that the state finance system "invidiously discriminates against the poor" in violation of the equal protection clause of the Fourteenth Amendment "because it makes the quality of a child's education a function of the wealth of his parents and neighbors." Education, the Court held, is a fundamental right "which cannot be conditioned on wealth." The fundamental problem with the California scheme was that it did not offer poor districts the same opportunity to choose their educational priorities. Although, theoretically, districts with lower tax bases can simply tax themselves at higher rates to produce more revenue, no conceivable means would permit the East Los Angeles district to produce the same amount of money as the one in Beverly Hills. Rejecting the argument that the state finance system enhances local autonomy, the Court agreed that the system actually lessens the choice of the poor district, which "cannot freely choose to tax itself into an excellence which its tax rolls cannot provide."

As the then-director of the Western Center on Law and Poverty housed at the University of Southern California Law School in Los Angeles, I helped finance research on the California suit and, of course, was quite pleased when several years' litigation resulted in a favorable decision. The state legislature procrastinated, however, and watered down its obligations to revise its school funding formula. A decade later, little of substance had changed.

Unimpressed by the California Supreme Court's findings, the U.S. Supreme Court, in 1973, closed the door to federal challenges of school financing.[2] The Court upheld the constitutionality of a Texas financing scheme that unfairly allocated educational resources across the state. The Texas system permitted wide variations in funding among school districts since it was funded, in part, by revenues realized from wildly disparate local property tax bases. As in California,

Texas maintained a minimum foundation program that ensured districts the funding necessary for basic expenses, but did not significantly ameliorate disparities in inter-district per-pupil wealth and expenditures.

Rejecting the petition of Mexican-American parents of children attending public schools in an urban school district in San Antonio, who were poor and resided in school districts with a low property tax base, the Court majority refused to treat the Texas system as racially discriminatory. In addition, it held that the Constitution affords no "explicit or implicit" right to a public education, and thus education may not be considered one of the fundamental rights protected under the Fourteenth Amendment's equal protection clause.

Suits brought to challenge school finance arrangements in several state courts have relied on their own constitutional provisions to invalidate school finance schemes that have the effect of discriminating against black or Latino students. Several states have declared education to be a fundamental right, subject to strict judicial scrutiny under the state constitution's equal protection provisions. Others have based state constitutional challenges on state provisions guaranteeing an efficient, adequate, or thorough system of public education to all residents. As a result, courts in at least eighteen of thirty-eight states where suits have been initiated—including Texas—have struck down school finance schemes either on state equal-protection grounds or under state constitutional provisions mandating equal or adequate education. As in California, though, it has proven easier to obtain court orders invalidating state school funding programs than it has in getting legislatures to revamp those systems in order to provide funding equity.

The various school finance litigations, whatever the state, have two things in common: First, courts generally do not make the connection between unequal funding and race; and second, there is reason to doubt that equalizing funding without additional funds will always make a substantive difference. The latter problem should come as little surprise. Schools in poor, segregated neighborhoods that have been marginalized for decades will not suddenly achieve high-quality education and produce students competitive with those of the traditionally privileged schools just because they are now given equal funding. That is like expecting a Pinto to keep up with a Porsche simply because their engines both burn gasoline. Remediation for present-day inequities cannot alone compensate for ancient injuries.

It is, though, a start. In June 2003, New York's highest court determined, in litigation begun eight years earlier, that the state's funding process shortchanged the schools in New York City and failed to provide them as required by the state constitution with "a sound basic education."[3] At the time of trial, the New York public school system comprised nearly twelve hundred schools serving 1.1 million children and employing a staff of over 135,000, including 78,000 teachers. Some 84 percent of the schoolchildren were racial minorities, and 16 percent were classified as Limited English Proficient, or LEP (persons who speak little or no English). Upward of 73 percent were eligible for the federal free or reduced lunch program; 442,000 city schoolchildren came from families receiving Aid to Families with Dependent Children; and 135,000 were enrolled in special education programs.

The court found that tens of thousands of the city's students are assigned to overcrowded classrooms led by unqualified, inexperienced teachers. More than a third of these students are functionally illiterate and only half of them graduate on time. Thirty percent never finish high school. As of the 1996–1997 school year, the state provided 39.9 percent of all public school funding—$10.4 billion out of a total of $26 billion—while districts provided 56 percent and the federal government 4 percent. These figures represented an investment of $9,321 per pupil, $3,714 of it by the state. Per-pupil expenditures in the New York City public schools, at $8,171, were lower than in three-quarters of the state's other districts, including all the other "large city" districts. The state's dollar contribution to this figure was also lower, at $3,562, than its average contribution to other districts; and the city's, at about $4,000, was likewise lower than the average local contribution in other districts.

The court gave the governor and the legislature four hundred days to ascertain the actual cost of providing a sound basic education and then ensure that every school district has the resources necessary to provide it. The court deliberately left unclear who will pay for any needed budget increases, but added that the distribution of the tax burden between the city and the state is "now in the realm of politics and not law." It appears that years of litigation in the courts and predictable foot-dragging in the legislature lie ahead.

The Texas Supreme Court tried a new approach when it ruled in a finance-equity suit that the state legislature had to establish a system of student assessment geared to broadly defined education goals and then had to determine the accreditation of each school district based on its progress in meeting the goals.[4] Cutting through the barrier of whether equal funding would result in equally effective schooling, the court found that an "efficient" education (as required by the Texas Constitution) requires more than elimination of gross disparities in funding; it requires the inculcation of an essential level of learning by which each child in Texas is enabled to live a full and productive life in an increasingly complex world. Thus the Court held the legislature must articulate the requirements of an efficient school system in terms of educational results, not just in terms of funding.[5]

According to Professors James S. Liebman and Charles F. Sabel, this "efficient education" approach dramatically shifted the emphasis of the lawsuit and the remedy from the definition of inputs to outputs: Instead of simply requiring an equalized or adequate level of financing, the court required the state to provide an adequate education for each child. And it assumed that the definition of adequacy would emerge from continual revision of the broad goals of education.[6] At the same time, the decision shifted the role of the court in relation to the other actors concerned with education and reform. In previous reform cycles, the courts were unrealistically expected to function as, in effect, a purpose-built administrative agency, establishing detailed rules for reformed schools and monitoring compliance with them. Now, the court oversees the standards set by the legislature and the Texas Education Agency under which the performance of schools in meeting those standards is measured.

How well this will work, particularly as aspects of the approach have been incorporated in the Bush Administration's No Child Left Behind Act of 2001, is too early to tell. Measuring a school's performance based on how students fare on standardized tests is an approach that is attractive to some educators and condemned as worse than irrelevant by others.[7]

"Inner-City" Independent Schools

Many advocates of nonpublic schools serving urban black children maintain that *Brown*'s integrative mandate is essentially assimilative.

Black students are sent to white schools where teaching, curricula, and conceptions of merit express the homogeneity of their history. Because little attention is given to multiracial, multicultural, or multi-class issues, black students often feel their school environment is alien to their experience. This institutional closed-mindedness makes inclusion as stigmatizing as exclusion. To be immersed in and judged by a system that fails to recognize the history, culture, and needs of black students may, indeed, be worse than being excluded.

The problem of low achievement and high drop-out rates—endemic in segregated and integrated settings—stems, black independent school supporters claim, from the schools themselves. The racism that appears to be entrenched in American public schools is especially rampant in many black and Latino public schools, where the unique and difficult concomitants of poverty can overwhelm even committed and competent personnel. Often, though, these schools have inadequate resources, poorly trained teachers, and ineffective leadership. These and probably other factors have convinced many that the only option for black children is for them to leave the system entirely.

The ineffectiveness of existing schools tends to become institutionalized by bureaucratic school administrators, blame-shifting politicians, and status quo–protecting teacher's unions. Seeking new approaches, educators and parents have looked to the establishment of black schools or academies either within the existing school system, or through charter schools, tuition voucher programs, or independent schools that are geared specifically toward the needs and experiences of the mainly black children they serve.

Dr. Gail Foster, a leading advocate for independent schools,[8] reports African Americans created close to four hundred schools nationally, enrolling some fifty-two thousand students.[9] She has studied seventy independent black schools in the New York–New Jersey area, serving twelve thousand students, most in elementary grades, although some schools cover the intermediate grades. They have survived, Foster found, both because of the inadequacy of public schools and because parents view them "as models of the type of curriculum and pedagogy—infused with community values, culture, and expectation for children—that should be a fundamental part of any school reform effort."

On a visit to a Solomon Schechter School in the New York City borough of Queens, part of a nationwide network of seventy Conservative Jewish schools, Foster found that students come from a range of observant families. Visiting classes and speaking to the principal, she found that Conservative Jewish schools that emphasize culture, Jewish heritage, and the Israeli homeland are much like independent black schools that emphasize the role of African ancestry and the contributions of black people.

This emphasis spurs some black parents to choose black independent elementary schools out of concern for the psychological well-being of their children. Foster explains that parents are frightened by the "crisis of self-hatred" so prevalent among African-American youth attending neighborhood public schools, even where preparation for and interest in learning is minimal, students adhere to a street culture in dress, language, and manner.

To avoid this environment, those black parents who are able move to the suburbs or enroll their children in expensive private schools. Even in these settings, black parents have reason for concern that, while they have escaped the ghetto, they will find little of African-American affirmation or role models in the school's outlook or its curriculum. Indeed, their children may be victimized by racism that is not less damaging because it is unthinking. That was the experience of C. Madison and Paula Penn-Nabrit. After frequent discriminatory incidents while their three sons, Charles, Damon, and Evan, were enrolled in Jacksonville, Florida, schools, they moved to Columbus, Ohio, and enrolled them in an outstanding country day school for boys. The Nabrit boys did well during their two-year stay and were well-liked, well-behaved, and well-adjusted.

There were incidents, though, that finally led the Nabrits to decide to home-school their sons, an undertaking requiring ability, patience, and courage that few parents have.[10] When Damon, who is darker than his fraternal twin, Charles, was in the fourth grade, a group of schoolboys began surrounding him at recess, teasing him and calling him "blacky" and "dukey." The twins told the boys to stop and complained to the teachers on recess duty, all to no avail. On the fourth day of the bullying, Damon beat up three of the boys and was immediately taken to the office for violating the school's policy against fighting. Initially, school officials refused to see the verbal violence to which Damon had been subjected as a problem, asserting that "teasing" was a natural occurrence with which boys must learn to deal. They never acknowledged the racial motivations for the "teasing."

On another occasion, a teacher wrote on Charles' research paper, "Be careful of plagiarism." In a meeting with the teacher, Charles was able to convince her that he knew all the words he had used, and the teacher admitted to Paula that she probably would not have been as surprised at the advanced level of Charles' work had he not been black. Black students and their parents could easily fill a book with stories of racial bias, subtle and not so subtle, that they have experienced in premier schools.

Most independent schools that are primarily African American eagerly welcome children of other cultures and races. Some have even given their schools names such as "Learning Tree Multi-Cultural School," or "Mrs. Black's School for All Children." Foster points out that blacks are accused of segregation when whites avoid their private schools, but the fact that such schools tend to be 100 percent black is a white parental choice, and not the result of a racially exclusive policy by the schools.

These schools are designed to respond to the social ills disproportionately visited upon blacks—discrimination, joblessness, poverty, and crime, to name a few—by fostering a sense of cultural pride, providing students with positive black role models, and teaching the particular skills black children need to survive using pedagogical models that will attract and hold their interest. The different life histories of black children raised in the inner cities require specialized approaches. Otherwise, as UCLA law professor Kenneth Karst warned: "To shift from a system of group discrimination to a system of individual performance is to perpetuate the effects of past discrimination into the present and future."[11]

In addition to ongoing funding difficulties and the opposition coming from several sources, not all of them white, the advocates of single-race schools have had to allay fears that encouraging racial separation will encourage both racism and separatism. In positive response, advocates point to an aspect of schooling lost sight of during the long years of desegregation efforts: the role of school in sustaining a community. Mrs. Hall, a teacher at the Fairmont Elementary School in St. Louis, explains: "A community is only as good as the school that is in it. The basis of the black community used to be the black Church. Fairmont has served an essential role, just as the black Church has played in the African American community."[12]

Many black independent schools operate out of churches, community centers, or rented buildings. They may be coed or open to only boys or girls. Despite their potential and the enthusiastic community support they engender, these schools have faced some opposition. Often the resistance has come from those who remain committed either to the *Brown* ideal of integration or to the maintenance of the status quo. Opponents from traditional civil rights groups and the ACLU have challenged some of the single-sex schools in court for, in their view, discriminating on the basis of race and gender.

Supporters believe that single-sex schools can better address problems of violence so endemic to some inner-city communities. Dr. Deborah Prothrow-Stith has diagnosed inner-city violence as a major "public health" problem and, in response, has developed an intervention program for the public-school system to help prevent teenage violence.[13] Although programs such as these need not necessarily be instituted in single-sex schools, some educators insist that these reforms will be more effective if targeted at males, the most frequent perpetrators of street violence. Although young girls may also benefit from violence intervention programs, their roles in the perpetuation of violence suggest that different programs, tailored to their specific needs, might be more appropriate.

High levels of violence, teenage pregnancy, and other social problems correlate with low academic performance. To the extent that single-sex education can improve academic performance, supporters maintain that such schools can be an important method of addressing these correlated problems. Beyond the issue of the value of separating by sex as well as race, several reasons explain why single-sex schools may serve elementary and secondary school children better than do coeducational classrooms. Research indicates that teachers are biased against boys in elementary grades and against girls in secondary grades. According to this theory, girls in elementary school are asked to read aloud more than are boys, perhaps from the sexist notion that reading is a feminine activity, whereas in high school, boys are encouraged to participate more actively in science and math. Furthermore, teachers praise girls for good manners in elementary school in a way that might dampen active learning skills later in their education. The rebellious spirit that teachers tolerate from elementary school boys, however, later serves them well when they become more active class-room participants. The availability of role models in single-sex elementary and secondary schools may well counter these tendencies, leading boys to see reading as more "masculine" and girls to see science and math as more accessible.

None of these arguments persuades those who view single-sex schools as an invidious form of gender segregation, even though some of the most prestigious prep schools in the country are single-sex. Simply referring to them as African-American schools, whether for girls or boys or both, also engenders negative reactions. But, as Professor Pamela Smith notes, Catholic schools or Jewish yeshivas are not labeled segregative. Like these schools, the schools attended by African-American children are characterized by the communities they serve. The label "all African American" is not a racial classification; it merely refers to the community served by the school. A better label, she admits, might be "inner-city schools," but Smith contends, the label alone should not trigger heightened constitutional scrutiny simply because the schools cater to African Americans.[14]

Independent black schools, while facing a host of economic and educational issues, continue to flourish because, as Foster explains, the curriculum and instruction reflect school leaders' assumption of the responsibility to provide students with the skills and attitudes they will need to improve themselves and their communities. They view setting high standards for their students as a critical part of the solution to the problems that plague their communities. Expulsion of students is more rare than at other schools, for part of their commitment is an expression of the schools' underlying reverence for their students, even those who are difficult and slow.

Charter Schools

Legislation, now enacted in at least thirty states, enables a designated granting body or "agency" to give permission and public funds to entities that apply for charters with the purpose of establishing and operating primary and secondary schools not burdened by many of the statutory and regulatory constraints of the existing education code. This means such schools are free from the centralized control and bureaucracy of the existing public school district. Charter schools, representing a new way of fulfilling various state constitutional mandates to provide free public education to the young, will probably play a prominent role in public education during the coming decade. They appear to further the political agendas of many and, according to supporters, hold great promise for developing innovative approaches to public education while challenging school systems to improve their performance.[15]

Charter advocates contend that such schools provide parental choice, eliminate bureaucratic and contractual regulations that inhibit change and innovation, and place competitive pressure on public school systems to reform themselves. Administrators urge that charter schools should be provided with a budget equal to the average per-pupil expenditures prevailing in the district or state in which their schools are chartered, but state charter laws generally provide charter schools with about 15 percent less money than regular public schools. Even so, the laws expect higher performance in exchange for fewer regulations. Advocates accept this responsibility, but urge that charter schools should be given about five years to justify the charter by demonstrating improvement in student performance.

Supporters contend that, with these resources, charter school teachers and staff will be more motivated than their counterparts at traditional public schools to produce effective educational results. All families, not just the wealthy, should be able to choose the schools their children will attend, advocates argue, dismissing as paternalism the concern that low-income parents will not make appropriate choices for their children.

Public school supporters generally view charter school movements with alarm. They fear they will simply increase school choice for privileged students and their parents, those who have the information and social savvy to exploit the new schooling opportunities. This concern seems unfounded. According to one study, nearly two-thirds of charter-school students nationwide are nonwhite, and more than half come from low-income families.[16] Opponents also predict that charter schools will discriminate, either explicitly or implicitly, by race or socioeconomic status and, if necessary, to further the movement, will harm disadvantaged students as they drain already-strapped school systems of needed funds and support. Court challenges to charter schools have been difficult because current judicial standards require proof that discrimination is intentional.

In summary, charter schools are options that allow students to exit schools that do not serve them. Parents, regardless of race, seek schools providing a high-quality education in a setting with shared community values, safety, proximity, and respect for parents. Indeed, shared values and proximity are more important to parents than educational outcomes, a reason Foster suggests why voucher and charter schools get consistently high marks from parents, even when academic performance is moderate or low.

Specialized Public Schools

Few major studies have attempted to answer the question of how these alternative, mainly minority, schools work. Successful inner-city schools, whether public, private, charter, secular, or sectarian, reflect similar qualities. The Frederick Douglass Academy (FDA) in Harlem, New York, is an archetype of such schools. Considered one of the top high schools in the country, its attributes are set out in its website:[17]

> The goal of the school is to provide a rich, vigorous and challenging academic curriculum that will enable our students to enter the college of their choice. College preparation begins in the 6th grade. Students in the middle school study Japanese or Latin, music, art and dance in addition to academic classes. Students take New York State Regents classes starting in 8th grade, and many students will have completed the requirements for a high school diploma by the end of the 11th grade. Students then take Advanced Placement Courses, and in some cases, introductory college courses. We offer Advanced Placement courses in Calculus, Physics, Chemistry, English, American/Global History and Foreign Language.
>
> Each student and family must make a commitment to becoming part of the dream of attending college. Students are expected to strive for excellence in every part of their lives. Students are required to wear a plain white shirt/blouse, blue navy pants/skirts and black shoes. Emphasis is placed on one's intellect and not on one's appearance. Students are accepted at FDA based on the results of an interview, and two written recommendations. Eighty percent of the accepted students must reside in the Harlem community and twenty percent of the students come from outside of District Five.
>
> The values and beliefs that influenced Dr. Martin Luther King when

he studied at Morehouse College are the exact same ones that each Frederick Douglass scholar is expected to exemplify. Every student is expected to learn The Frederick Douglass Student Creed (based on the Morehouse [College] Student Creed) and the 12 Non-Negotiable Academy Rules. Four hours of homework is expected of our students. Entering students are required to attend our summer enrichment program (three weeks for grades 6 and 7 and six weeks for grade 9).

The Academy is fortunate to have developed partnerships with many organizations. A few of the major collaboratives are: Ithaca College (staff development, scholarships and visiting professors); HBO (internships, mentorships, computers and SAT Preparation); GAP (internships, mentorships, jobs, scholarships and "Little Shop of Horrors" school store); PriceWaterhouseCooper (mentorships); Con Edison (computer staff development); Columbia University, ILT (staff development and Internet capability); American Ballet Theater ("Make A Ballet" program) and Sumitomo Bank and JAL, Japan Airlines (travel opportunities).

Benefactors have sponsored trips for our students to Italy, France, Israel, Japan, South Africa, England, and Canada. In addition, The Frederick Douglass Academy has been featured in numerous articles in the press. In the January 1999 *U.S. News and World Report*, FDA was included in the list of 100 top Schools in the nation. The school has been featured on all local television stations. The school provides over 25 clubs and teams to supplement the courses of academic studies that are offered in the school. These activities may take place before class, after school, and/or on Saturdays.

Data about F.D.A. in the New York Public Schools 2001–2002 Annual School Report provides detailed information about the school's makeup and achievements.[18] Eighty-three percent of the student body is black, 14 percent Hispanic, and 2 percent Asian and white. Males are 37.5 percent and females 62.5 percent of the approximately one thousand students in the school staffed by sixty teachers and fourteen administrators. Ninety-nine percent of FDA graduates go on to college.

As to performance on standardized tests in the class of 2002, 88 percent of the students scored 65 or above on the English Graduation Assessment Requirement and 95.4 percent performed as well on the Mathematics Graduation Assessment Requirement. On New York

Regents examinations after three years, the percentage of FDA students scoring 65 or above was 75.3 percent in English, 92.6 percent in mathematics, 85.8 percent in global history, and 85.8 percent in science. These scores are substantially higher than those in the general New York City high schools that must accept all students living in their zones.

Consider the African American Academy in Seattle. After a rocky start a decade ago, it is now a public school model, as its staff and 465 students now occupy a new $23.3 million, 100,000-square-foot building located on a twelve-acre site. Currently 90 percent black (most of these schools have no racial admissions criteria), the Academy uses the same curriculum as the Seattle public schools but blends African and African-American history into daily lessons. The gap in achievement with white schools is closing, albeit slowly, a sign that the school is meeting a major challenge, given that 84 percent of its students are eligible for free and reduced-price lunches; only 19 percent of the students live with both parents, the lowest rate in the district; and, the school estimates, 40 percent of the students live with relatives or foster parents.[19]

The alternative school programs described here vary greatly in make-up and effectiveness. Special academic settings within public schools may better meet the needs of some poor students and their parents than others. Charter and voucher programs, in particular, vary greatly from state to state. Black educators seeking to gain state approval for such programs often experience serious political obstacles. It is thus better not to favor voucher or charter programs in general, but rather to support or oppose them after reviewing the enabling laws. For example, a voucher law that allows a school to charge more tuition than the amount of the voucher is quite different from one that prohibits such charges.

Tuition Vouchers

Tuition voucher arrangements, probably the most controversial of educational alternatives to emerge in the last decade, allow parents to select a public or private school of their choice.[20] Voucher programs allow a state to write checks to parents for all or part of the private- or public-school tuition for elementary or secondary schooling. In some cases, parents endorse the check to the public or private school of their choice; in other cases, states send a check, payable to the parent, directly to the school. Voucher legislation is under consideration in at least twenty-three states and has been adopted in Arizona, Maine, Wisconsin, Ohio, Pennsylvania, and Vermont.

Supporters of voucher programs hold that, by allowing parents to choose the schools for their children, a more market-oriented educational system will be created. This system will bring both private and public schools into competition, thus increasing the quality of education for all.[21] Opponents respond by arguing that vouchers will not alter the educational advantages available to well-off parents but, rather, will enhance them by siphoning needed resources from schools already poorly funded. Vouchers will mislead black parents in their continuing quest for equal educational opportunity in a still-racist world. One critic writes:

> Private school tuition vouchers alone can not create educational equity, but they might provide a guilt-assuaging illusion of equity that would encourage those who already have educational advantages to maximize those advantages and ignore the collective responsibility to educate all of the citizens in a democracy.[22]

Opponents contend that the real beneficiaries of vouchers are the pervasively sectarian schools, funding of which, they argue, would violate the First Amendment's establishment clause. Using this argument, opponents have challenged plans that would permit the use of vouchers at religion-related schools in Milwaukee and Cleveland. Each system has taxpayer-funded voucher programs allowing public funds for religious schools.

The Milwaukee Parental Choice Plan (MRCP) survived a court challenge.[23] It permits states to give selected students $2,500 per year to use at private schools. Tuition checks made out to parents are mailed directly to the participating schools at which the parents have enrolled their children. Participating schools must comply with federal antidiscrimination provisions in Title VI and must follow state reporting requirements. Students are chosen through a lottery from families with incomes below 175 percent of the poverty level, a level that allows fifteen thousand Milwaukee students (about 15 percent of the school population) to leave public schools for private schools. Of the private schools participating, 89 percent are sectarian. The

Wisconsin Supreme Court found that the state's voucher program is a "neutral" effort to help parents pay for education and is not seeking to advance religion, since poor parents are given money to send their children to either a sectarian or a nonsectarian school. Thus, funds reach sectarian schools only through intervening choices made by individual parents.

The Cleveland plan is similar to Milwaukee's in that eligible parents with an average income of under $10,000 per year receive vouchers of up to $2,500 per year, and may use them in sectarian schools. In May 1997, about 80 percent of the two thousand students in the program used the vouchers to attend religious schools, most of them Catholic. The state courts blocked the Cleveland plan, but the Supreme Court gave its approval in a 5 to 4 vote, even though, by this point, 96 percent of the students taking part in the program used the vouchers to attend religious schools.[24] A factor was that the voucher program was one of a number of efforts over the years to provide options for Cleveland's poor parents in a demonstrably failing public system. Among the fifty largest school districts in the country, Cleveland had the lowest overall graduation rate with 28 percent.[25]

Writing for the majority, Chief Justice Rehnquist concluded that the program was enacted for a valid secular reason and did not violate the establishment clause by promoting religion, the decision on where to spend the vouchers being left to the parents. In a concurring opinion, Justice O'Connor expanded further on the theme of "parental choice," noting the array of options that Cleveland offered to parents who preferred to stay in the public school system. Writing in dissent, Justice Souter, joined by the three other moderate members of the Court, argued that public school options could not be considered in assessing parental choice or else "there will always be a choice and the voucher can always be constitutional." He also stressed that the Court had never before upheld such a substantial transfer of taxpayer dollars to religious institutions, transfers he deemed a "dramatic departure from basic Establishment Clause principle."

Catholic Schools

In urban areas, many black and Hispanic parents have chosen Catholic schools over the public schools. They have done so despite the tuition costs and the fact that neither they nor their children are members of the Roman Catholic Church. Parents expect that these schools will provide disciplined learning and positive academic outcomes that they fear are not found in the public schools.

Church-related schools in general and Catholic schools in particular welcomed the Supreme Court's voucher decision that has been a major factor in school growth in cities like Milwaukee where vouchers are available.[26] The Catholic Messmer High School, located in one of the city's poorest neighborhoods and once nearly closed, is now flourishing beyond all expectations with voucher students. Eighty percent of Messmer's four hundred students are non-Catholic, and more than half are there because of the voucher program that covers much of the $3,100 a year tuition. The school's president, Brother Bob Smith, is a Capuchin monk of the Franciscan order, whose goal is to give the students a religious foundation. To this end, students pray every day, go on spiritual retreats, and attend four masses a year. And while Messmer does not "cherry- pick" the best students, and there is no admissions test for entry, 85 percent of the graduates go on to college—three times the rate of neighboring public high schools.

Supplemental School Programs

A major part of the educational challenge today goes beyond curriculum, trained teachers, decent facilities, and adequate resources: that is, the motivation to learn which is so sadly lacking in many children, particularly those from lower-income areas. Many educators do not see how providing motivation is a prerequisite to effective teaching and learning.

Those schools and youth programs able to provide motivation tend to be successful. In New York City, the Harlem Boys' Choir is a well-known example of using music as the incentive to motivate youngsters to learn and grow. Others are the All Stars Talent Show Network and the Joseph A. Forgione Development School for Youth.[27] Both programs, supervised by Dr. Lenora Fulani, are privately funded supplementary-education ventures that serve tens of thousands of inner city kids each year. Fulani believes that her out-of-school programs and projects help to motivate the children.

Researchers and practitioners in the field of supplementary

education—often referred to as after-school programs—have made important discoveries over the last decade that bear directly on the achievement gap. These findings show that poor kids, who may have few enriching experiences outside of school, do not develop as learners in the ways that more privileged kids do. The All Stars Project creates those experiences for young people of all ages using a performance-cultural model.

Fulani explains that her programs focus on issues of development and motivation. They relate to the young people as people who have the capacity to perform ahead of themselves—meaning as more than, or other than, who they are. In the All Stars, they are taught how to create performances on stage as a way of learning to perform in life. In the Development School for Youth, she says:

> We teach young people to use performance skills to become more cosmopolitan and sophisticated—to interact with the worlds of Wall Street, with business and the arts. In becoming more cosmopolitan— in going beyond their narrow and parochial and largely nationalistic identities—they acquire a motivation to learn as a part of consistently creating and recreating their lives.

Fulani reports that it doesn't take long, for example, for the young people in the Development School to grasp that they have to learn new ways of speaking, reading, and writing to sustain themselves in the interactions with corporate executives they are meeting with as part of the curriculum. This developmental approach is specifically designed to address the academic failure of poor kids. Children of well-to-do families receive supplementary education as a matter of course. Their parents expose them to the workings of the world, to travel, culture, dialogues at home about current events, government, and the arts. Study after study, at one university after another, have shown that these kinds of supplementary experiences enhance, if not determine, the children's learning capability.

In this brief summary of schooling alternatives, the solutions offered by Gail Foster, Lenora Fulani, and other educators share common principles. They believe deeply that children can learn. They recognize how barriers of poverty, cultural deprivation, and the lack of positive life models and experiences can block learning potential. They know that effective teaching begins with creating and building motivation to learn by involving students in sports, artistic endeavor, or other skills-development activities that serve as "door openers" to overcome insecurities and antilearning attitudes. In effect, to quote John Holt, a school principal and, for many years, the director of the summer camp I attended as a child: "Accept children as you find them, and then take them as far as they can go."

15

MOVING BEYOND RACIAL FORTUITY

A GOSPEL SONG ASKS: "What do you do when you've done all you can and it feels like it's never enough?" The answer, "Just stand," seems so passive, but as interpreted by those who framed those words out of the difficulties of their own lives, it means to keep on, to not give up in the face of seemingly fruitless struggle. It draws on a necessary maxim of the oppressed: to "make a way out of no way."

Those of us who have labored for decades in racial-justice campaigns can identify with that gospel lyric, particularly civil rights lawyers whose primary mission was trying to desegregate school systems. The school issues of today grow out of societal conditions that affect educational efforts across the economic spectrum. They can't all be laid at the doorsteps of *Brown*'s failure, but looking back over the decades, I wonder whether the long school desegregation effort was an unintended but nonetheless contributing cause of current statistical disparities that some critics angrily attribute to the continuing effects of racism. Others, not all of whom are white, assert with equal vehemence that blaming failure on racism is an excuse; that we need to get up off our dead asses, drop the welfare tit, stop having "illegitimate" babies, and find jobs like everybody else.

More objective observers of black distress view the source as the lack of employment, the bedrock of survival and success in this society. In the post–World War II years, racial reformers felt that gaining racial equality would eliminate the barriers that underlay the economic disparities between blacks and others. While a powerful symbol, the call for equality was easier to make than for a great many blacks to realize. Just as the *Brown* decision in 1954 did not open up law-firm jobs when I graduated from law school in 1957, the hard-fought litigation to erode public manifestations of segregation meant little to those black people far less fortunate than I as they looked in vain for openings in schools, jobs, and housing. We should have recognized that the banner of "equal opportunity" increased rather than made obsolete the need to "make a way out of no way." Here, I want to assess the current condition of black people at many levels, take a hard look at the striving for racial equality as a concept, and suggest how our strategies and tactics, both as individuals and groups, may move us forward in the face of barriers that are not less formidable because so many in the society tell us that they are no longer there.

Assessing Current Conditions

As former National Urban League president Hugh Price observed, "work is essentially the activity through which human beings define themselves and their relationship to, not merely society, but to life itself."[1] Sociologist William Julius Wilson makes this point in his book, *When Work Disappears*. In his view, it is massive unemployment and not the lack of family values that has devastated our inner-cities and placed one-third of our young men—denied even menial jobs when they lacked education and skills—in prison or in the jaws of the criminal court system, most of them for nonviolent drug offenses.[2]

Based on data from three research projects on the urban poor of Chicago, Professor Wilson portrays a devastating picture of the nation's urban centers where jobs have virtually disappeared, leaving residents jobless or in search of employment in neighboring suburbs. This search poses problems of transportation and negative employer perceptions. Without jobs to support their families, the jobless men, often low-skilled and uneducated, can spiral into cycles of crime, domestic violence, alcoholism, and despair. In an annual report that reviews some positives in job growth for blacks as well as the adverse effects of the recession, economist Bernard Anderson expresses concern "about the future employment prospects for black workers [stemming] from their continuing concentration in depressed areas of major cities, and the challenges facing black youth in the public schools."[3]

During the 1990s, blacks made substantial gains in employment, both in numbers and in the range of jobs from which we had been excluded. With the downturn in the economy, the "last hired, first fired" syndrome is cutting into these gains. In mid-2003, the *New York Times* reported: "Unemployment among blacks is rising at a faster pace than in any similar period since the mid-1970s, and the jobs lost have been mostly in manufacturing, where the pay for blacks has historically been higher than in many other fields."[4]

As an instance, a seat-belt maker in Indianapolis closed a plant and laid off 350 workers, more than 75 percent of them black. Many of them were hired in the late 1990s when unemployment was quite low, and to expand production, the company hired young men without high school diplomas. They went from the streets to making $12–$13 an hour, wages that enabled them to start families, lease apartments, and purchase cars. After their up-from-the-street experience, given the current job market, they face the possibility of being returned to their old environment.

It is true that, despite racial barriers and the ups and downs of the job market, a growing number of black people—and not just sports and entertainment celebrities—are achieving what by current standards of income and status can be called success. Too often, though, their achievement comes at a price, and sometimes a price not worth paying. As they climb the ladder of success, they leave their values on the rungs and arrive well-heeled and moderately respected by nearly everyone but themselves. They learn the hard way that success does not shield them from the myriad forms of racial subordination. *The Rage of a Privileged Class*, by journalist Ellis Cose,[5] is based on dozens of interviews with educated black people holding impressive positions in corporate and government offices. They are embittered because success does not shield them from slights and even blatant instances of racial discrimination.

Wallace Ford, one of those Cose interviewed, is a former student of mine at the Harvard Law School. He had come there from Dartmouth College, and has held a number of high-level positions in business and government. Even so, Ford told Cose that he had underachieved in comparison with many whites who, while brilliant and extremely well educated, were not so bright that he was "blinded from across the table." Ford asked himself:

> Why can they do fifty-million-dollar deals with little more than projections on the back of an envelope? And why were others, blacks who were 'offering up mom, dad, and all their kids,' able to get only crumbs? . . . My mind cannot accept the fact that of all the [black] people I went to law school with, only half a dozen of them achieved partnerships in any of the New York law firms.

Reading his alumni publications, Ford learned of many whites who were succeeding spectacularly. He knew blacks who, although their degrees got them jobs and opportunities, are frustrated that they are not able to achieve the pinnacles they compete for. "You end up suspecting that race is a factor," but, he told Cose, the truth is hard to know. "People aren't saying 'You black son of a bitch.' "[6]

Those blacks seeking success in the business world may decide not to protest the discrimination that cloud their lives. No such options are available to many young black males who, despite having more opportunity for success than any of their forebears, are stumbling through life. In *The Envy of the World*,[7] Ellis Cose surveys their status. Overcome by the obstacles of poverty and racism they view as insurmountable, they determine to flout social conventions and, as they put it, live so as to "keep it real." For many, the results are a disaster that inevitably leads to death or imprisonment.

If brought together in one incorporated region, the black males who are now in prison would instantly become the twelfth-largest urban area in the country. A recent study shows that in 2002, 10.4 percent of black men aged twenty-five to twenty-nine, or 442,300 people, were in prison. By comparison, 2.4 percent of Hispanic men and 1.2 percent of white men in the same age group were in prison. This large racial disparity had not increased in the past decade. But Marc Mauer, the assistant director of the Sentencing Project, a prison-change research and advocacy group, said of the continuing high number of young black men in prison that "the ripple effect on their communities, and on the next generation of kids growing up with their fathers in prison, will certainly be with us for at least a generation."[8]

When Cose adds to the prison population the black males ravished by AIDS, murder, poverty, and illiteracy, the widening gap separating the black elite from the so-called underclass makes for a paralyzing pessimism. Out of his many interviews, Cose constructs a mosaic of the temptations of the street, its powerful allure, its seduction: Young black males feel it is "offering us a place to belong, the only place—or so we are made to believe—that we alone can own." "From the moment our brains are capable of cognition, we are primed to embrace our presumed destiny." Their perception of reality is shaped by movies, television, and radio, all portraying the black man as a "street-wise, trash-talking operator, as the polar opposite of the refined, cerebral white male, who, coincidentally, may control the world but lacks our style and soul."[9]

For many raised in inner-city poverty and some in middle-class surroundings, education becomes a casualty of the street mind-set. Black males who lose interest in school at an early age seldom complete even high school. And for many years, the disproportionate number of black women vis à vis black men in college and graduate schools has been a distressing proof of what is happening to males at an early age. This situation is all too apparent at historic black colleges. A friend who teaches at one black college in the deep South reports that of the 280 students who graduated in the spring 2003 class, all but 50 were women. The disparities are not quite as severe at the professional school level. Admissions officers report, though, that the pool of qualified black men is significantly smaller than that of black women.

Of course, the pattern of increasing percentages of women graduating from college is a general phenomenon.[10] Professor Andrew Hacker reports that in 2002, women were awarded 57 percent of all bachelor's degrees, compared with only 35 percent in 1960. Hacker says that "the tangle of pathology" once used to describe unstable conditions in black families is now emulated in white families: "Divorce, decamping fathers, and births to unmarried women are nearly as common in white suburbs as they once were in the predominantly black inner cities."[11] It is another reminder that society's ills dramatically affect both blacks and whites.[12]

Cose concludes his powerful book with a set of instructions, literally a means of survival he feels young black men must know to survive and thrive in America. As a former civil rights lawyer, however, I find it hard to contemplate that, while the conditions that placed these men in such jeopardy were developing, my priority, and that of so many others, was in forcing southern school systems to enroll black children in white schools where we assumed, with far more faith than evidence, they would get a better education.

In these pages, I condemn the racism that causes whites to reflexively oppose civil rights programs they believe will help unworthy blacks when, in fact, they will be of greater benefit to whites. Affirmative action is the contemporary example. But black civil rights advocates' impassioned opposition to white racism can sometimes confuse our priorities, causing us to expend our resources on issues far less important than how to address the systematic destruction of so many young black men and the women who are associated with them.

These are not the thoughts I envisioned for the fiftieth anniversary of *Brown v. Board of Education*. The alternative decision I imagined in chapter 3 was intended less to avoid what has already occurred than to provide an explanation of what went wrong. In the light of all that has happened in the wake of the much-wished-for and then greatly heralded decision, I wanted to explore Professor Alexander Bickel's prediction that *Brown* would remain on the books and yet become, "dread word, irrelevant."

By this point, I hope it is clear that the answer is obvious. *Brown* is the definitive example of the fate of civil rights policies that were sought with too little regard for either the variables of racial fortuity or the tremendous obstacles those we hoped to help were actually facing in their lives.

Racial Equality: A Goal Too Vulnerable

An understandable but, in retrospect, serious misjudgment was our over-reliance on court orders to achieve racial equality. In our school desegregation campaigns, equality would be realized when schools were no longer identifiable by race. This equality by "definitional fiat" limitation is circumscribed, as Brandon Lofton, a student in my constitutional law class points out, because we designated the U.S. government as maker and guarantor of the promise of equality.[13] Lofton cites the speeches of Martin Luther King, Jr., and other black leaders who insisted that the government must honor its commitment to racial equality.

By so doing, Lofton argues, "the civil rights leadership limited its conception of African-American identity and freedom to the American legal and social context." This tactic helped the movement dismantle segregation at the point when the blatant "Jim Crow" system threatened the nation's policymakers' designs for world leadership after World War II. Thus when, with persistent pleading from the State and Justice Departments, the Supreme Court proclaimed that separate facilities were now to be inherently unequal, as Michael Seidman noted:

> the demand for equality had been satisfied and blacks no longer had just cause for complaint. The mere existence of *Brown* thus served [to] legitimate current arrangements. True, many blacks remained poor and disempowered. But their status was no longer a result of the denial of equality. Instead, it marked a personal failure to take advantage of one's definitionally equal status.[14]

Equality by proclamation not only failed to truly reflect the complexity of racial subordination, it also vested the government and the courts with the ultimate moral authority to define African-American freedom. When the *Brown* decision was followed by civil rights laws, mostly motivated by black activism that highlighted the continuing racism that undermined our Cold War battles with the Soviet Union, policymakers and much of white society easily reached the premature conclusion that America was now fair and neutral. With implementation of the moderate civil rights laws, the trumpets of "reverse discrimination" began sounding the alarm. In quick response, the government and the courts began giving priority to the rights of "innocent whites" caught in the remedial web of civil rights laws that, to be effective, had to recognize and correct the priorities of race that some whites had deemed vested and permanent.

Soon the cacophony settled into a virtual orchestra playing a melody that in this century resembles the song that begins: "The party's over." I am not sure what that policy-activated orchestra was playing in the nineteenth century when the nation abandoned Reconstruction policies. In both eras, though, there is the readiness to mute any sound of the racial remedies earlier and solemnly promised to blacks in order to maintain stability and solidarity among whites whose own social and economic status varies widely.

Today, black people and many Hispanics are trapped in a racial time warp. We are buffeted by the painful blows of continuing bias as the law upon which we relied for remedies is reinterpreted with unsupported assurances that the disadvantages we suffer must be caused by our deficiencies because, we are told without even a trace of irony, racism is a thing of the past. The hypocrisy so apparent in the claims of a color-blind society illustrate the harsh and disconcerting truth about racial progress. We prefer to ignore or rationalize rather than confront these truths because they disrupt our long-settled expectations of eventual racial equality.

Given the setbacks in civil rights suffered in recent decades, and the decline in the relative well-being of so many people of color, civil rights adherents need to reconsider our racial goals. We need to examine what it was about our reliance on racial remedies that may have prevented us from recognizing that these legal rights could do little more than bring about the cessation of one form of discriminatory conduct that soon appeared in a more subtle though no less discriminatory form. I hope that this examination leads us to redefine goals of racial equality and opportunity to which blacks have adhered for more than a century.

Stanford professor Robert Gordon explained the need for this redefinition. Interpreting the writings of the Critical Race Theory adherents, he referred to the writings of Italian Marxist Antonio Gramsci and his notions of "hegemony." Gordon explained that:

> the most effective kind of domination takes place when both the dominant and dominated classes believe that the existing order, with perhaps some marginal changes, is satisfactory, or at least represents the most that anyone could expect, because things pretty much have to be the way they are.[15]

Views of this kind afflict the working classes who, though recognizing they are ill-treated and poorly paid, toil on in silence, concluding that nothing can be done and "making waves" about their condition will only make things worse.

We civil rights professionals are not immune to the hegemonic syndrome. Even as we fight through the courts to improve conditions, our actions represent a major denial of reality about the nation's history and how and when it addresses even the most severe racial inequities. Thus, as Gordon asserts, we civil rights lawyers are a key cog in "legitimating" class society by providing it an opportunity from time to time to appear "approximately just." While the law functions as a tool of the dominating class, it must function so as to induce both the dominant and dominated classes to accept the hierarchy. It accomplishes this result by appearing to be universal and operating with a degree of independence by making "it possible for other classes to use the system against itself . . . and force it to make good on its utopian promises." In so acting, Gordon maintains, the law can serve as an agent for positive gains by disadvantaged groups.

But there is a catch. The very process of realizing a gain sought through the courts ultimately serves to deepen the legitimacy of the system. Gordon and other critical legal scholars are correct in asserting that the effort to gain rights and even the discussion of rights serve to co-opt and legitimize the very concept of rights and equality, leaving them empty of dependable substance.

Professor Kimberle Crenshaw saw the dilemma a dozen years ago, but concluded that as long as race consciousness thrives, blacks will have to rely on rights rhetoric to protect their interests.[16] There are, though, limited options to those deemed the Other in making specific demands for inclusion and equality. Doing so in the quest for racial justice, though, means that "winning and losing have been part of the same experience."

Crenshaw recognized race and racism as playing key roles in the maintenance of hegemony, adding: "until whites recognize the hegemonic function of racism and turn their efforts toward neutralizing it, African-American people must develop pragmatic political strategies—self-conscious ideological struggle—to minimize the costs of liberal reform while maximizing its utility." Given racism's critical role in providing an outlet for white frustrations caused by economic exploitation and political manipulation, one wonders whether American society could survive as we know it if large numbers of whites ever realized what racism costs them and decided to do something about it.

The obsession with white dominance renders that much-needed recognition unlikely. Can it be that at some unacknowledged level racial equality advocates know we are living an impossible dream? And as a shield against that awful truth, can it be that we hold tightly to our belief in eventual racial justice and the litigation and legislation we hope will give meaning to that belief? Remaining faithful to the racial-equality creed enables us to drown out the contrary manifestations of racial domination that flourish despite our best efforts.

Long ago, in a major denial of reality, the racial-equality commitment had to survive the undeniable fact that the Constitution's framers initially opted to protect property, which included enslaved Africans. That commitment had to overlook the political motivations for the Civil War amendments, self-interest motivations almost guaranteeing that when political needs changed, the protection provided the former slaves would not be enforced. In conformity with past practice, protection of black rights is now predictably episodic. For these reasons, both the historic pattern and its contemporary manifestations require review and replacement of racial-equality ideology with specific programs leading to tangible goals.

Racism translates into a societal vulnerability of black people, whose exploitation few politicians—including those at the presidential level—seem able to resist. And why not? The unwillingness to remedy even the most serious racial injustices, if those remedies will appear detrimental to the expectations of whites, is now settled. The effectiveness of "racial bonding" by whites requires that blacks must seek a new and more realistic goal for our civil rights activism. African Americans need a rationale based on what we can gain for ourselves rather than on what we can obtain from courts or other government entities.

Forging Fortuity

The danger with our commitment to the principle of racial equality is that it leads us to confuse tactics with principles. The principle of gaining equal educational opportunity for black children was and is right. But our difficulties came when we viewed racial balance and busing as the only means of achieving that goal. At a much earlier point than we did, we should have recognized that our tactic was making it harder rather than easier to reach our goal. I fear that the tactic of using racial classifications as the vehicle for affirmative action programs will endanger those programs, if not by the Court, then by the political process.

Surely the courts can serve as a defense against the retaliatory actions that government and other entities will launch to halt racial-justice programs, but even then, defeats are more likely than protection. A more activist approach, though, will provide insulation against the frustration of rejection. Strategies can be planned that will recognize when the self-interests of both society and African Americans will probably be in accord. The interest-convergence theory should not remain a seeming fortuity we recognize only after the fact. And we may even need to initiate and support actions that seemingly fly in the face of interest-convergence principles when those actions make life more bearable for blacks in a society where blacks are a permanent, subordinate class. Recognition of our true status will serve as a gateway to an era where we forge fortuity, that is, defy the workings of the involuntary sacrifices and interest-convergence determinants of racial policies and practices.

Many blacks already understand and incorporate this approach in interchanges with whites on the job, and in their commercial and community dealings. My parents were typical of many who drilled into me at an early age that because you are black, you have to be twice as good to get half as much. Unspoken in that advice is that whites are presumed competent until they prove the contrary. Blacks are assumed to be mediocre and certainly no intellectual match for whites until their skills and accomplishments gain them an often-reluctant acceptance. Success for the black person requires effective functioning achieved with the knowledge that his or her work will not be recognized or rewarded to the same degree as a white person doing the same thing. A black person may be a fortuitous beneficiary, but it is usually necessary to push the dynamics of fortuity hard to become so.

Those who took part in the sit-ins were forging fortuity. By their nonviolent protests to dramatize the justice of their cause, they overcame traditional laws of trespass and breach of the peace. Their leaders were able to think and plan within a context of "what is" (the existing problem) rather than simply rely on the abstract concept of equality. The sit-ins taught us that a great many whites would not maintain discriminatory policies if the cost was too high. Employing tactics based on this knowledge will lift the sights, providing a bird's eye view of discriminatory situations and how best to address them. From this broadened perspective on events and problems, we can recognize, understand, and thus be better able to cope with the various stages of racial subordination.

A prime example of forging fortuity is the resurgence of a range of single-race schools discussed earlier. Educators and parents have ignored the siren song that only integrated schools are worth fighting for. Going against the resistance of public school officials and teachers' unions, they have worked in a number of settings to provide children with effective educations based on the needs those children present, turning negative outside influences into positives for learning and development. Beyond official schools, there are hundreds of after-school or supplemental school programs, such as I described in the previous chapter, where dedicated individuals volunteer to establish and train young people with natural talents in the arts or sports that can become vehicles for learning and stepping stones to college and brighter futures than these young people would otherwise have enjoyed.

Beyond schools, we need professionals able to articulate racially realistic positions that touch some whites in the pocketbook, expecting that their sense of justice will follow. My example is the late William Robert Ming, a black lawyer from Chicago of marvelous skills and supreme self-confidence. In the early 1960s, he along with several other black lawyers were retained to go to Alabama and defend Martin Luther King, Jr. King, who had been charged with violating the state's income tax laws, a charge based on a presumption that all funds belonging to his organization, the Southern Christian Leadership Conference, represented his own taxable income.[17] In his defense, Ming did not raise an issue of jury discrimination because all the jurors were white. Rather, he used his voir dire objections to maximize the number of white businessmen on the jury. At trial, he made sure the jury understood that the state was threatening King with prison for not reporting income that was not his.

In his summary, Ming did not mention race or suggest that the state was prosecuting King because of his civil rights leadership. Instead, he simply reviewed the state's evidence and warned the jury: "If you want to set a precedent in which the state of Alabama can calculate your income taxes based on the total monies you have in your checking accounts, you find this man guilty." After almost four hours, the jury returned. The verdict: "Not guilty."[18]

Admittedly, forged fortuity tactics intended to achieve goals of racial justice will not find favor with either the media or large entities to which civil rights groups look for funding and endorsement. In order to reach masses of people, local and national organizations should seek to revitalize and support black newspapers that once played a major informational role when their white counterparts refused to carry any black news their readers might deem threatening or even uncomfortable. The coverage is much better today, but the white media's stories on black leaders and their activities, particularly if what they say or do is deemed upsetting or threatening, is often negative and sometimes hostile.

In addition, it is possible to make effective use of the Internet as both a communications and an organizing mechanism to present issues of concern that either do not interest the media or are published in forms that distort the message. Antiwar groups have used the Internet to great advantage in organizing major protest marches, petition-signing, and fundraising, and for sending messages to elected representatives intended to spur passive leaders into taking stands they fear may harm their chances for reelection.

While a cliché, speaking truth to power can discourage those who hope to act against the public's interest and convince most people to support them. Articulating our differences publicly may not win individuals or groups any popularity awards, but protests and the expression of opposition are forms of power we can enlist in campaigns for reforms, including those not recognized by courts or of interest to those individuals we helped elect.

We must recognize and acknowledge (at least to ourselves) that our actions are not likely to lead to transcendent change and, despite our best efforts, may be of more help to the system we despise than to the victims of that system we are trying to help. That realization and the dedication it engenders can lead to policy positions and campaigns that are less likely to worsen conditions for those we are trying to help, and that can serve as reminders to the establishment that they must contend with strong opposition. But beyond that, continued struggle can bring about unexpected benefits and gains that in themselves justify continued endeavor.

I am convinced that America offers something real for black people. It is not though, the romantic love of integration—though, like romance, we may seek and sometimes experience it. It is surely not the long-sought goal of equality under law—though we must maintain the struggle against racism lest the erosion of rights become even worse than it now is. The pragmatic approach that we must follow is simply to take a hard-eyed view of racism as it is, and of our subordinate role in it. We must realize with our slave forebears that the struggle for freedom is, at bottom, a manifestation of our humanity that survives and grows stronger through resistance to oppression even if we never overcome that oppression.

Just as the *Brown* decision's major contribution to the freedom struggle was the nation's response to the violent resistance of its opponents, so we who were its intended beneficiaries can learn from the myriad ways in which the relief we deserved was withheld. *Brown*, in retrospect, was a serious disappointment, but if we can learn the lessons it did not intend to teach, it will not go down as a defeat.

CONCLUSION

Booker T. Washington was hailed by whites and despised by many blacks for his accommodationist policies on race as reflected in his 1895 "Atlanta Compromise" speech, urging blacks to concede disenfranchisement and segregation in order to gain white support for progress in business and education.[1] Whatever Washington's intentions, the surrender of basic citizenship rights in the hope that hostile whites would reciprocate with schooling and better jobs, deserved the condemnation it received from black leaders, particularly W. E. B. Du Bois. Even so, in his speech, Washington used a parable to convey his philosophy of Negro self-sufficiency that has contemporary significance.

A lost ship has sailed for many days before finally sighting a friendly vessel. Frantically, the lost ship's crew signal their need for water, for they are dying of thirst. The rescue boat signals back: "Cast down your bucket where you are." The crew does so and brings them up filled with the fresh water of the Amazon River into which they have unknowingly sailed.

Whatever the wisdom of Washington's advice to a people whose dire physical plight was the result, not of storms abroad, but of an overwhelming racial hostility at home, the admonition "Cast down your buckets where you are" can be a solution if not the salvation for those working to reform and revitalize the ongoing crusade to overcome the debilitating effects of racism. To benefit from this resource in our midst, blacks must supplement the forms and patterns of striving for racial equality with innovative forms of personal self-image, group organization, resource collection and distribution, and strategic planning, using the concept of racial fortuity as a guideline.

Such efforts are underway in countless areas across the country. They go forward in the face of a racial history in America that raises the question whether unacknowledged forces—stronger than the authority of the Civil War amendments and the civil rights statutes of both the nineteenth and twentieth centuries—will dilute the protection from discrimination people of color can expect from laws and policies nominally intended for this purpose.

Social reformers in any area face opposition and frequent rejection, but black people seem uniquely burdened with the obligation to repeat history whether or not they earlier learned its lessons. The first Reconstruction experience, as bitter as it was, did not teach us to avoid a similar withdrawal of the rights and opportunities gained during the second Reconstruction of the 1960s. The statistics of black subordination in income, unemployment, prison, education, and health disparities, indicate that they are presently undergoing a period of redemption quite like the one that erased the gains they had made during Reconstruction.

No, blacks are no longer murdered by lynch mobs, but the disabilities wrought by poverty can also be deadly. Who is to argue that the high percentage of blacks facing the death penalty or lengthy prison sentences, all too often because they have lacked competent legal representation, is any more fortunate? I am not ignoring the black middle-class and the countless black people serving in positions that were impossible to imagine at the time *Brown* was decided in 1954.

Beyond the ebb and flow of racial progress lies the still viable and widely accepted (though seldom expressed) belief that America is a white country in which blacks, particularly as a group, are not entitled to the concern, resources, or even empathy that would be extended to similarly situated whites. Within this truth lies the foundation for the two-sided coin of racial fortuity. It validates today the theologian Reinhardt Niebuhr's prediction in 1932 that:

> It is hopeless for the Negro to expect complete emancipation from the menial social and economic position into which the white man has

forced him merely by trusting in the moral sense of the white race. . . .
However large the number of individual white men who do and who
will identify themselves completely with the Negro cause, the white
race in America will not admit the Negro to equal rights if it is not
forced to do so. Upon that point one may speak with a dogmatism
which all history justifies.[2]

As I have tried to show, the decision in *Brown v. Board of Education*
and its unassertive and finally failed implementation were in tune
with, rather than a departure from, this history. It was a perfect precedent precisely because it spoke in reformist tones that lifted the spirits
of blacks and raised the ire of whites whose leaders' overreaction to
civil rights protests led to public support and congressional action
that might not otherwise have occurred for some time. At bottom,
though, *Brown* helped maintain a stable society by moving it forward,
far less than civil rights advocates had hoped but far more than opponents felt was needed or necessary.

In effect, the fate of *Brown* mirrored the experience of the black
people the decision was intended to assist in their centuries-long
struggle for equality. Motivated in part by the nation's domestic and
international needs, the opinion's recognition of racial injustice for
blacks stirred whites to its forceful rejection. Few could even conceive
that what blacks sought as a matter of law, many whites needed as a
matter of fact. The Supreme Court accepted the civil rights lawyers'
argument that because of segregation, black children and, through
them, black people had been deeply harmed. The unintended but
readily assimilated side effect of that argument was that whites were
not harmed, and their dominant position in all things important was
right, just, and appropriate.

Since whites in general were not held responsible for harm to
blacks, it followed that only those whites who were found liable for
intentional discrimination should be penalized. As I suggested earlier,
the *Brown* decision substituted one mantra for another: where "separate" was once equal, "separate" would be now categorically unequal.
Rewiring the rhetoric of equality (rather than laying bare *Plessy*'s
white-supremacy underpinnings and consequences) constructs state-
supported racial segregation as an eminently fixable aberration. And
yet, by doing nothing more than rewiring the rhetoric of equality, the

Brown Court foreclosed the possibility of recognizing racism as a broadly shared cultural condition. In short, the equality model offered reassurance and short-term gains, but contained within its structure the seeds of its destruction.

The inscription on the gravesite of Whitney Young, the former head of the National Urban League, reads: "Where injustice reigns, all are unequal."[3] Evidently, the very truth of this message renders its recognition so difficult. And yet, the vision remains of an America that recognizes the values of racial difference—and those values, countless in number, would be no less worthy without the obsessive need to dominate and discriminate based on race. Absent the barriers based on race, the history of public education during the last two centuries would certainly be a more positive story featuring a better-educated and thus a more enlightened citizenry. The *Brown* decision failed to remove these barriers. The hopes that it would do so have been replaced by a reluctant recognition that it unintentionally replaced overt barriers with less obvious but equally obstructive new ones. The campaign must continue for the sake of our children.

* * *

I attended Justice Thurgood Marshall's funeral in the magnificent Washington Cathedral. Listening to the eulogies of his life, some delivered by members of the Court who steadfastly opposed his efforts to make the law more humane and caring, I considered the well-settled process whereby when black civil rights leaders die—or are killed—the nation transforms their memories. Though in life they were feared and hated because of their bold speech and audacious actions, upon their deaths they are borne on rhetorical wings, a thousand eulogies lifting them to a special place in that uniquely American racial pantheon. There, blacks have been accorded in death a distinction usually reserved for those who in life have achieved rather than failed to accomplish the goals to which they committed their lives.

In this vein, the Rev. Jesse Jackson wrote that:

those who have fought for the highest and best principles of our country, the true patriots, have been vilified and crucified [for they] invariably disturb the comfortable and comfort the disturbed, and are persecuted in their lifetimes even as their accomplishments are applauded after their deaths.[4]

Deserved or not, the nation has managed to find a place in this pantheon of heroes for its memory of *Brown v. Board of Education*, a decision that promised much and of which, I am willing to assume, the Supreme Court expected much. I have tried here to explain why it fell so far short of achieving its goals. In this effort, I am aided by the Rev. Peter Gomes, minister of the Memorial Church at Harvard University. Gomes wrote about Martin Luther King in terms that apply as well to the *Brown* decision:

> In death he was able to claim the loyalty denied him in life, for it is far easier to honor the dead than to follow the living, and so we take the dead to our bosoms, for there they can no longer do any harm; and we can translate a living, breathing, both noble and fallible human being into a heroic impotence, satisfying our need to both admire and be protected from something larger than ourselves.[5]

Gomes's words give meaning to the event described at the beginning of this book, when, at a Yale University commencement, applause followed the reminder that the *Brown* decision would soon be fifty years old. It was a dramatic instance of how readily this society assimilates the myriad manifestations of black protest and achievement. In that process, the continuing devastation of racial discrimination is minimized, even ignored, while we in the civil rights movement who gained some renown as we labored to end those injustices are conveniently converted into cultural reinforcements of the racial status quo. We become irrefutable proof that black people can make it in America through work and sacrifice.

Work and sacrifice, as important as they are, have never been sufficient to gain blacks more than grudging acceptance as individuals. They seldom enjoy the presumption of regularity, the sense that they belong or are competent, which whites may take for granted. Of course, at some point on the ladder of achievement, blacks are no longer deemed black by those whites who know them. We are told point-blank that we are "different." Sadly but understandably, there are black people who view such statements as compliments.

The psychic damage done by unofficial long-term exclusion is impossible to measure. None of us are immune, not even those who fight to end racism or try hard to understand, describe, and record it. Boston College law professor Anthony Farley, who views the quest for racial equality as an almost romantic longing for acceptance, writes:

> Everybody at some level believes in it. It's a deeply seductive image. The image that we all want, as oppressed people, is an image of our masters finally loving us and recognizing our humanity. It is this image that keeps prostitutes with their pimps, the colonized with their colonizers and battered women with their batterers. Everybody dreams of one day being safe." [6]

In an analogy to F. Scott Fitzgerald's novel that is almost too revealing in its implications, Farley suggests that:

> *The Great Gatsby* is the Great American Novel for a reason. Gatsby believed in the green light and that was his undoing—rich girls don't marry poor boys. And yet the compound where Daisy lived was across the bay. At night, it was marked by a green light on its pier—far away, but not Gatsby felt unattainable.

Concluding the novel, Fitzgerald wrote:

> Gatsby believed in the green light, the orgastic future that year by year recedes before us. It eluded us then, but that's no matter—tomorrow we will run faster, stretch out our arms farther. . . . And one fine morning—so we beat on, boats against the current, borne back ceaselessly into the past. [7]

"Well," Farley suggests, "that's what we do, we're borne back ceaselessly into the past. Gatsby doesn't get it . . . [and neither do] we, the intellectuals. We actually produce the seductive literature of the green light." To carry Farley's analogy further, the wealthy society crowd that the beautiful Daisy epitomizes is shallow and uncaring, floating through life on the things money can buy. Gatsby, totally consumed by Daisy, nevertheless says with exasperation, "Her voice is full of money. . . . That was it. . . . It was full of money—that was the inexhaustible charm that rose and fell in it, the jingle of it, the cymbals' song of it. . . . High in a white palace the king's daughter, the golden girl. . . ."[8]

In our anxiety to identify, we are attracted to the obvious and the superficial, the least worthy characteristics of the dominant group. It is that unconscious component of quest that gives even hard-earned progress a mirage-like quality. The decision in *Brown* and all the civil rights recognitions that came before—for there were far more recognitions of racial injustices than meaningful remedies—seemed more real than they could possibly be. We hardly noticed that the advances we hailed actually marked those periods when policymakers realized that remedies for racial injustice and the nation's needs coincided. Fortuity was more important than any national commitment to "freedom and justice for all."

Myth, though, can be revealed and transformed into useful strategy. Despite its limited benefit, those who defended the University of Michigan affirmative action plans utilized diversity as a self-interest strategy planned for in advance rather than a happy coincidence recognized in retrospect. Utilizing the racial-fortuity model in planning and implementing civil rights strategies may mean relying less on the courts to advance racial justice goals. As individuals and groups, blacks must challenge the assumptions of white dominance and the presumptions of black incompetence and inferiority. By refusing to accept white dominance in our schools, places of work, communities, and, yes, among those whites who consider us friends, we both show a due regard for our humanity and often convey enlightenment to whites deeply immersed in the still-widespread, deeply held beliefs of a white-dominated society.

Professor Robert Gordon offers encouragement when he reminds us that:

Things seem to change in history when people break out of their accustomed ways of responding to domination, by acting as if the constraints on their improving their lives were not real and that they could change things; and sometimes they can, though not always in the way they had hoped or intended; but they never knew they could change them at all until they tried. [9]

Preston Wilcox, a longtime Harlem activist, restates Gordon's words in the form of a grass-roots challenge: "Nobody can free us but ourselves." His admonition has meaning for every aspect of life for African Americans and all those deemed the "others." Nowhere does it have greater relevance than in the education of our children. Wilcox's truth is easier to acknowledge than to act on, and this, of course, is usually both the measure and the challenge of truth.

NOTES

Introduction

1. *Brown v. Board of Education*, 347 U.S. 483 (1954).
2. Derrick Bell, "Serving Two Masters: Integration Ideals and Client Interests in School Desegregation Litigation," 85 Yale L. J. 470 (1976).
3. Derrick Bell, "*Brown v. Board of Education* and the Interest-Convergence Dilemma," 93 Harv. L. Rev. 518 (1980).
4. 163 U.S. 537 (1896).
5. Michael Seidman, "*Brown* and *Miranda*," 80 Calif. L. Rev. 673, 717 (1992).

Chapter 1: *Plessy*'s Long Shadow

1. *Plessy v. Ferguson*, 163 U.S. 537 (1896).
2. John Hope Franklin, *History of Racial Segregation in the United States*, 34 Annals of the American Academy of Political and Social Science 6–8 (1956).

Chapter 2: *Brown*'s Half Light

1. Lerone Bennett, *Confrontation: Black and White* (Chicago: Johnson Publishing Co., 1965), 221–22.
2. Peter Bergman, *The Chronological History of the Negro in America* (New York: Harper & Row, 1969), 352, 357–58.
3. *Buchanan v. Warley*, 245 U.S. 60 (1917). The ordinance denied blacks the right to occupy houses in blocks in which whites were the predominant race, and denied whites the right to occupy housing in mainly black areas.

The Court saw the measure as an effort to bar blacks from acquiring property on the basis of color in violation of the Fourteenth Amendment.

4. *Moore v. Dempsey*, 261 U.S. 86, 91 (1923). The Court found that racial prejudice so reduced the trial to a "mask,—that counsel, jury, and judge were swept to the fatal end by an irresistible wave of public passion. . . ."

5. Mark Tushnet, *The NAACP's Legal Strategy Against Segregated Education, 1925–1950* (Chapel Hill: University of North Carolina Press, 1987).

6. Id., 5–6.

7. *Missouri ex re. Gaines v. Canada*, 305 U.S. 337 (1938); *Sipuel v. Board of Regents of the University of Oklahoma*, 332 U.S. 631 (1948). See Robert Carter, "The NAACP's Legal Strategy Against Segregated Education," 86 Mich. L. Rev. 1083 (1988) (discussing the organization's gradual and incremental approach).

8. *Sweatt v. Painter*, 339 U.S. 629 (1950).

9. *Brown v. Board of Education*, 347 U.S. 483 (1954). The cases consolidated for this appeal came from Kansas, South Carolina, Virginia, and Delaware. A fifth case, *Bolling v. Sharpe*, 347 U.S. 487 (1954), challenged segregation in the District of Columbia schools as unconstitutional in violation of due process clause of the Fifth Amendment

10. *Plessy v. Ferguson*, 163 U.S. 537 (1896).

11. 347 U.S. 483, 492–93.

12. Id., 494.

13. 349 U.S. 294 (1955).

14. Id., 299.

15. Loren Miller, *The Petitioners: The Story of the Supreme Court and the Negro* (New York: Pantheon, 1966), 351.

16. J. Harvie Wilkinson III, "The Supreme Court & Southern School Desegregation, 1955–1970: A History and Analysis," 64 Va. L. Rev. 485, 507 (1978).

Chapter 3: *Brown* Reconceived

1. *Giles v. Harris*, 189 U.S. 475, 488 (1903).

2. *Plessy v. Ferguson*, 163 U.S. 537, 552 (1896).

3. Argument, *The Oral Argument Before the Supreme Court in* Brown v. Board of Education of Topeka, *1952–55*, Leon Friedman, ed. (New York: Chelsea House Publishers, 1969), 215.

4. *Cumming v. Richmond Co. Board of Education*, 175 U.S. 528 (1899).

5. *Berea College v. Kentucky*, 211 U.S. 45 (1908). See also *Gong Lum v. Rice*, 275 U.S. 78 (1927) (the Court rejected the challenge of Chinese parents whose child was assigned to a Negro school).

6. C. Vann Woodward, *The Strange Career of Jim Crow*, 2d rev. ed. (New York: Oxford University Press, 1966).

7. *Sweatt v. Painter*, 339 U.S. 629 (1950). See also *Mclaurin v. Oklahoma*

State Regents, 339 U.S. 637 (1950); *Sipuel v. Oklahoma*, 332 U.S. 631 (1948); *Missouri ex re. Gaines v. Canada*, 305 U.S. 337 (1938).

8. W. E. B. Du Bois, "Does the Negro Need Separate Schools?" 4 J. Negro Educ. 328 (1935); See generally Derrick Bell, "The Legacy of W. E. B. Du Bois: A Rational Model for Achieving Public School Equity for America's Black Children," 11 Creighton L. Rev. 409 (1977).

9. 163 U.S. 537, 559.

10. Jerome McCristal Culp, "An Open Letter from One Black Scholar to Justice Ruth Bader Ginsburg: Or How Not to Become Justice Sandra Day O'Connor," 1 Duke J. Of Gender L. & Policy 21, 27 (1994).

11. Id., 28.

Chapter 4: The Racial-Sacrifice Covenants

1. Edmund Morgan, *American Slavery, American Freedom: The Ordeal of Colonial Virginia* (New York: Norton, 1975).

2. Staughton Lynd, *Slavery and the Founding Fathers*, in *Black History*, Melvin Drimmer, ed. (New York: Doubleday & Co., 1968), 115. See also Staughton Lynd, *Slavery, Class Conflict, and the Constitution* (Indianapolis: Bobbs-Merrill, 1967).

3. W. E. B. Du Bois, *The Suppression of the African Slave Trade to the United States of America, 1638–1870* (New York: Schocken, 1969), 49.

4. Id., 48–51.

5. Donald Robinson, *Slavery in the Structure of American Politics: 1765–1820* (New York: Harcourt Brace Jovanovich, 1971), 92, quoting from Thomas Jefferson, *Notes on the State of Virginia*.

6. Staughton Lynd, *Slavery and the Founding Fathers*, 181–82.

7. Id., 131.

8. Id.

9. See, e.g., William M. Wiecek, *The Sources of Antislavery Constitutionalism in America, 1760–1848* (Ithaca, N.Y.: Cornell University Press, 1977), 62–105, pointing out that the original Constitution included up to ten slave clauses, including U.S. Const. art. I, sec. 2, cl. 3 (apportioning Congressional representatives among states based on population, determined by all free persons and three-fifths of the slaves); U.S. Const. art. I, sec. 8, cl. 15 (vesting power in Congress to suppress insurrections, including those by slaves); U.S. Const. art. IV, sec. 2, cl. 3 (prohibiting states from freeing runaway slaves); and U.S. Const. art. IV, sec. 4 (obligating the federal government to protect states from domestic violence, including slave insurrections). See also Mary Francis Berry, *Black Resistance/White Law: A History of Constitutional Racism in America* (Englewood Cliffs, N.J.: Prentice-Hall, 1971).

10. Mary Francis Berry, "Slavery, The Constitution, and the Founding Fathers," in *African Americans and the Living Constitution*, John Hope Franklin and Genna Rae McNeil, eds. (Washington, D.C.: Smithsonian Institution Press, 1995), 14–15.

11. Leon Litwack, *North of Slavery: The Negro in the Free States, 1790–1860* (Chicago: University of Chicago Press, 1961), 74, 79, 576.

12. *United States ex re. I Goldsby v. Harpole*, 263 F.2d 71, 79, n.21 (5th Cir. 1959), quoting Alexis de Tocqueville, *Democracy in America*.

   Evidently to conform the law with practice, the Pennsylvania Supreme Court ruled in *Hobbes v. Fogg*, 6 Watts 553 (1837), that blacks did not have the right to vote even though there was no express prohibition in the state's constitution or laws. Relying on reasoning foreshadowing that used by Chief Justice Taney two decades later in *Dred Scott v. Sandford*, 60 U.S. (19 How.) 393 (1857), the court found that provisions entitling "every freeman" to vote could not include blacks who were slaves when the provisions were adopted and were not freed thereby. Thus, the founders must not have intended to include blacks among citizens entitled to all the rights and privileges of citizenship. The political limbo into which blacks were cast by the *Hobbes v. Fogg* decision was made certain the following year when the Pennsylvania constitution was amended to give "the rights of an elector" to "every white freeman of the age of twenty-one . . . " (Pa. Const. 1838, art. Ill. sec. I). The era is reviewed in Eric Springer, "The Unconquerable Prejudice of Caste-Civil Rights in Early Pennsylvania," 5 Duq. L. Rev. 31, 47–50 (1966–1967).

13. *Dred Scott v. Sandford*, 60 U.S. (19 How.) 393 (1856).

14. *Emerson v. Scott*, 15 Mo. 576 (1852).

15. 60 U.S. 393, 407.

16. The case and its era are covered in Don E. Fehrenbacher, *The Dred Scott Case: Its Significance in American Law and Politics* (New York: Oxford University Press, 1978).

17. Mark A. Graber, "Desperately Ducking Slavery: Dred Scott and Contemporary Constitutional Theory," 14 Constitutional Commentary 271, 280–81 (1997).

18. Peter Bergman, *The Chronological History of the Negro in America* (New York: Harper & Row, 1969), 212.

19. In the more recent literature on Reconstruction, there are many views on radical Republican motivations, the accomplishments of the experiment, and the reasons for its failures. For a fair sample of these views, with special focus on the myriad of factors contributing to the Hayes-Tilden Compromise, see Lerone Bennett, *Black Power USA: The Human Side of Reconstruction* (Chicago: Johnson Publishing Co., 1967); Hodding Carter, *The Angry Scar: The Story of Reconstruction* (Garden City, N.Y.: Doubleday, 1959); W. E. B. Du Bois, *Black Reconstruction in America* (New York: Atheneum, 1992); Paul Haworth, *The Hayes-Tilden Disputed Presidential Election of 1876* (Cleveland, Ohio: Borrows Brothers, 1906); Rayford Logan, *Betrayal of the Negro from Rutherford Hayes to Woodrow Wilson* (New York: College Books, 1965); Kenneth Stampp, *The Era of Reconstruction: 1865–1877* (New York: Knopf, 1965); John Hope Franklin, *Reconstruction: After the Civil War* (Chicago: University of

Chicago Press, 1961); C. Vann Woodward, *Reunion and Reaction: The Compromise of 1877 and the End of Reconstruction* (Boston: Little, Brown, 1966).

20. Charles H. Wesley, *Negro Labor in the United States, 1850–1925: A Study in American Economic History* (New York: Vanguard Press, 1927), 138–47.

21. See, e.g., Joel Williamson, *After Slavery: The Negro in South Carolina During Reconstruction, 1861–1877* (Chapel Hill: University of North Carolina Press, 1965), 161–63.

22. Samuel Denny Smith, *The Negro in Congress, 1870–1901* (Chapel Hill: University of North Carolina Press, 1940), 4–5.

23. W. E. B. Du Bois, *Black Reconstruction in America: 1860–1880* (New York: Atheneum, 1992), 638–42.

24. Id., 664.

25. John Hope Franklin and Alfred A. Moss, Jr., *From Slavery to Freedom: A History of Negro Americans*, 6th ed. (New York: Knopf, 1988), 231–35.

26. Tom Watson, "The Negro Question in the South," in Stokeley Carmichael and Charles Hamilton, *Black Power: The Politics of Liberation in America* (New York: Vintage Books, 1992), 67–68.

27. Franklin and Moss, *From Slavery to Freedom*, 231–35.

28. C. Vann Woodward, *Origins of the New South, 1877–1913* (Baton Rouge: Louisiana State University Press, 1971), 211–12.

29. Woodward, *Reunion and Reaction*.

30. *NAACP Legal Defense Fund, Death Row USA Report* (Apr. 1999).

31. See David Baldus and George Woodworth, "Racial Discrimination and the Death Penalty in the Post–*Furman* Era: An Empirical and Legal Overview, With Recent Findings from Philadelphia," 83 Cornell L. Rev. 1638 (1998).

32. *McCleskey v. Kemp*, 481 U.S. 279 (1987).

33. Id., 340–41.

34. See Paul Butler, "By Any Means Necessary: Using Violence and Subversion to Change Unjust Laws," 50 U.C.L.A. L. Rev. 721, 734 (2003).

35. Id., 735.

36. See Susan Sturm and Lani Guinier, "The Future of Affirmative Action: Reclaiming the Innovative Ideal," 84 Calif. L. Rev. 953, 957 (1996).

37. See Ian Ayres, "Further Evidence of Discrimination in New Car Negotiations and Estimates of its Causes," 94 Mich. L. Rev. 109 (1995); Ian Ayres, "Fair Driving: Gender and Race Discrimination in Retail Car Negotiations," 104 Harv. L. Rev. 817 (1991).

38. Derrick Bell, *Faces at the Bottom of the Well: The Permanence of Racism* (New York: Basic Books, 1992), 158.

39. Id., 194.

Chapter 5: The Interest-Convergence Covenants

1. Mary Dudziak, *Cold War Civil Rights: Race and the Image of American Democracy* (Princeton: Princeton University Press, 2000).

2. Leon Litwack, *North of Slavery: The Negro in the Free States, 1790–1860* (Chicago: University of Chicago Press, 1961), 3–20.

3. Alexis de Tocqueville, *Democracy in America* (New York: Anchor Books, 1969), 344.

4. For a discussion of the historical import of the *Quack Walker* case, see David B. Davis, *The Problem of Slavery in the Age of Revolution: 1770–1823* (New York: Oxford University Press, 1999), 508. See also Elaine Mac-Eacheron, "Emancipation of Slavery in Massachusetts: A Reexamination, 1770–1790," 55 J. Negro Hist. 289 (1970).

5. Pennsylvania Act, Mar. 1, 1780, ch. 146.

6. Arthur Zilversmit, *The First Emancipation: The Abolition of Slavery in the North* (Chicago: Chicago University Press, 1967), 4, 124–32.

7. See Robert Fogel and Stanley Engerman, *Time on the Cross: The Economics of American Negro Slavery* (Boston: Little, Brown, 1974). See also Donald L. Robinson, *Slavery in the Structure of American Politics, 1765–1820* (New York: Harcourt Brace Jovanovich, 1971), 29–38.

8. Winthrop D. Jordan, *White Over Black: American Attitudes Toward the Negro, 1550–1812* (Chapel Hill: University of North Carolina Press, 1968), 345.

9. Lorenzo Greene, *The Negro in Colonial New England, 1620–1776* (Port Washington, N.Y., Kennikat Press, 1966), 332–33.

10. Litwack, *North of Slavery*,

11. Lincoln's motivations are reviewed in Dillard, "The Emancipation Proclamation in the Perspective of Time," 23 Law in Transition 95 (1963).

12. Id., 96.

13. Id. A joint resolution for compensated emancipation was passed by Congress in early 1862, but by that point in the hostilities, there was little interest in it. Congress did approve a measure freeing slaves in the District of Columbia and providing funds to send them abroad if deemed advisable.

14. Id., 97–98.

15. John Hope Franklin has reviewed Lincoln's changing viewpoint on the Emancipation Proclamation and the effect of the document on blacks, the nation, and the world in John Hope Franklin, *The Emancipation Proclamation* (Garden City, N.Y.: Doubleday, 1963).

16. Dillard, *The Emancipation Proclamation in the Perspective of Time*, 98.

17. Proclamation of January I, 1863, No.17, 12 Stat. 1268 (1863).

18. Frederick Douglass, *Life and Times of Frederick Douglass* (New York: Crowell-Collier, 1962), 351–55.

19. See Leon Litwack, *Been in the Storm So Long: The Aftermath of Slavery* (New York: Knopf, 1979), 117–25.

20. James Garfield Randall, *Constitutional Problems Under Lincoln* (New York: Appleton, 1951), 100.

21. Id., 316–17.

22. Franklin, *From Slavery to Freedom*, 279.

23. Slaughter-House Cases, 83 U.S. (16 Wall.) 36 (1873).

24. *Santa Clara County v. Southern Pac. R.R.*, 118 U.S. 394 (1866).

25. See, e.g., *Allgeyer v. Louisiana*, 165 U.S. 578 (1897); *Lochner v. New York*, 198 U.S. 45 (1905); *Adkins v. Children's Hospital*, 261 U.S. 525 (1923).

26. Usually in cases of more symbolic than substantive value, the Court did recognize the Civil War amendments' protection against exclusion of Negroes from juries; see *Strauder v. West Virginia*, 100 U.S. 303 (1880); Ex parte Virginia, 100 U.S. 339 (1880). During the first few decades of the twentieth century, the Court found that Negro rights had been violated in *Bailey v. Alabama*, 219 U.S. 219 (1911) (striking down state peonage laws that coerced primarily black labor); *United States v. Reynolds*, 235 U.S. 133 (1914) (invalidating an Alabama law criminalizing breach of surety agreements whereby private parties paid the fines to liberate convicted criminals from jail in exchange for promises to labor for a specific time.); *McCabe v. Atchinson*, T.&S.F.R. Co., 235 U.S. 151 (1914) (striking down a state law permitting railroads to exclude blacks from first-class service rather than offer separate but equal accommodations); *Guinn v. Oklahoma*, 238 U.S. 347 (1915) (invalidating Oklahoma's "grandfather clause" under the Fifteenth Amendment); and *Buchanan v. Warley*, 245 U.S. 60 (1917).

27. 109 U.S. 3 (1883).

Chapter 6: *Brown* as an Anticommunist Decision

1. Mary Dudziak, *Cold War Civil Rights: Race and the Image of American Democracy* (Princeton: Princeton University Press, 2000), 18–78. For a detailed review of the Dudziak book, see Richard Delgado, "Explaining the Rise and Fall of African-American Fortunes—Interest Convergence and Civil Rights Gains," 37 Harv. Civ. Rts. Civ. Lib. L. Rev. 369 (2002).

2. Id., 3–17.

3. Id., 18–20.

4. Id., 24.

5. Id., 44–45.

6. Id., 31–32.

7. Id., 66–67.

8. Id., 77–78.

9. See *Shelley v. Kraemer*, 348 U.S. 1 (1948) (holding that restrictive covenants barring sales to nonwhites were unenforceable in courts). The

government argued that in conducting its foreign relations, it had been embarrassed by racial discrimination at home. Dudziak, *Cold War Civil Rights*, 91–92.

Henderson v. United States, 339 U.S. 816 (1950) (segregated dining facilities on railroad trains violated the Interstate Commerce Act [ICC], at least in situations where blacks were delayed in receiving service because of limited accommodations, while seats were available in areas reserved for whites). The Justice Department had taken the stronger position that segregation was not authorized under the ICC, and if it was authorized, it violated the Fourteenth Amendment. Dudziak, *Cold War Civil Rights*, 92–93.

10. *McLaurin v. Oklahoma*, 339 U.S. 637 (1950), and *Sweatt v. Painter*, 339 U.S. 636 (1950). Both cases struck down laws barring the admission of or segregation of blacks in the state's graduate schools.

11. Dudziak, *Cold War Civil Rights*, 95–96.

12. Id., 100.

13. Id., 101.

14. Id.,101–2.

15. Id.,104–6.

16. *Dennis v. United States*, 341 U.S. 494, 547 (1951).

17. Alfred Blaustein and Clyde Ferguson, *Desegregation and the Law: The Meaning and Effect of the School Desegregation Cases* (New Brunswick, N.J.: Rutgers University Press, 1957), 11–12.

18. W. E. B. Du Bois, *The Autobiography of W. E. B. Du Bois: A Soliloquy on Viewing My Life from the Last Decade of its First Century* (New York: International Publishers, 1968), 333.

Chapter 7: The Role of Fortuity in Racial Policy-Making

1. See, *Williston on Contracts*, ch. 37.1, Richard A. Lord, ed. Database updated May 2003.

2. See, e.g., *Cherry for Use of Trueblood v. Aetna Cas. & Sur. Co.*, 300 Ill. App. 392, 21 N.E.2d 4 (3d Dist. 1939), judgment aff'd, 372 Ill. 534, 25 N.E.2d 11 (1939), citing *Carson Pirie Scott & Co. v. Parrett*, 346 Ill. 252, 178 N.E. 498, 81 A.L.R. 1262 (1931).

3. Id.

4. Lerone Bennett, *Before the Mayflower*, 5th ed. (Chicago: Johnson Publishing Co., 1982), 366–70.

5. *Smith v. Allwright*, 321 U.S. 299 (1944) (party nominating candidates deemed agency of the state and exclusion of blacks violated their rights under the Fourteenth and Fifteenth Amendments); *Terry v. Adams*, 345 U.S. 461 (1953) (selection of candidates by a "private" all-white Jaybird primary, whose selections then appeared on the Democratic Party primary, held a violation of the Fifteenth Amendment).

6. See, e.g., Alfred Brophy, "Some Conceptual and Legal Problems in Repa-

rations for Slavery," 58 NYU Annual Survey of American Law 497 (2003); Chad Bryan, "Commentary: Precedent for Reparations? A Look at Historical Movements for Redress and Where Awarding Reparations for Slavery Might Fit," 54 Ala. L. Rev. 599 (2003); Robert Westley, "Reparations and Symbiosis: Reclaiming the Remedial Focus," 71 Univ. Missouri at Kansas City L. Rev. (2002): Robert Westley, "Many Billions Gone: Is It Time to Reconsider the Case for Black Reparations?" 19 B.C. Third World L. J. 429 (1998); Watson Branch, "Reparations for Slavery: A Dream Deferred," 3 San Diego L. J. 177 (2002); Edberto Roman, "Reparations and the Colonial Dilemma: The Insurmountable Hurdles and Yet Transformative Benefits," 13 Berkeley La Raza L. J. 369 (2002); Kevin Hopkins, "Forgive the U.S. Our Debts? Righting the Wrongs of Slavery," 89 Geo. L. J. 2531 (2001).

7. Randall Robinson, *The Debt: What America Owes to Blacks* (New York: Dutton, 2000).

8. Note, "Bridging the Color Line: the Power of African-American Reparations to Redirect America's Future," 115 Harv. L. Rev. 1689 (2002).

9. See, e.g., Vincene Verdun, "If the Shoe Fits Wear It: An Analysis of Reparations to African Americans," 67 Tul. L. Rev. 597 (1993).

10. Boris Bittker, *The Case for Black Reparations* (New York: Random House, 1973).

11. *Alexander v. Oklahoma*, Civ. No. 4:03cv00133 (N.D. Oklahoma). See Tatsha Robertson, "Quest for Vindication: Survivors of 1921 Tulsa Race Riots Hail Suit for Reparations," *Boston Globe* (Feb. 26, 2003), A1.

12. See Derrick Bell, *Gospel Choirs: Psalms of Survival in an Alien Land Called Home* (New York: Basic Books, 1996),125–27.

13. Robinson, *The Debt*, 206.

Chapter 8: Racism's Economic Foundation

1. See, generally, Derrick Bell, *Faces at the Bottom of the Well: The Permanence of Racism* (New York: Basic Books, 1992).

2. See Amy L. Chua, *World on Fire: How Exporting Free Market Democracy Breeds Ethnic Hatred and Global Instability* (New York: Doubleday, 2003); see also Amy L. Chua, "The Paradox of Free Market Democracy: Rethinking Development Policy," 41 Harv. Int'l. L. J. 287 (2000); and Amy L. Chua, "Markets, Democracy and Ethnicity: Toward a New Paradigm for Law and Development," 108 Yale L. J. 1 (1998).

3. Chua, "The Paradox of Free Market Democracy," 287, 288.

4. Id., 289.

5. Id., 306.

6. Id.

7. David Roediger, *The Wages of Whiteness: Race and the Making of the American Working Class* (New York: Verso, 1991).

8. Cheryl Harris, "Whiteness As Property," 106 Harv. L. Rev. 1707 (1993).

9. Id., 1759.

10. See, e.g. Ken Emerson, *Doo Dah! Stephen Foster and the Rise of American Popular Culture* (New York: Simon & Schuster), 96–98.

11. Morrison, *The Pain of Being Black*, Time (May 22, 1989), 120.

12. Tilden J. LeMelle, foreword to Richard M. Burkey, *Racial Discrimination and Public Policy in the United States* (1971), 38.

13. Roediger, *The Wages of Whiteness*, 12–13.

14. Richard Kluger, *Simple Justice* (New York: Knopf, 1976), 679.

15. See, e.g., Roediger, *The Wages of Whiteness*; Howard Winant, *Racial Conditions: Politics, Theory, Comparisons* (Minneapolis: University of Minnesota Press, 1994); Noel Ignatiev, *How the Irish Became White* (New York: Routledge, 1995); Karen Brodkin, *How Jews Became White Folks & What That Says About Race in America* (New Brunswick, N.J.: Rutgers University Press, 1999).

16. See Jamaica Kincaid, "The Little Revenge from the Periphery," 73 Transition 68, 73.

17. 198 U.S. 45 (1905).

Chapter 9: School Litigation in the Nineteenth Century

1. 59 Mass. (5 Cush.) 198, 201–4 (1850).

2. Id., 209.

3. See White, "The Black Leadership Class and Education in Antebellum Boston," 42 J. Negro Educ. 513 (1973).

4. Mass. Laws 1855, ch. 256, sec. 1. See Stanley Schultz, *The Culture Factory: Boston Public Schools, 1789–1860* (New York: Oxford University Press, 1973), 204–5.

5. *Board of Education of Ottawa v. Tinnon*, 26 Kan. 1, 19 (1881).

6. 163 U.S. at 544.

Chapter 10: The School Desegregation Era

1. Robert Carter, "The Warren Court and Desegregation," 67 Mich. L. Rev. 237, 243 (1968).

2. *Cooper v. Aaron*, 358 U.S. I (1958).

3. 5 U.S. (Cranch) 137 (1803).

4. *Covington v. Edwards*, 264 F.2d 780 (4th Cir. 1959), cert. denied, 361 U.S. 840 (1959) (pupil placement law validated and procedures established); *Carson v. Warlick*, 238 F.2d 724 (4th Cir. 1956), cert. denied, 353 U.S. 910 (1957) (exhaustion of administrative remedies required); *Hood v. Board of Trustees*, 232 F.2d 626 (4th Cir. 1956), cert. denied, 352 U.S. 870 (1956) (exhaustion of administrative remedies required); *Shuttlesworth v. Birmingham Bd. of Educ.*, 162 F. Supp. 372 (N.D. Ala. 1958), aff'd. (on the limited ground on which the district court rested its decision), 358

U.S. 101 (1958); accord, *Holt v. Raleigh City Bd. of Educ.*, 265 F.2d 95 (4th Cir.), cert. denied, 361 U.S. 818 (1959) (requirement that parent and child follow procedures established by pupil placement board sustained); *DeFebio v. County Bd.*, 199 Va. 511, 100 S. E.2d 760 (1957), appeal dismissed and cert. denied, 357 U.S. 218 (1958).

5. Carter, "The Warren Court and Desegregation," 247.

6. Id., 247.

7. 377 U.S. 218, 234 (1967). In the following year, the Court stated that "[d]elays in segregating school systems are no longer tolerable." *Bradley v. School Bd. of Richmond*, 382 U.S. 103 (1965). See also *Rogers v. Paul*, 382 U.S. 198 (1965).

8. *Cisneros v. Corpus Christi Independent School District Civ. A. No. 68-C-95* (Jun. 4, 1970). See Margaret E. Montoya, "A Brief History of Chicana/o School Segregation: One Rationale for Affirmative Action," 12 Berkeley La Raza L. J. 159, 170 (2001).

9. 78 Stat. 252, 42 U.S.C. sec. 2000d–2000d-4 (1964).

10. Aaron Henry with Constance Curry, *Aaron Henry: The Fire Ever Burning* (Oxford: University of Mississippi Press, 2000).

11. *Roberts v. City of Boston*, 59 Mass. (5 Cush.) 198, 209 (1850).

12. Burke Marshall, "Professional Responsibility and Constitutional Doctrine," 48 Tul. L. Rev. 465 (1973).

13. Id., 471.

14. Id., 474.

15. 402 U.S. 1 (1971).

16. 413 U.S. 189 (1973).

17. 418 U.S. 717 (1974). The Detroit public school population was already 63.8 percent black in 1970 and was growing at a rate greater than the city's black population. Given the prospect of an increased white exodus, a remedial plan consolidating the Detroit system with the fifty-three surrounding suburban districts was deemed the only solution by the district court. *Bradley v. Milliken*, 345 F. Supp. 914 (E.D. Mich. 1972), aff'd., 484 F.2d 215, 250 (6th Cir. 1973).

18. "Half of Blacks in Poll Question Busing's Value," *New York Times* (Mar. 2, 1981), B4. See also Lena Williams, "Controversy Reawakens as Districts End Busing," *New York Times* (Mar. 25, 1986), A24. In DeKalb County, Georgia, a poll of black residents commissioned by the DeKalb Chamber of Commerce found that 87.6 percent of black parents surveyed would not support mandatory busing to achieve racial balance in the schools. See Robert Jordan, "Is Desegregation Working for Blacks?" *Boston Globe* (Jul. 1, 1990), 89.

19. See Note, "Teaching Inequality: The Problem of Public School Tracking," 102 Harv. L. Rev. 1318 (1989).

20. W. E. B. Du Bois, "Does the Negro Need Separate Schools?" 4 J. Negro Educ. 328 (1935).

Chapter 11: The End of the *Brown* Era

1. Robert Carter, "A Reassessment of Brown v. Board," in *Shades of Brown: New Perspectives on School Desegregation*, Derrick Bell, ed. (New York: Teachers College Press, 1980), 21, 27.

2. *Calhoun v. Cook*, 362 F. Supp. 1249, 1251 n.5 (N.D. Ga. 1973). The plan included provisions that there would not be less than 20 percent of blacks in already integrated "stabilized" schools nor less than 30 percent in other schools. The district court found the plan reasonable, "considering the small percentage of white children (21 percent) now remaining in the system . . ." (id., 1251 & n.7).

3. Benjamin Mays, "Comment: Atlanta: Living with *Brown* Twenty Years Later," 3 Black L. J. 184, 190, 191–92 (1974).

4. *Calhoun v. Cook*, 525 F.2d 1203 (5th Cir. 1975).

5. *Milliken v. Bradley*, 433 U.S. 267, 282 (1977).

6. *Liddell v. Caldwell*, 546 F.2d 768 (8th Cir. 1976).

7. See 59 Mass. (5 Cush.) 198, 201–4 (1850).

8. Derrick Bell, "The Legacy of W. E. B. Du Bois: A Rational Model for Achieving Public School Equity for America's Black Children," 2 Creighton L. Rev. 409, 419 (1977).

9. W. E. B. Du Bois, *Dusk of Dawn: An Essay Toward an Autobiography of a Race Concept* (New York: Harcourt, Brace & Co., 1940), 303.

10. Derrick Bell, "Serving Two Masters: Integration Ideals and Client Interests in School Desegregation Litigation," 85 Yale L. J. 470 (1976).

11. Bell, "Serving Two Masters," 471–72.

12. Dean Campbell, "Defining and Attaining Equal Educational Opportunity in a Pluralistic Society," 26 Vand. L. Rev. 461, 478 (1973).

13. Ray Rist, *The Invisible Children: School Integration in American Society* (Cambridge, Mass.: Harvard University Press, 1978), reviewed in Derrick Bell, "The School Integration Battle: Leaders and Losses in Year 25," 92 Harv. L. Rev. 1826 (1979).

14. Daniel Monti, *A Semblance of Justice: St. Louis School Desegregation and Order in Urban America* (Columbia: University of Missouri Press, 1985).

15. Jill Nelson, "Retired Educators Recall 50 Years of Change in D.C. Schools," *Washington Post* (Apr. 22, 1989), B1.

16. See *Board of Education of Oklahoma City Public Schools v. Dowell*, 498 U.S. 237 (1991).

17. See, e.g., William Taylor, "*Brown*, Equal Protection, and the Isolation of the Poor," 95 Yale L. J. 1700, 1710–11nn.36–42 (1986).

18. Erica Frankenberg, Chungmei Lee, and Gary Orfield, *A Mutiracial Society with Segregated Schools: Are We Losing the Dream?* (Cambridge, Mass.: Harvard University Press, 2003).

19. Jonathan Kozol, *Ordinary Resurrections: Children in the Years of Hope* (New York: Crown Publishers, 2000), 31. For a depressing review of segregation and inadequacies in schools across the country, see Jonathan Kozol, *Savage Inequalities: Children in America's Schools* (New York: Crown Publishers, 1991).

20. College Entrance Examination Board, *Equality and Excellence: The Educational Status of Black Americans* (1985), 12.

21. N. Francis, "Equity and Excellence in Education," in *Association of Black Foundation Executives Conference Proceedings* 73 (Apr. 26, 1985).

22. *Keyes v. School District No. 1*, Denver, Colorado, 413 U.S. 189 (1973).

23. See *United States v. Texas*, 466 F.2d 518 (5th Cir. 1972).

Chapter 12: *Brown* as Landmark

1. Statement by Stacie Hendrix at the Black, Latino, Asian Pacific Alumni Association (BLAPAA) annual dinner, New York University Law School, April 12, 2003.

2. See., e.g., Herbert Wechsler, "Toward Neutral Principles of Constitutional Law," 73 Harv. L. Rev. 1 (1959), and a response by Charles Black, "The Lawfulness of the Segregation Decisions," 69 Yale L. J. 421 (1959). *Brown II* was more generally criticized, and in particular by those who defended *Brown I*. See, e.g., Charles Black, "The Unfinished Business of the Warren Court," 46 Wash. L. Rev. 3 (1970).

3. Michael J. Klarman, "*Brown*, Racial Change, and the Civil Rights Movement," 80 Va. L. Rev. 7 (1994). See also Michael J. Klarman, *From Jim Crow to Civil Rights: The Supreme Court and the Struggle for Racial Equality* (New York: Oxford University Press, 2003).

4. Harry Belafonte, "My Soul Speaks," *Essence* (Jan. 2003), 148.

5. Gerald N. Rosenberg, *The Hollow Hope: Can Courts Bring About Social Change?* (Chicago: University of Chicago Press, 1991).

6. Id., 156.

7. Id.

8. Robert Carter, "A Reassessment of *Brown v. Board*," in *Shades of Brown: New Perspectives on School Desegregation*, Derrick Bell, ed. (New York: Teachers College Press, 1980), 148.

9. Michael Seidman, *Brown and Miranda*, 80 Calif. L. Rev. 673, 717 (1992).

10. Id.

11. John Charles Boger, "Willful Colorblindness: The New Racial Piety and the Resegregation of Public Schools," 78 North Car. L. Rev. 1719, 1794 (2000).

12 Kevin Brown, "The Legal Rhetorical Structure for the Conversion of Desegregation Lawsuits to Quality Education Lawsuits," 42 Emory Law Journal 791, 816 (1993).

Chapter 13: Affirmative Action and Racial Fortuity in Action

1. *Regents of the University of California v. Bakke*, 438 U.S. 265, 404 (1978) (Justice Blackmun concurring).

2. William Bowen and Derek Bok, *The Shape of the River: Long-Term Consequences of Considering Race in College and University Admissions* (Princeton, N.J.: Princeton University Press 1998).

3. *Regents of the University of California v. Bakke*, 438 U.S. 265 (1978).

4. Michael Selmi, "The Life of Bakke: An Affirmative Action Retrospective," 87 Geo. L. J. 981–82 (1999).

5. See, e.g., Charles Lawrence and Mari Matsuda, *We Won't Go Back: Making the Case for Affirmative Action* (Boston: Houghton Mifflin, 1997); Alex M. Johnson, Jr., "Defending the Use of Quotas in Affirmative Action: Attacking Racism in the Nineties," 1992 U. Ill. L. Rev. 1043, 1073 ("considering the black experience in a historical and contextual framework that focuses not only on the past, but [also on] the future of American society, the use of quotas is the most efficacious method for achieving racial equality in contemporary American society").

6. See, e.g., Stephan Thernstrom and Abigail Thernstrom, *America in Black and White: One Nation, Indivisible* (New York: Simon & Schuster, 1997).

7. See Janine Jackson, "White Man's Burden: How the Press Frames Affirmative Action," *EXTRA!*, (Sept.–Oct. 1995), 7 (describing press tendency to define affirmative action using the "hot-button" term "quota"; to ignore the continuing discrimination against women and people of color; and to portray questions of discrimination "as most importantly the concern of white men").

8. Susan Sturm and Lani Guinier, "The Future of Affirmative Action: Reclaiming the Innovative Ideal," 84 Calif. L. Rev. 953, 957 (1996).

9. Ben Jackson, "The Other Candidate," *Chronicle of Higher Education* (Jul. 4, 2003), C3.

10. *Hopwood v. Texas*, 78 F.3d 932 (5th Cir. 1996), cert. denied, *Hopwood v. Texas*, 518 U.S. 1033 (1996).

11. 78 F.3d 932 (5th Cir. 1996), cert. Denied, *Hopwood v. Texas*, 116 S. Ct. 2580 (1996).

12. Tex. Educ. Code Ann. 51.803 (1998).

13. David Orentlicher, "Affirmative Action and Texas's Ten Percent Solution: Improving Diversity and Quality," 74 Notre Dame L. Rev. 181 (1998).

14. See, Sara Hebel, "'Percent Plans' Don't Add Up," *Chronicle of Higher Education* (Mar. 21, 2003), A22.

15. Jacques Steinberg, "Using Synonyms for Race, College Strives for Diversity," *New York Times* (Dec. 8, 2002).

16. Id.

17. Amy Argetsinger, "Supreme Court Case Prompts Some area Colleges to Make Subtle Changes in Policy," *Washington Post* (Mar. 12, 2003), A 1.

18. Marvin Krislov, "Open the 'Black Box' of College Admissions," *Chronicle Review* (Aug. 1, 2003), B16. Krislov is vice president and general counsel of the University of Michigan at Ann Arbor.

19. Jacques Steinberg, "3 Look to College Suit to Show Their Merits," *New York Times* (Feb. 23, 2003), A 32.

20. *Grutter v. Bollinger*, 288 F.3d 732 (6th Cir. 2002).

21. See, e.g., *City of Richmond, Va. v. J.A. Croson*, 488 U.S. 469 (1989) (striking down a city's set-aside program intended to ensure that a percentage of contracts would be awarded to minority-owned businesses); *Wygant v. Jackson Board of Education*, 476 U.S. 267 (1986) (refusing to approve a union contract specifying that in case of teacher lay-offs, a certain percentage of minority teachers would be retained without regard to their seniority); *Shaw v. Reno*, 509 U.S. 630 (1993) (a congressional electoral reapportionment plan creating two black districts held invalid as structured on racial basis).

22. Diana Jean Schemo, "Doctors, Soldiers and Others Weigh In on Campus Diversity," *New York Times* Week in Review (Feb. 23, 2004), 7.

23. *Gratz v. Bollinger*, 123 S. Ct. 2411, 2427–28 (2003).

24. *Grutter v. Bollinger*, 123 S. Ct. 2325, 2342 (2003).

25. 123 S. Ct. 2339.

26. See, e.g., Joan Tarpley, "A Comment on Justice O'Connor's Quest for Power and its Impact on African American Wealth," 53 S.C. L. Rev. 117 (2001); Jerome McCristal Culp, Jr., "An Open Letter from One Black Scholar to Justice Ruth Bader Ginsburg: Or, How Not to Become Justice Sandra Day O'Connor," 1 Duke J. Gender L. & Pol'y 21 (1994) (arguing that Justice O'Connor's jurisprudence of race has been dismissive of black people's concerns).

27. See, e.g., *Johnson v. Santa Clara Transportation Agency*, 480 U.S. 616, 647 (1987) (Justice O'Connor concurring) (approving affirmative action under Title VII for women).

28. Culp, "An Open Letter," 31.

29. *Shaw v. Reno*, 509 U.S. 630, 644 (1993) (5–4 decision, Justice O'Connor concurring)("a racial classification, regardless of purported motivation, is presumptively invalid and can be upheld only upon an extraordinary justification").

30. *Wygant v. Jackson Board of Educ.*, 476 U.S. 267, 286 (1986) (5–4 decision, Justice O'Connor concurring) ("the analysis and level of scrutiny applied to determine the validity of [a racial] classification do not vary simply because the objective appears acceptable to individual members of the Court").

31. See *Local 28 of Sheet Metal Workers v. EEOC*, 478 U.S. 421, 497 (1986) (6–3 decision, Justice O'Connor concurring) ("The creation of racial preferences by courts, even in the more limited form of goals rather than

quotas, must be done sparingly and only where manifestly necessary to remedy violation of Title VII").

32. *City of Richmond v. J.A. Croson*, 488 U.S. 469, 494, 495–96 (1989) (6–3 decision, Justice O'Connor plurality opinion) ("the standard of review applied is not dependent on the race of the party burdened or benefited by the classification").

33. *Adarand Constructors v. Pena*, 515 U.S. 200, 227 (1995) (5–4 decision, Justice O'Connor concurring) ("all racial classifications, imposed by whatever federal, state, or local governmental actor must be analyzed by a reviewing court under strict scrutiny"). The decision overturned Metro Broadcasting, Inc. v. FCC, 497 U.S. 547 (1990).

34. *Wygant v. Jackson Board of Educ.*, 476 U.S. 284, 287 (1986).

35. Sheet Metal Workers, 478 U.S. 496; see also *U.S. v. Paradise*, 480 U.S. 149, 199–200 (1987) (5–4 decision, Justice O'Connor dissenting) ("The District Court had available several alternatives that would have achieved full compliance with the consent decrees without trammeling on the rights of nonminority troopers").

36. Tarpley, "A Comment on Justice O'Connor's Quest," 119.

37. Melvin L. Oliver and Thomas M. Shapiro, *Black Wealth/White Wealth: A New Perspective on Racial Inequalities* (New York: Routledge, 1995), 182.

38. 123 S. Ct. 2325, 2369 (Chief Justice Rehnquist dissenting).

39. Id., 2325.

40. 123 S. Ct. 2350 (Justice Thomas dissenting).

41. 123 S. Ct. 2411 (Justice Ginsberg dissenting).

42. 123 S. Ct. 2325, 2349 (Justice Scalia dissenting).

43. 123 S. Ct. 2411, 2442 (Justice Souter dissenting).

44. Peter Schmidt, "Affirmative-Action Fight Is Renewed in the States," *Chronicle of Higher Education* (Jul. 18, 2003), A19

45. Susan Sturm and Lani Guinier, "The Future of Affirmative Action: Reclaiming the Innovative Ideal," 84 Calif. L. Rev. 953, 957 (1996).

46. See Tony Schwartz, "The Test under Stress," *New York Times* (Jan. 10, 1999). During the summer of 1999, the *Princeton Review* rented a beach house in the Hamptons for a group of its star coaches so they could tutor students at a rate of $300 per hour. Jane Gross, "Multiple Choice and Margaritas," *New York Times* (Aug. 9, 1999), B1.

47. 123 S. Ct. 2325, 2359–2360 (Justice Thomas dissenting).

48. Carol Swain, "Affirmative Action Ruling Makes It Easy for Elites," www.temmesseam.com

49. Daniel Golden, "Family Ties: Preferences for Alumni Children in College Admission Draws Fire," *Wall Street Journal*, 2003 WL-WSJ 3956563 (Jan. 15, 2003).

50. Jamilah Evelyn, "The 'Silent Killer' of Minority Enrollments," *Chronicle of Higher Education* (Jun. 20, 2003), A17.

Chapter 14: Searching for Effective Schools in the Post-*Brown* Era

1. *Serrano v. Priest*, 96 Cal. Rper. 601, 487 P.2d 1241 (Cal. 1971).

2. *San Antonio School District v. Rodriguez*, 411 U.S. 1 (1973).

3. *Campaign for Fiscal Equity, Inc., v. State of New York*, 2003 WL 21468502, N. E.2d (Jun. 2003).

4. *Edgewood Indep. Sch. Dist. v. Meno*, 917 S.W.2d 717, 730 (Tex. 1995).

5. J. Steven Farr and Mark Trachtenberg, "The Edgewood Drama: An Epic Quest for Education Equity," 17 Yale J. L. & Pol'y 607 (1999).

6. James S. Liebman and Charles F. Sabel, "The Federal No Child Left Behind Act and the Post-desegregation Civil Rights Agenda," 28 N.Y.U. Rev. L. & Social Change (2003).

7. See Pamela M. Prah, "Rules May Guarantee F's For Many Schools," *Focus* (Jan.–Feb. 2003), 8.

8. Gail Foster, "Historically Black Independent Schools," in *City Schools*, Diane Ravitch and Joseph Viteritti, eds. (Baltimore: John Hopkins University Press, 2000), 291.

9. School Directory, Institute for Independent Education, ii (Washington, D.C., 1995).

10. Paula Penn-Nabrit, *Morning by Morning: How We Home-Schooled Our African-American Sons to the Ivy League* (New York: Villard, 2003).

11. Kenneth Karst, "Paths to Belonging. the Constitution and Cultural Identity," 64 N.C. L. Rev. 303,343 (1986).

12. Jerome E. Morris, *A Pillar of Strength: An African American School's Communal Bond with Families and Community since* Brown, 33 Urban Education 10 (1999).

13. Deborah Prothrow-Stith and Michaele Weissman, *Deadly Consequences* (New York: Harper Collins, 1991), 163–64.

14. Pamela J. Smith, "All-Male Black Schools and the Equal Protection Clause: A Step Forward Toward Education," 66 Tul. L. Rev. 2003 (1992).

15. See, e.g., Karla A. Turekian, "Traversing the Minefields of Education Reform: the Legality of Charter Schools," 29 Conn. L. Rev. 1365 (1997); Kevin S. Huffman, "Charter Schools, Equal Protection Litigation, and the New School Reform Movement," 73 N.Y.U. L. Rev. 1290 (1998).

16. See Richard C. Seder, "Allow Charter Schools to Reach Their Full Potential," *Christian Science Monitor* (Oct. 3. 1997), 18.

17. The Frederick Douglas Academy, 2581 Adam Clayton Powell, Jr., Boulevard, New York, New York 10039. http://aolsearch.aol.com/aol/ search?=query=Frederick+Douglass+Academy

18. Detailed data about the Academy can be found at http://www.nycenet.edu/daa/schoolReports/

19. Sara Gonzales, "For African Americans, A School to Call Home," *Seattle*

Times (Jun. 16, 1999); Linda Shaw, "Seattle's African American Academy: Rescuing the Dream," *Seattle Times* (Feb. 14, 1999).

20. See Frank R. Kemerer, "The Constitutionality of School Vouchers," 101 Ed. Law. Rep. 17 (1995); Carol L. Ziegler and Nancy M. Lederman, "School Vouchers: Are Urban Students Surrendering Rights for Choice?" 19 Fordham Urb. L. J. 813 (1992); Greg D. Andres, "Private School Voucher Remedies in Education Cases," 62 U. Chi. L. Rev. 795 (1995).

21. See Milton Friedman, *Capitalism and Freedom* (Chicago: University of Chicago Press, 1962), 93–96.

22. Molly Townes O'Brien, "Private School Tuition Vouchers and the Realities of Racial Politics," 64 Tenn. L. Rev. 359 (1997).

23. The Milwaukee plan is *Jackson v. Benson*, 578 N.W.2d 602 (Wis. 1998), cert. denied, 119 S. Ct. 466 (1999).

24. *Zelman v. Simmons-Harris*, 536 U.S. 639 (2002).

25. Jay P. Greene, ed., *High School Graduation Rates in the United States* (Black Alliance for Educational Options [BAEO]), Nov. 2001.

26. Timothy Egan, "The Changing Face of Catholic Education," *New York Times* (Aug. 6, 2000), 4A, 28.

27. For a detailed study of the programs, see Edmund Gordon, Carol Bowman, and Brenda Mejia, eds., *Changing the Script for Youth Development: An Evaluation of the All Stars Talent Show Network and the Joseph A. Forgione Development School for Youth* (Institute for Urban and Minority Education (IUME)), Teachers College, Columbia University (Jun. 2003).

Chapter 15: Moving Beyond Racial Fortuity

1. Hugh Price, "Still Worth Fighting For: America After 9/11," in *The State of Black America, 2002*, Lee Daniels, ed. (New York: National Urban League, 2002), 9.

2. William Julius Wilson, *When Work Disappears: The World of the New Urban Poor* (New York: Vintage Books, 1996).

3. Bernard Anderson, "The Black Worker: Continuing Quest for Economic Parity," in *The State of Black America, 2002*, Lee Daniels, ed., (New York: National Urban League, 2002), 51, 65.

4. Louis Uchitelle, "Blacks Lose Better Jobs Faster As Middle-Class Work Drops," *New York Times* (Jul. 12, 2003), A1.

5. Ellis Cose, *The Rage of a Privileged Class* (New York: HarperCollins, 1993).

6. Id., 74–75.

7. Ellis Cose, *The Envy of the World: On Being a Black Man in America* (New York: Washington Square Press, 2002). See also, Haki Madhubuti, *Black Men: Obsolete, Single, Dangerous?* (Chicago: Third World Press, 1991).

8. Fox Butterfield, "Study Finds 2.6 percent Increase in U.S. Prison Population," *New York Times* (Jul. 28, 2003), http://www.nytimes.com

9. Id., 42.

10. Andrew Hacker, *Mismatch: The Growing Gulf Between Women and Men* (New York: Scribners, 2003).

11. Id., 149.

12. See Lani Guinier and Gerald Torres, *The Miners' Canary: Enlisting Race, Resisting Power, Transforming Democracy* (Cambridge, Mass.: Harvard University Press, 2002).

13. Brandon Lofton, *Victories and Limitations of the Civil Rights Movement: The Need for an Empowering African-American Ideology* (unpublished paper on file with the author).

14. Michael Seidman, *Brown and Miranda*, 80 Calif. L. Rev. 673, 717 (1992).

15. Robert Gordon, New Developments in Legal Theory, in *The Politics of Law*, 2nd ed., David Kairys, ed. (New York: Pantheon Books, 1990), 413, 418.

16. Kimberle Crenshaw, "Race, Reform, and Retrenchment: Transformation and Legitimation in Antidiscrimination Law," 101 Harv. L. Rev. 1331 (1988).

17. David Garrow, *Bearing the Cross: Martin Luther King, Jr. And the Southern Christian Leadership Conference* (New York: Morrow, 1986), 129–30.

18. Id., 136.

Conclusion

1. Booker T. Washington, "The Atlanta Compromise (Sept. 18, 1895)," in *Ripples of Hope: Great American Civil Rights Speeches*, Josh Gottheimer, ed. (New York: Perseus, 2003), 132.

2. Reinhold Niebuhr, *Moral Man and Immoral Society* (New York: C. Scribner's Sons, 1932), 252–53.

3. Franklin Raines, "What Equality Would Look Like: Reflections on the Past, Present and Future," in *The State of Black America, 2002*, Lee Daniels, ed., (New York: National Urban League, 2002), 13.

4. Jesse Jackson, "On Patriotism," *The Nation* (Jul. 15/22, 1991), 101.

5. Peter Gomes, *Sermons: Biblical Wisdom for Daily Living* (New York: Morrow, 1998), 47.

6. Anthony Paul Farley, "8th Story: Illness and Its Interlocutors in Thirteen Stories," 15 Touro L. Rev. 543, 621 (1999).

7. F. Scott Fitzgerald, *The Great Gatsby* (New York: Scribner, 1925), 182.

8. Id., 144.

9. Robert Gordon, "New Developments in Legal Theory," in *The Politics of Law*, 2nd ed., David Kairys, ed. (New York: Pantheon, 1990), 413, 424.

INDEX